The Rape of the Peasantry

ERNEST FEDER is an agricultural economist who has taught at several U.S. and Latin American universities. He has many years of field experience in Latin America (notably in Colombia, Brazil, Chile, Peru and Mexico), where he has worked with the Economic Commission for Latin America and the Food and Agriculture Organization of the United Nations.

THE RAPE OF THE PEASANTRY

LATIN AMERICA'S LANDHOLDING SYSTEM

BY ERNEST FEDER

ANCHOR BOOKS
DOUBLEDAY & COMPANY, INC., GARDEN CITY, NEW YORK

The Anchor Books edition is the first English language publication of THE RAPE OF THE PEASANTRY

Anchor Books edition: 1971

EDITORS' STATEMENT

This volume is part of a publishing program on Latin America, under the general editorship of Otto Feinstein and Rodolfo Stavenhagen. The purpose of these books is to present an inter-American dialogue on Latin American affairs, from history and culture to economics, politics and sociology. This program is designed to make the best scholarship from Latin America available to readers in the U.S.

OTTO FEINSTEIN is a Professor in the Science of Society Division of Monteith College, Wayne State University. He is editor of *New University Thought*. Professor Feinstein has written articles for numerous publications, and is the editor of *Two Worlds of Change: Readings in Economic Development*.

RODOLFO STAVENHAGEN is a Mexican who studied sociology and social anthropology at the University of Chicago, the National University of Mexico and the University of Paris. Since 1956, he has been teaching at the National University of Mexico, and is currently affiliated with the International Institute of Labor Studies in Geneva. He is the author of many articles on Latin America, including "Seven Erroneous Theses about Latin America," which appears in *New University Thought*, as well as *Agrarian Problems and Peasant Movements in Latin America*, also published by Anchor.

Foreword

Two groups with almost irreconcilable views confront each other today on the subject of agricultural development: the Technocrats and the Reformers. Although both wish to improve the performance of Latin American agriculture, as well as the welfare of the farm population, they propose diametrically opposite policies. The Technocrats are in favor of stimulating output and the efficiency of production by channeling more resources, including (and perhaps mainly) modern machinery and innovations, into agriculture and improving farm management, but without making major changes in the agrarian structure. They are advocating dynamic changes in the production processes, but want to maintain the status quo in the economic, social and political institutions which make up the Latin American agricultural sector. They are sponsoring costly irrigation and drainage schemes, equally expensive colonizations of uninhabited jungle areas or deserts, the import or domestic assembly of modern machinery and equipment, the distribution of improved seeds and fertilizers, and increased credit. They are also in favor of more education for farm people, on the theory that people with higher levels of education earn larger incomes. Of course, this education is thought to be needed only by the rural poor, not by the rich landlords.

Most national and international policies and programs for agricultural development are inspired by these views and they are well financed. Since the majority of all agricultural resources are controlled by a small number of owners of large estates, it would seem obvious that such policies and programs would benefit primarily this landed elite, and only secondarily the peasants, through the "trickle-down effect" (although, as we shall show later, there may be no such effect at all). Hence the Technocrats are consciously or unconsciously *elite-oriented*.

The Reformers have a different approach. They are of course not opposed to modern technologies. But they see in the existing agrarian structure an almost absolute barrier to an efficient use of technologies, and a drastic increase in agricultural production which would reverse nutritional trends or an adverse foreign exchange situation, and, more important, a barrier to the early elimination of poverty. Hence, as a prerequisite for a rapidly expanding agricultural sector able to distribute much greater benefits to the peasants, they propose to do away with the existing agrarian structure. The Reformers, then, can be said to be *peasant-oriented*. Because of their political content, the Reformers' views are sometimes popular and sometimes unpopular, depending on the political situation. They do not command strong support among the rank-and-file politicians, or, obviously, among those who have a strong stake in the preservation of the status quo (and this includes many people in the Americas who have a strong voice in the decision-making processes), although they appeared to have gained a greater appeal in the early 1960's. After the Cuban revolution and land reform, which established for the first time in Latin American history a large socialist sector in agriculture, and after the Alliance for Progress of 1961, it appeared for a while that the 1960's would become the decade of the liberation of the peasants, through systematic and peaceful land reforms. The Cuban land reform did away with the privately owned estates almost with one stroke. The Charter of Punta del Este, which organized the Alliance, was a warning that without the elimination of the existing inequalities in the distribution of agricultural resources and incomes, rural poverty and the oppression of the peasants, development could not be expected to take place at the desired rate of speed, and political conflicts would become inevitable. But if the peasants and the Reformers expected this liberation, they have been sadly disappointed. By the latter half of the decade, a strong reaction to structural reforms had set in.

Given the economic, social and political structure of Latin American agriculture today, it is probable (although of course not certain) that the Reformers' approach to agricultural development is the correct one. During the past decade—partly in response to an intellectual stimulus provided by the now defunct and never very viable Alliance for Progress—such a large amount of detailed information on the agrarian structure and its relation to agricultural development has become available that it would almost appear self-evident that under present conditions Latin America's peasants cannot look toward a better future without a real land reform.

Numerous analyses have demonstrated convincingly that the latifundio is firmly entrenched in Latin America and has even gained ground in recent years at the expense of the peasants. As it has in the past, latifundismo is still able to perform well for the benefit of the big landlords—the landed elite—but it is now unable to meet the demands of a growing and restless peasantry. Furthermore, it seems to represent the most important single obstacle to rapid economic, social and political development.

The following chapters contain a basic analysis of the characteristics and functioning of Latin America's latifundio agriculture and of the meanderings of the so-called land reforms of the 1960's. An attempt has been made to look at agricultural problems from the standpoint of the peasants, although it is perhaps impossible for an outsider to appreciate how peasants, whose experience has been nothing but poverty and humiliation for generations, actually feel. Some readers might object that so much of this book is devoted to a criticism of a small landowning class and so little to that of the peasantry. Perhaps it is accurate to say that this book is somewhat one-sided. But so is Latin American agriculture, controlled as it is to such a large extent by this small landed elite.

In preparing this book, I have drawn extensively on the inexhaustible material prepared by CIDA,[1] particularly on its

---

[1] CIDA (the Spanish initials for the Inter American Committee for Agricultural Development) was organized in 1962 by mandate of the Charter of Punta del Este of 1961; its members were the Food and Agriculture Organization

detailed land tenure studies, which are still largely unknown by the general public.[2] Taken together, the CIDA reports could be called *Latin American Drama*, because they are presently the greatest contribution to the knowledge of Latin American agriculture, comparable to Gunnar Myrdal's *Asian Drama* for the Asian continent. The CIDA reports are unique because they are based in large part on innumerable field studies and therefore are able to present a detailed picture of the conditions under which Latin America's peasants live and work, and to elucidate the effect of rural institutions on agricultural performance.[3]

But I cannot begin this analysis without a note of thanks to

(FAO), the Economic Commission for Latin America (ECLA), the Inter-American Development Bank (IDB), the Organization of American States (OAS) and the Inter American Institute for Agricultural Sciences (IIAS). Between 1965 and 1966 it published seven reports—one for each of seven countries —entitled *Land Tenure Conditions and Socio-Economic Development in* (1) *Argentina*, (2) *Brazil*, (3) *Chile*, (4) *Colombia*, (5) *Ecuador*, (6) *Guatemala* and (7) *Peru*. The reports can be obtained through the Pan American Union, Washington, D.C. In the text, reference to the reports are as follows: CIDA, (country) Report, op. cit.

A summary (regional report) for the seven country reports was published by S. Barraclough and A. Domike, "Agrarian Structure in Seven Latin American Countries," in *Land Economics* (Madison, Wisc.), November 1966, pp. 391 ff, and in Spanish in *El Trimestre Economico* (Mexico), Vol. 33 (130), pp. 235 ff.

Country reports on Mexico, Venezuela, Bolivia and the Central American countries are to be published by CIDA in the near future. Several appendices to the regional report on the seven countries are also forthcoming.

[2] The CIDA studies were carried out during the first half of the decade of the 1960's and some of the statistical information is based on the censuses available at that time. Where possible I have brought the statistical information up to date. In some cases, I have used CIDA data without adjustments to improve uniformity of presentation. Since the fundamental relationships in Latin American agriculture have not changed significantly, this does not seem to affect the conclusions at which I have arrived.

[3] This book is devoted to conditions prevailing in Latin American agriculture at the present time. For students of history, the following references might be useful: Andrew Pearse, "Agrarian Change Trends," in *Agrarian Problems and Peasant Movements in Latin America*, ed. Rodolfo Stavenhagen (New York: Doubleday Anchor Books, 1970); CIDA, "The Origins of Present Tenure Systems," prepared by Andrew Pearse (to be published shortly by CIDA); Sergio Bagú, *Estructura de la Sociedad Colonial* (Buenos Aires: Ateneo, 1946); J. M. Ots-Capdequi, *El Estado Espanol en las Indias* (Mexico: Fondo de Cultura Economica); Antonio Garcia, *Bases de la Economia Contemporanea, Capitalismo y Feudalismo en la America Colonial Espanol* (Bogotá: R.F.I.O.C., 1948); Celso Furtado, *La Formacion Economica del Brasil* (Mexico: Fondo de Cultura Economica, 1962); Jose Carlos Mariategui, *Siete Ensayos de Interpretacion de la Realidad Peruana* (Lima: Amauta).

the small group of colleagues and friends whose insights and work this little volume partly reflects. They are Solon Barraclough, C. Clyde Mitchell, Arthur Domike, Edmundo Flores, Andrew Pearse, Rodolfo Stavenhagen, Carlos Alberto de Medina, Gerrit Huizer, Peter Dorner, Eric Jacoby, Juan Ballesteros, Rafael Baraona and Marion Brown.

The views expressed in this book are my own, and do not necessarily represent the views of the organizations with which I am or have been associated.

Contents

Glossary

Minifundios
Farms which have insufficient land to satisfy the minimum needs of a family or to allow the utilization of their work through the year (up to two workers).

Family Farms
Farms which have sufficient land to support a family through the work of its members, using the farming methods prevailing in the area (up to four workers).

Medium-Sized Multi-Family Farms
Farms which have sufficient land to employ a number of workers outside the family (five to twelve workers).

Large-Sized Multi-Family Farms (Latifundios)
Farms which have sufficient land to give employment to a group of workers much larger than the family of the owner (over twelve workers).

Administrator
Farm manager, usually on an estate.

Estates
Used in the text to refer to all multi-family farms.

Farm Workers
Members of the farm labor force, including both hired and family workers (including working members of the estate owners' family). May be owners or producers, tenants, sharecroppers or wage workers.

Landed Elite
Used in the text as general reference to owners of estates.

PART I

LATIFUNDISMO: AN UNEMPLOYMENT AGRICULTURE

If whole masses of the peasantry held out against the preponderant teaching of conservatism, and presently showed themselves once more to be anything but conservative, the basic reason is most probably to be found in the economic and political conditions of their life, and in their own direct response to these conditions. . . . and there is at least the flavor of plausibility in the testimony on the question of propaganda given by one of the peasants brought before a magistrate after the disturbances of 1902: "No rumors came to me about any little books," he said. "I think that if we lived better, the little books would not be important, no matter what was written in them. What's terrible is not the little books, but this: that there isn't anything to eat."

G. Tanquary Robinson, *Rural Russia under the Old Regime* (Berkeley: University of California Press, 1969), Chapter IX, "The Revolution of 1905: The Rising Tide," p. 144.

A. HUMAN ASPECTS

CHAPTER 1

A Summary View of Rural Poverty

The latifundio agriculture of Latin America is an unemployment agriculture. It does not fully employ, or it employs wastefully, the available land and capital resources, and the available manpower.

Unemployment or underemployment of manpower is reflected in the large number of poor who represent a very high proportion of the total rural population. The rural poor are of two kinds. They are the millions of *smallholders,* who are poor by definition, because they barely eke out a subsistence living on plots of land too small to provide for full employment and an adequate family income. Some of the plots —called in some countries "microfincas"—are so tiny that on a cadastral map of any respectable scale, they would have to be drawn in with the help of a microscope. In 1960, of 17.2 million rural families in nineteen Latin American countries, approximately 5.7 million were families of smallholders.

Then there are the *landless workers*. They represent another 6.9 million poor families. They receive for their labor extremely low wages in cash or in kind. Often they receive no remuneration whatever, because in many regions peasants still have to put in days of work free or nearly free of charge in "homage" to the big landlords. That is, they must show their gratitude for being allowed to work the rest of the time at near-starvation wages.

The estimated 12.6 million poor rural families represented in 1960 about 73 per cent of the total of 17.2 million farm families. The net annual increase in the number of farm families is estimated at about 271,000 families. By 1970, therefore, the number of poor farm families must have risen from about

12.6 million to around 15.0 million, on the assumption (which we shall test below) that most of the new families will be added to the lowest strata of the rural population. In other words, out of a total rural population of 114 million in 1970, about 86 million will be living at subsistence levels. In 1980, there will be 18 million poor rural families.

Rural Poverty in 19 Latin American Countries
in 1960

Countries	Rural Families (in millions)	Poor Rural Families (in millions)	New Families Annually (in thousands)
10 Countries with Good Estimates[a]	12.0	8.7	185
2 Countries with Fair Estimates[b]	3.5	2.7	50
7 Remaining Countries[c]	1.7	1.3	27
All 19 Countries	17.2	12.6	271

[a] Argentina, Brazil, Chile, Colombia, Ecuador, Guatemala, Peru, El Salvador, Honduras, Nicaragua.
[b] Dominican Republic, Mexico.
[c] Bolivia, Costa Rica, Haiti, Paraguay, Panama, Uruguay, Venezuela. The number of poor families in these countries was estimated on basis of relationships found in the countries enumerated in [a].

Brazil and Guatemala are evidence of the truth of the assumption that most new families in agriculture are poor. According to the Brazilian census statistics of 1950 and 1960, a conservative estimate is that 65 per cent of the 1.2 million rural families that made up the net rural population increase were poor. Apparently this came about in the following manner: Between 1950 and 1960 the number of smallholdings (minifundios) increased sharply from 465,000 to 1,056,000—much in excess of the possible natural increase of the smallholders' families during this decade. Many small units sprang up in Brazil's frontier regions; others in old established communities. Subdivision of older smallholdings also accounts for many new minifundios. Since these new smallholders could not all originate from the old smallholders' families, they come no doubt from the ranks of the landless workers. In fact, the number of landless workers did apparently decline slightly during this decade. The settlement of landless workers on minifundios does not indicate much of an improvement in their living standards, although it may represent in many cases a slight increase in security. The expansion of minifundios is in reality only an expansion of rural slums and in some cases, as shall be explained later, it is only a prelude to a new generation of landless workers.

If the census data are accepted at face value, the proportion of the poor rural families of all rural families declined in Brazil from 65 per cent in 1950 to about 61 per cent in 1960. Census statistics must, however, be interpreted with caution. In the first place, there are excellent reasons to believe that the number of landless workers was larger than the last census reported and not about the same as in 1950, because there has been a marked tendency in recent years for large landowners and employers of rural labor to underreport both their land and their labor force to make it appear that latifundismo is not as widespread as it really is. But the fault is not all with the owners of latifundios. Agricultural censuses systematically underreport the lowest level of farm workers, partly because many of them do not have a fixed residence. Since the mobility of farm workers has sharply increased, it is likely that a growing proportion of the rural labor force is not accounted for by the last census. Also, some rural workers without land live in urban areas where they continue to be dependent on farm work, but are not included in the enumeration.

A more important factor indicating that the proportion of poor families has not fallen is that many so-called family farms do not in fact provide incomes and levels of living beyond those found on minifundios, although they have slightly more land and a family-sized labor force.[1] Producers on

---

[1] This was found to be the case in one important northeastern farm community and is typical for areas where small farms predominate. See CIDA, Brazil Report, op. cit., pp. 452 ff.

these family farms cannot utilize all their land because they cannot obtain sufficient capital and technical assistance. An estimate of the number of such family farms which ought to be classified with the minifundios can be obtained in the following manner:

The natural (net) increase in the total number of poor families between 1950 and 1960 is estimated at 807,000 families, on the realistic assumption that the offspring of poor families who remain in agriculture must remain poor, as they have at best access only to small plots of land. If these 807,000 families are added to the 3.5 million poor families existing in 1950, the total number of poor families in 1960 would be about 4.3 million, or 65 per cent of all rural families. Of course, the 807,000 families exceeded by about 307,000 the number of all poor rural families in the categories of smallholders and landless workers that were actually added during the decade (keeping in mind that the unskilled landless workers' families declined slightly by about 100,000, according to census figures).[2] What happened to these 307,000 families? If the number of landless workers did not increase, then they are no doubt included in the family farms, mainly the smallest ones, whose number also increased (like the minifundios) significantly during the decade.

If these interpretations are correct, then, the proportion of poor families in Brazil has not declined. This is an important conclusion.

In Guatemala, trends were different, but with similar results. The number of families without land increased sharply between census years (1950 and 1964) partly because the natural (net) increase in the number of families living on smallholdings exceeded sharply the number of new smallholdings established during the fourteen-year period. As a result the agrarian structure deteriorated in two ways from the point of view of the campesinos: through an increase in smallholdings and through an increase in landless workers. Note

[2] The computation is as follows: Estimated natural increase in the families of smallholders and landless workers, 1950–60, was 807,000 families. Actual increase in the number of smallholders and landless workers (after deducting the skilled workers) was from 3,531,000 to 4,025,000 families, or nearly 500,000 families.

that about 92 per cent of the new farm families in Guatemala were poor families and that the proportion of poor families rose from 90 per cent in 1950 to 91 per cent in 1964.

The Changing Structure of Rural Poverty in Brazil and Guatemala

(figures in thousands)

Status of Farm Family	Brazilian Families 1950	1960	Guatemalan Families 1950	1964
Producers				
Minifundios	465	1,056	308	365
Family Farms	807	1,281	33	44
All Multi-Family Farms[a]	792	997	8	8
All Producers	2,064	3,334	349	417
Landless Workers	3,340[b]	3,306[b1]	69	149
TOTAL	5,404	6,640	416	566

[a] Medium-sized and large multi-family farms.

[b] [b1] Including 274,000 and 337,000 skilled workers respectively.

Since Brazil and Guatemala appear to be representative cases for Latin American agriculture, and although there were significant differences in the manner in which the structure of poverty changed in the two countries, it is clear that rural poverty in Latin America increased in absolute terms and remained at best stationary in relative terms. In countries where there has not been a notable geographic expansion of agriculture, the natural increase in rural families has to lead to more families without land. Where agriculture expanded, smallholdings could increase and, as in Brazil, absorb a portion of families without land. In practically no country has there been a systematic and effective program to wipe out poverty, as we shall see later.

CHAPTER 2

What Is "Rural Poor"?

It is necessary now to explain in some more detail what is meant by rural poverty, which affects about fifteen million rural families in the hemisphere. In other words, we must briefly delve into the problem of the inequality of wealth and incomes within the rural sector (the problem of land distribution will be dealt with separately), and the extent and seriousness of low living levels encountered among farm workers and smallholders.

Income inequality is not *per se* unjust or an impediment to economic development. Differences in individuals' abilities, tastes and responsibilities can explain and justify income differences. But inequalities are not so easily condoned when the differences are great and persistent, where the mass of the population lives without even food and shelter necessary to life, and where the disparities are perpetuated by systematic exclusion of most of the population from the means of livelihood, education and political power needed to improve their status. In most of rural Latin America, the income distribution is a problem precisely because of the unequal access of the population to the opportunities for progress and personal achievement.

The source of the income inequalities and the means for their perpetuation lie in control over land and other essential factors of production. Those who hold the land in underdeveloped economies, where few employment opportunities exist outside agriculture, control the keys to power and even to existence. The low incomes of the bulk of the population have obvious consequences beyond the individuals who suffer them. The markets for all types of goods, other than those needed for simple subsistence, cannot be large where incomes of so many people are so low. Rural poverty bears directly on productive efficiency because the conditions under which the campesinos' returns are earned provide them with no incentives for improving their performance.

For seven countries for which relatively detailed data are available—Argentina, Brazil, Chile, Colombia, Ecuador, Guatemala and Peru—it was estimated that two thirds of the active agricultural population (exclusive of the non-working members of the farm families) were small producers on minifundios and rural hired workers of various types, but in some countries the proportion was considerably higher. For example, in Chile, 73 per cent; Ecuador, 87 per cent; Guatemala, 83 per cent; and Peru, 89 per cent. Rural poverty has obviously assumed alarming proportions.

In analyzing the distribution of income in the rural sector it is important to distinguish between the distribution of income among "producers"—the usual measure—and that among "all farm workers." In the former, the hired workers' incomes are excluded. But in both cases the income earned from non-farm activities is excluded from the statistics, which tends to diminish the income disparities between the various classes of rural people. This is because small producers and farm workers only in rare cases obtain returns from the non-farm activities—and then only in small amounts—whereas the non-farm returns of large producers are often much in excess of their farm incomes. Hence income distribution measures do not adequately reflect the differences in bargaining power and status which are so intimately related to monetary returns of individuals. But even the disparities in farm incomes alone are understated by the available data, because they do not account, or account only partially, for multiple ownership of estates, which is a widespread phenomenon throughout the hemisphere. Although these factors tend to cover up the real extent of income inequalities, it remains clear that the differences in the amounts of land controlled by large and small producers alone are sufficient to generate extreme differences in incomes earned.

The pattern of income distribution in rural Latin America

on an aggregate basis is not readily available through adequate statistics and we must rely on a few examples which appear to reflect realistically the maldistribution of income at least for the seven countries mentioned. It is to be kept in mind that the importance of the data cited lies not so much in the demonstration of sharp income gaps as in the extremely low level of incomes earned by the farm workers and small producers. In Chile, for example, the rural workers, representing about 87 per cent of the people in agriculture, earned as a class an estimated 34 per cent of the total agricultural income in 1954, while the upper 12 per cent earned close to 66 per cent of the total agricultural income. But the situation has not changed much in that country, according to more recent estimates. Producers on small lots and farm workers (about 71 per cent of all people active in agriculture) earned in 1960 33 per cent of the agricultural income (including both cash and imputed incomes), whereas the large producers (3 per cent) earned nearly 37 per cent of the total income. As a result it was estimated that the small producers and farm workers in Chile would have to work on the average 26 years in order to earn the annual farm income of one large producer. The income gap apparently tends to increase with the quality of the farming area. For example, in the region of Valdivia, in southern Chile, on eight large farms which were studied in detail, the *inquilinos* have to work between 80 and 218 years to earn the annual income of their employers. The annual family income of the workers in 1962–63 varied between 300 and 485 escudos, while that of the employers ranged from 32,500 to 80,800 escudos.[1] In Colombia, the distribution of the value of the aggregate agricultural output, an approximation of gross agricultural income among farm producers, was used to estimate income distribution for the country as a whole. Producers on sub-family farms (64 per cent of all producers) accounted for 21 per cent, whereas the latifundistas (1 per cent) accounted for almost 15 per cent of the total value of production. The gross farm income of the smallest producer families averaged one forty-fifth of that of the families on

[1] CIDA, Chile Report, op. cit., pp. 33, 181–84, 211–13. One escudo equals $.95 U.S.

latifundios. However, the averages taken for the country as a whole obscure the fact that there are larger differences in income, and very low incomes for small producers, in the country's best agricultural areas. In one community of the rich valley of the Cauca, 1,054 small producers on farms of less than ten hectares earned on the average an estimated 1/480 of the net income of 22 estate owners each controlling an average of about 1,220 hectares. The average annual farm income of the former was less than 1,700 pesos (about $170), which was considered inadequate for sustaining a farm family.[2] In three communities in the same general area, in which a broad sample study has been carried out, the annual net income of families on farms up to .96 hectares (20 per cent of all farms in the sample) averaged 568 pesos, and on farms between .96 and 4.8 hectares (46 per cent of all farms), 2,080 pesos, or 1/473 and 1/127 respectively of the net income of farms exceeding 96 hectares. Small farms up to 9.6 hectares (78 per cent of all farms) earned only 9.3 per cent, while large farms exceeding 96 hectares (less than 4 per cent) earned nearly 63 per cent of the total net income generated on the farms in these communities. It would seem that, as in Chile, the largest disparities in income distribution exist in the best agricultural areas of Colombia.

The total family incomes of thirty-five Colombian farm workers interviewed in various case studies fluctuated for most of them between 3,000 and 5,000 pesos annually. The lowest annual per capita family income of these workers was 216 pesos, and in most cases it did not exceed 800 pesos when the family was large.[3] The exceptions were the organized sugar cane workers, who earned more satisfactory incomes.

In Guatemala, the distribution of rural income was also estimated indirectly by the value of production of nine major products on the 349,000 farms in the various farm classes. The largest estates produced about 350 times more than the

[2] E. Feder and A. J. Posada, "Analisis Socio-Economico de Recuperacion de Zonas de Tierras en el Valle del Cauca," *Economia Colombiana* (Bogotá), November 1964, p. 41; December 1964, p. 24.

[3] CIDA, Colombia Report, op. cit., pp. 202 ff, 211, 371 ff, 517 ff. Ten pesos equal one U.S. dollar.

minifundios, numbering about 234,000; but 925 times more than the 74,300 microfincas, tiny plots on which mostly Indians reside. By far the greatest number of these small farms are located in the altiplano. The bulk of the farm population —i.e., the producers on the sub-family-sized farms, the workers and the members of their families—earn incomes which are barely sufficient for providing food and clothing, and many incomes appear to be too low even for that. The average annual gross product per microfinca was estimated at 45 quetzales, or 9 quetzales per capita per year. According to a number of case studies carried out in Guatemala, total gross income from sales and imputed home consumption of a typical minifundio in the altiplano amounted to about 324 quetzales annually, or 54 quetzales per capita per year for a family of six, i.e., about $4.50 U.S. per capita per month. Even if 196 quetzales per family is added as an average income from other sources, the total remains unimpressive. On the coast, a typical minifundio income amounted to an average of 967 quetzales, and varied from 110 to 4,700 quetzales, but the number of minifundios on the coast is relatively small. In most countries the incomes of workers tend to be lower than those of smallholders although in Guatemalan case studies the differences were not large. Of 35 workers interviewed, 18 earned an average of 248 quetzales, while the average income of the 35 families, inclusive of perquisites, was 327 quetzales annually. This did not include products produced on owned or rented plots of 10 workers, or those from plots allotted by employers to 6 workers. But average production of these plots was estimated at only 48 quetzales. This raised the average income of the 35 workers' families to 396 quetzales annually, with well over one half earning considerably less than 400 quetzales.[4] In this connection one must recall that in 1964, of 566,000 rural families, 514,000 were poor. Of those, nearly 30 per cent were families of workers without land, and about one fifth families on micro-plots, the remainder being families on minifundios.

For Brazil, aggregate national estimates on rural income

---

[4] CIDA, Gautemala Report, op. cit., pp. 59, 85, 104 f, 171. One quetzale equals one U.S. dollar.

distribution are hard to come by. Case studies throw light on conditions existing in a few selected rural communities. For example, in 1962, in Garanhuns in the Agreste of Pernambuco, which is the home of many small farms, eight out of nine small farms up to twelve hectares, including both minifundios and family farms, had a net farm income[5] which ranged from −52,000 cruzeiros to 189,000 cruzeiros, or from −187,000 to 63,000 cruzeiros per capita, with four farms having a per capita return considerably below 20,000 cruzeiros. The average income of the eight farms equaled about 66,000 cruzeiros but after taking into account all the producers' cash expenditures for food, clothes and other necessities, 4 out of the 8 farmers had cash deficits, and only one had a more significant positive cash balance. The low incomes of these farms seemed to be in large part the result of inadequate land or capital resources. A ninth farm of 4.2 hectares was well managed, had irrigated land and showed a net farm income of about 530,000 cruzeiros. The incomes of workers also fluctuated around a very low level. Take, for example, sharecroppers in the Northeast. In one community in the state of Ceará 10 sharecroppers on 4 latifundios—all with large families —earned a per capita cash income, after deducting farm operating expenses, of 12,000 cruzeiros, or 21,000 cruzeiros if items furnished by the landlord and home consumption are included. Since those interviewed had been allotted somewhat larger plots, they were slightly better off than their fellow workers on the same estates. After deducting expenses for food, medicine and clothing, average cash balance was 1,000 cruzeiros for the year (about $2.50 U.S.). If outside incomes of two croppers, one of whom worked as a carpenter, are excluded, the group's cash balance actually was negative.

Here is another case. Fourteen permanent resident workers in the rich cacao area of Itabuna in the state of Bahia earned an average annual cash wage of about 59,000 cruzeiros and earned 8,000 cruzeiros more cash income from off-farm work. After deducting expenses for necessities, their average cash balance was −37,000 cruzeiros and in fact 10

[5] Gross farm cash return less farm operating expenses, plus small amounts of other incomes.

of 12 workers had expenditures exceeding their cash income. The per capita cash income of 9 married workers with families was 15,000 cruzeiros per year. The homes furnished by the landlords and consumption of homegrown food from ceded plots were insufficient to prevent the workers from going into debt. Incomes of non-permanent, non-resident workers in the cacao plantations of the area are believed to be substantially lower, as they are only employed part time. In a community in Minas Gerais, the per capita cash income of 8 workers' families ranged from 14,600 cruzeiros for those living on the farm to 27,700 cruzeiros for those living on their own plots in a little village. But the benefits of the somewhat higher cash incomes in comparison to those of the workers in the North were offset by the higher living costs in Minas Gerais.

In the state of São Paulo, incomes of the bulk of the nearly one million sharecroppers, *colonos* and other hired workers are also very low. According to a government report, workers who receive their earnings from wages only earned in 1959/60 less than 50 per cent of the legal minimum wage. In evaluating this statistic it must be recalled that minimum wages are at a level which intends to provide the wage earners with a subsistence income. Even in the colonization areas of southern Brazil, as in Santa Cruz in Rio Grande do Sul, the incomes of small farmers and hired workers are by and large insufficient. With regard to colonization projects in general it has been observed that "the living conditions of the settlers are close to those of the poorest rural workers."[6] In this context it must be recalled that during the 1960's, the decline in real incomes in rural Brazil was very sharp.

On the other hand, estate owners reported incomes which were substantially higher. In the previously mentioned community of Garanhuns three large multi-family farms reported net incomes ranging from 880,000 to 3,700,000 cruzeiros. In all of the four communities mentioned, 7 farms with 500 hectares or more had an average gross income of 10.7 million

[6] CIDA, Brazil Report, op. cit., pp. 463 ff, 434 ff, 408 ff, 282, 546. The cruzeiro rose from 318 to 475 per U.S. dollar during 1962 at the official rate, but to 800 on the free exchange market.

cruzeiros and a net of 3.5 million cruzeiros, the two highest net incomes being 5.9 and 9.0 million cruzeiros. Obviously this did not include incomes from the other farms of the owners or from their non-farm sources.[7]

In Peru, no aggregate data are available on the distribution of farm incomes among various classes of producers or farm workers. A number of case studies of typical small producers and farm workers, however, throw some light on their economic and financial situation. For example, the annual average net income (gross farm income minus current farm expenditures) of 16 producers on minifundios on the coast amounted to about 14,000 soles; that of 27 independent small producers in the sierra, about 9,500 soles; that of 30 members of indigenous communities, about 8,000 soles; and that of colonos, 2,300 soles. The producers on the coast farmed an average of 1.8 hectares and those in the sierra, 2.5, 1.6 and 1.2 hectares respectively. Typical per capita net cash farm incomes in the sierra ranged from 831 to 1,313 soles annually for farm workers and small producers, but after accounting for their cash expenditures for food and other necessities, their per capita cash balances were effectively zero. A revealing picture is obtained also from the sixth population census in 1961, according to which 90 per cent of the rural hired workers earned yearly incomes of less than 10,400 soles, but about 55 per cent earned less than 5,200 soles. It is to be noted that these estimated annual earnings of the rural workers were based on weekly salary rates, which would normally overestimate the total earnings, since a large proportion of them are employed only part of the year.[8]

In Ecuador's sierra, as in Guatemala's altiplano, the incomes of the Indian farm families are extremely low. About 80 per cent of all minifundios—the bulk of the Indian farm population—live in the sierra and average annual farm production per minifundio, which is indicative of gross income earned, was estimated at 4,900 sucres; that of family farms at 34,000 sucres. In the coastal area it was 10,000 and 53,800

7 Ibid., pp. 459 ff.
8 CIDA, Peru Report, op. cit., pp. 71, 139, 266 and 273 f. 26.80 soles equal one U.S. dollar.

sucres respectively. Case studies of *huasipungueros* and other Indian workers in the sierra showed gross family incomes to be even less than 4,900 sucres. On one large hacienda, a typical *huasipungo* had a farm income of 1,788 sucres and approximately 2,700 sucres from cash wages earned by the huasipunguero and the people living with him. Per capita income was minimal, since families with 6–8 children are common. On another hacienda, the cash and imputed annual farm income of a huasipungo amounted to about 3,700 sucres plus 1,000 sucres from everybody's wages earned. According to a study recently undertaken by the United Nations Special Fund, the total annual incomes from all sources of two typical huasipungueros were 2,878 and 3,153 sucres respectively. Where farm workers obtained larger plots of land or had irrigated land, or where they could complement their income with other income earning activities, such as weaving, incomes tended to be slightly higher. For example, two small tenants, father and son, on 1.48 hectares of irrigated land belonging to an estate, produced principally tomatoes and had a net farm income (after farm cash expenses) of 24,515 sucres. Since this was a family of eleven, the per capita income was still only about 2,000 sucres. In one indigenous community, one "prosperous" member consumed the entire produce from his 7 tiny plots on poor eroded land and earned 5,400 sucres from the sale of weavings, saving about 2,000 sucres. But a poor family of four in the same community, with .35 hectare of land, did not raise enough food for its home consumption, sold 788 sucres worth of twine (*hilo de cabuya*) and had a deficit of 34 sucres after expenses for necessities of life, including additional food.[9]

If we summarize this dismal picture, it is clear that national statistics can only partially characterize the squalor in which millions of farm people in Latin America live. The available estimates from aggregate data and case studies in specific communities reveal income levels which imply a level of living at or even below mere subsistence for millions of peasants. If

[9] CIDA, Ecuador Report, op. cit., pp. 148 ff, 314 ff, 241 ff. 25 sucres equal one U.S. dollar.

ence crops without being included as "producers." Others are hired only for wages. The available evidence tends to support the view that pure wage workers, whose numbers are steadily growing throughout the hemisphere, are worse off than producers on sub-family farms, because of greater insecurity of employment and the lack of a certain, though often meager, supply of homegrown foods. However, they may be slightly better off in terms of access to cash. Obviously the averages in the above table obscure much larger income discrepancies in specific localities, such as in those where the Indians reside or in particularly fertile areas where speciality crops are grown.

It must be stressed again that the statistics on income distribution do not reveal the financial straitjacket in which small producers and hired farm workers normally find themselves. Not only are their incomes frequently no higher than their expenditures for subsistence, so that they have no savings, but they are frequently below their expenditures, leaving them with an annual cash deficit. Another indication is the importance of expenditures for necessities of life—particularly for food—even where food is grown for home consumption. It is not unusual to find that food expenditures run from 60–70 per cent of all cash expenditures, leaving little if anything for health, schooling or savings. Cash deficits are normally "financed" by loans or advances from employers, merchants or moneylenders, and renewed year after year. This perpetuates the vicious circle of low incomes, the urgency of buying food for survival and the need for contracting debts to buy them. A permanent debt situation intensifies the precarious financial situation of small producers and farm workers. It is obvious that the financial straits of the minifundistas and farm workers are not the result of extravagant living or abnormal appetites. They are the result of totally insufficient incomes.[11]

In addition, in most Latin American countries a rather

[11] Can farm peoples' incomes be at "less than subsistence" levels? In strict definition, incomes of this type would not permit their receivers to survive, at least not for long. If the minimum wages set by law are used as a criterion, then practically all wage workers have less than subsistence incomes. Minimum wage rates are defined as wages which give workers a bare subsistence income. Rural workers never receive the legal wage rates.

sharp inflation exerts a constant downward pressure on real incomes as increases in wage rates or in prices received by producers tend to be slower than increases in the prices of staple foods and other vital consumer goods.

CHAPTER 3

The Accumulation of Wealth and Its Distribution

The inability of small plot holders and farm workers to save a portion of their income for the purchase of durable or semi-durable household goods or for investments in the farm enterprise is reflected in their lack of material possessions. Since wealth reflects the accumulation of years of savings from incomes, it is to be assumed that the distribution of wealth in agriculture is significantly more unequal than the distribution of incomes. The scattered information available demonstrates that the bulk of poor farm families have few and primitive farm tools and few other belongings necessary for a comfortable homelife. Except for owners of minifundios, farm families do not generally own a home. Farm workers who are assigned a plot of land often find there a modest residence—usually an adobe or wood shack—which belongs to the landlord. If there is no home, it is customary for landlords to allow a worker to build one, using his and his family's labor. At times they have to buy the building materials with their own money, knowing fully that property in the construction lies with the landlords. But they still must agree to this condition because if they did not, they would be without a job. A few items of furniture and clothing and a few cooking utensils typically make up the total wealth in most farm workers' homes. At times, they own a sewing machine, which allows the wives to earn small extra incomes. Sometimes hired workers have to buy their farm tools out of their incomes, even if they work exclusively on the landlords' crops. If they are allowed by the employers to keep animals—a permission which is by no means always granted—they may have a few head of livestock, but these are limited to sheep, goats or hogs. In order to assure that their number is kept small, the landlords often require that part or all the offspring of this livestock is turned over to them.

We can give a few examples from recent field studies to illustrate the foregoing. In Ecuador, on a well-managed patriarchal hacienda, the farm "equipment" of a huasipunguero consisted of a few old tools and homemade utensils. His livestock consisted of a few sheep, hogs and chickens. The value of the fixed and variable capital, including the house, of an average huasipunguero on this estate amounted to 32,400 sucres, of which only 11,600 were for the operating capital; but this is a rough estimate because of the difficulty of estimating the value of very old assets. On another hacienda, 40 families of huasipungueros, of which 16 owned sheep, had among them a total of 1,444 head of sheep, apparently the major source of their farm income. The families occupied 180 hectares of heavily eroded land, on which they produced crops, and disposed of an unspecified but small amount of cattle and hogs. In another case, the total capital of two tenants (father and son) renting 1.48 hectares of land (and considered as having a slightly better than average income) was estimated at only 9,810 sucres, the operating capital consisting of a few tools, beehives and a sprayer. Another worker on the same farm, with an allotment of .74 hectare of land, had a total fixed and operating capital of 4,800 sucres.[1]

In Brazil the bulk of the farm workers with or without land, including small tenants and sharecroppers, have practically no assets whatever. The worst cases are the many thousands of homeless migrant workers who wander from farm to farm in search of employment with nothing but a small bundle (*bomba*) containing their belongings. Studies in eleven widely scattered communites reveal, for example, that the minifundios, which comprised up to 25 per cent of all farms, reported only 2 per cent of the total fixed and operating capital, while the latifundios (3 per cent of all farms) reported 33 per cent of the capital. These figures are based on the values reported to the Census of Agriculture of 1960 of the land,

[1] CIDA, Ecuador Report, op. cit., pp. 215, 286, 315, 320.

buildings, vehicles, animals, machinery and equipment. They underrepresent, however, the proportion of assets controlled by large estate owners because of the low values reported by them for the land and other capital items.[2] This underreporting completely distorts the available evidence of the distribution of wealth. An example was an estate owner who valued his 2,788 hectares at 5 million cruzeiros and his total assets at 8.1 million cruzeiros. A nearby small producer reported his 44 hectares also at 5 million and his total assets at 7 million cruzeiros. It is interesting to speculate in quantitative terms on the effects of the underreporting of land, the greatest source of a potential understatement of the disparities in the distribution of wealth, although by no means the only one. If the land of the large estates were valued at the same per-hectare figure as that reported by family farms, for the eleven communities, the value of all land in the estates would increase from 4 billion to about 9.5 billion cruzeiros.

Effect of Underreporting of Real Estate Values
on the Distribution of Wealth in Eleven
Communities in Brazil
(in million cruzeiros)
(1960)

Farm Tenure Class	Value of All Assets	Value of Land Alone	% Distribution of All Wealth (1)	(2)[a]
Minifundios	387	263	2	2
Family Farms	5,429	2,987	30	23
Medium Multi-Family	6,330	4,878	35	27
Large Multi-Family	5,909	3,963	33	——
Large Multi-Family[a]	11,437	9,491	——	48

[a] If land in large multi-family farms is valued at the same per-hectare value as on family farms.

It is to be noted that in nine communities included in the table (i.e., excluding two colonization areas) the minifundios

[2] The data also underrepresent the gap in the distribution of wealth because two of the eleven *municípios* are colonization areas where the distribution of wealth was significantly more equal.

did not report one single tractor, although one of the communities has thousands of minifundios. Less than 0.5 per cent of the jeeps and trucks and only 8 per cent of the tractors were on family farms. In four of the communities, there were no plows whatever on the minifundios, and all minifundios reported only 6 per cent of the plows. The latifundios alone, on the other hand, reported 73, 36 and 54 per cent of all tractors, plows and jeeps or trucks, respectively. None of these figures, of course, includes the possessions of hired workers.[3] A similar situation is found in Guatemala.[4]

It is interesting to observe that in Mexico, where the number of smallholdings is still excessively large, the distribution of farm equipment is also very unequal. Privately owned farms of less than five hectares reported only 2 per cent of the value of machinery, equipment and vehicles, while privately owned farms of over five hectares reported 67 per cent. Ejidatarios reported 31 per cent. As a result, average value of all operating capital on the larger farms (over five hectares) was about 8,000 pesos; of the smaller farms (less than five hectares), only 228 pesos; and of the ejidatarios, about 1,000 pesos.[5]

Value of Operating Farm Capital in the Private and Ejidal Sector of Mexico, 1960

Farm Sector and Size	No. of Producers	Value of Machinery, Equipment and Vehicles %	Value of Simple Farm Tools %
Private			
Farms over 5 ha	371,445	67	25
Farms less than 5 ha	756,915	2	27
All private Farms	1,128,360	69	52
Ejidatarios	1,455,225	31	48
All Farms	2,573,585	100	100

The available evidence tends to support the assumption that the distribution of wealth is considerably more unequal than

[3] CIDA, Brazil Report, op. cit., pp. 372, 348 ff.
[4] CIDA, Guatemala Report, op. cit., pp. 102, 73.
[5] 12.50 Mexican pesos equal one U.S. dollar.

CHAPTER 4

Living Standards and Income Distribution

The state of nutrition, clothing, housing and sanitation among the underprivileged people in rural communities is at substandard levels. But, as one Brazilian sociologist observed, no description can adequately render the squalor in which most of them live. In Colombia, for example, the majority of the population suffers from an "alarming chronic underconsumption of food" compared to diets which are considered adequate by Colombian experts, although due to the favorable tropical climate, there are no large areas of sharp undernutrition. However, 46 per cent of the rural and urban families have an inadequate intake of calories, and 48 per cent have an inadequate intake of protein. According to studies undertaken by the Ministry of Public Health, average per capita intake was 1,907 calories (2,300 recommended) and protein consumption, 46.3 grams (69 grams recommended). In one rural community near Bogotá, protein intake was 50 grams, of which two thirds were of vegetable origin. In another community, in Nariño, at an altitude of 3,000 meters, the per capita intake of calories was 2,036, of protein, 47 grams, with two thirds from vegetable sources. These averages hide substantial differences between the diets of lower and higher income groups. For example, in a community in Caldas, the average diet consisted of 1,863 calories, but the poor consumed only 1,401 calories, while the upper income groups consumed 2,889 calories. Meat consumption was minimal.[1]

In Ecuador, the diet of the Indian population is appallingly poor and monotonous. According to some case studies, the

[1] CIDA, Colombia Report, op. cit., pp. 217 f, 219.

consumption of alcoholic beverages, encouraged by village merchants and employers, is relatively high in the food budget although the actual amounts spent on alcoholic beverages are very small. (Alcoholic beverages are high in calories and offer some protection against cold weather.) The food produced by the farm workers on their small plots is insufficient to provide an adequate diet for their families. Often part of the produce has to be sold to provide cash for urgent needs and repurchased later at higher prices. Most of the foods are of the starchy type. One poor family of four in an indigenous community had an annual expenditure of 822 sucres for necessities of life, of which nearly two thirds went for food and alcoholic beverages, the remainder going for clothing, religious holidays and charity.[2]

In Brazil, official estimates indicate an adequate total supply of food in terms of calories per person. However, these statistics contradict research findings and field observations on the state of nutrition to the effect that there is real hunger and undernourishment in large parts of the country, perhaps particularly in the rural sector. This strange contradiction in a country with over 260 million hectares in farmland and another 600 million hectares of unexplored land can only be the result of an extremely unequal distribution of income. Instances where farm families have to go periodically without food are not rare. For example, a small farmer interviewed in the state of Pará had nothing available to eat at home on the day he was interviewed. The common diet reported for large parts of the country consists of coffee (no food value), yucca meal, sweet potatoes and, very occasionally, dried meat. In the state of São Paulo, farm families reported coffee for breakfast (no food value); rice, beans and vegetables for lunch; and for dinner, a soup made from the leftovers from lunch. Occasionally, there is meat, but this consists only of the cheapest cuts (mostly bones). In Paraíba, doctors reported that 80 per cent of the population is undernourished. In the state of Espírito Santo, depending on the area, 35 to 80 per cent of the population suffer from diseases caused by lack of

---

[2] CIDA, Ecuador Report, op. cit., p. 243. In parts of the Andean region, farm people are forced to contribute a portion of their earnings to the priests.

food or lack of vitamins; 50 to 80 per cent of the people do not eat meat frequently (in general only once a week). In Rio Grande do Norte a large part of the population eat once or at the most twice a day, and their diet is based (during the harvest) on brown sugar and meal in the morning, and beans and meal and occasionally sun-dried meat. It is noteworthy that Brazil, which according to official statistics has a surplus of carbohydrates, still found it necessary to supplement its reportedly sufficient supplies of calories with imports of more carbohydrates over a period of several years. It is estimated that the overall deficit of proteins and fats which now exists according to the official statistics, is likely to increase if food production and therefore the composition of domestic food supplies does not undergo radical changes. Furthermore, it was estimated that in 1963 a family of four to five people in Rio de Janeiro earning the minimum salary established by law and spending 50 per cent of its income on a diet consisting of 74 per cent carbohydrates, 11 per cent proteins and 15 per cent fat would, at the prices prevailing on June 1, 1963, be supplied with a daily average of only 1,200 to 1,500 calories. Since rural workers normally earn considerably less than the legal minimum wages, their diet must accordingly be considered inadequate. Even in the colonization area of Rio Grande do Sul, it was found that the situation of hired rural workers is compelling; they live in great misery and have hardly enough to eat and to clothe themselves though they toil from sunrise to sunset.[3]

These poor conditions with respect to diet throughout Latin America are equaled by conditions of housing, clothing, sanitation and education. The bulk of the farm population live in huts which are windowless earthen or straw shacks with dirt floors. Adults and children crowd into one or two rooms. There is no direct water supply and drinking water is frequently drawn from canals or brooks that double as sewers. Normally the water supply is relatively far from the house. There are no indoor or outdoor toilet facilities, and few doc-

[3] CIDA, Brazil Report, op. cit., pp. 33 ff, 550 ff, 296. The example of Rio de Janeiro is based on the average national diet. See also CIDA, Guatemala Report, op. cit., pp. 113 f.

tors or hospitals in the communities to which the rural population has access. Rarely do workers benefit from insurance and medical services. Witchcraft is still widely practiced in case of sickness, and usually the most primitive "medicines" are used, if any. Small producers and landless laborers rarely send their children to school except, in the best cases, for a couple of years to elementary school. In many regions there is not even this opportunity.

The distorted distribution of land is a fundamental cause of the sharp social stratification dating from the period of the colonial conquest and slavery, and characterized by a distorted distribution of income and wealth. In turn, the extremely unequal distribution of income reinforces the maintenance of a rigid class structure. Except in the very few regions where alternative employment opportunities exist or tenure arrangements are unusually good, annual incomes of the equivalent of about $250 U.S. are common; in some areas they average less than $100. In parts of the sierra of Peru, income per capita is reported as $15–$20 U.S. per annum, creating one of the lowest living levels in the whole world. One half to three quarters of the incomes of the poor goes for food, leaving little for clothing and other necessities. There is effectively no surplus (savings) from which to buy products of handicraft or of domestic infant industries whose growth depends on expanding internal markets.

CHAPTER 5

Rural Unemployment and Its Manifestations

In the Latin American context, employment (in its broadest sense) is the principal institutional mechanism for distributing income and opportunities among the masses of the people.[1] In other words, rural poverty is to a considerable extent, if not almost exclusively, attributable to rural unemployment and underemployment in the Latin countries, all of which are endowed with ample natural resources and a rich landed elite. In the following paragraphs, we shall briefly examine the extent of unemployment or underemployment and its manifestations, and subsequently establish why unemployment and underemployment are inseparable from a latifundio agriculture.

Although the concepts of unemployment or underemployment have caused considerable anxiety and endless academic controversy, it is now widely admitted that a large proportion of the rural population of Latin America is not gainfully employed full time or even part time, and that in the face of an increasing rural labor force, employment opportunities are scarce, and probably getting scarcer. Excess supplies of manpower are evident in practically all agricultural regions of Latin America. They are difficult to measure precisely, but there are a few quantitative and several qualitative indices which reflect their magnitude.

One approximate index of unemployment is the overcrowding of the rural labor force on smallholdings. It is significant that there exists in Latin American agriculture a

[1] Solon Barraclough, "Employment Problems Affecting Latin American Agricultural Development," *Monthly Bulletin of Agricultural Economics and Statistics* (FAO, Rome), July–August 1969.

highly uneven distribution of the labor force in relation to the farmland. In seven countries, for example, representing approximately two thirds of all Latin American agriculture, about 10.6 million rural workers, including family and hired workers, were reported by smaller farms (minifundios and family farms) totaling about 113.5 million hectares of farmland, including about 37 million hectares of cultivated land. The minifundios alone reported 5.3 million workers, although they controlled only about 11.4 million hectares, of which 6.3 million hectares were cultivated land. On the other hand, less than 10 million workers were reported by the multi-family farms, controlling about 376 million hectares of farmland and 80 million hectares of cultivated land. In fact, the large multi-family farms which controlled about 40 per cent of all farmland (probably a gross underestimate) only reported 3.7 million rural workers. It is therefore estimated that of the largest *producers* each has at his disposal on the average over 400 times more land than a smallholder and that each *farm worker* on the largest farms has on the average 44 times more land than a worker on the smallholdings. Thus land is a scarce resource only for the smallholders. If the relation between land and workers had been about the same on the larger farms as on the smaller farms, and assuming the same average quality of land,[2] levels of farm management and technology in both categories of enterprises, the multi-family farms could have employed 35.1 million workers instead of the 9.7 million they actually employed. The smaller farms obviously contribute more to rural "employment" than the large farms, considering their resources. The overcrowding of people on small farm units has no doubt increased during the 1960's.

It is also noteworthy that nearly 80 per cent of the hired workers were employed on the multi-family farms and that on the largest estates the hired workers outnumber the family workers by about eight to one.

[2] This assumption is not realistic, since the large farms generally occupy the best land. Much unemployment or underemployment is in fact attributable to the fact that the land on minifundios is usually of poor quality, exhausted and eroded from years of intensive cultivation.

Distribution of Land and Labor on Various
Farms and Composition of the Labor Force[a]

Farm Class	Farm-land (million hectares)	Cultivated Land (million hectares)	Total Labor Force (millions)	Family Workers (millions)	Hired Workers (millions)
Minifundios	11.4	6.3	5.3	4.4	.9
Family Farms	102.1	29.4	5.3	3.9	1.4
Multi-Family Medium	118.1	39.5	6.0	2.5	3.4
Multi-Family Large	257.9	40.7	3.7	.4	3.3
TOTAL	489.5	115.9	20.3	11.2	9.0

[a] In Argentina, Brazil, Chile, Ecuador, Guatemala, Colombia and Peru. The data refer to the 1950–60 period, based on CIDA statistics. More recent censuses show that the distribution of land and labor has tended to become still more uneven. For more up-to-date data on the labor force, see Part II, Chapter 10.

The excess supply of labor on the smallest plots can be estimated roughly by comparing their land/worker ratio with that of family farms, on the assumption that on family farms, workers are employed more nearly full time throughout the year with present techniques of farming.[3] Using this criterion, then, of the 5.3 million workers (exclusive of non-working members of their families) living on minifundios, 4.2 million, or about 79 per cent, were "in excess" in the seven countries.

Approximate Measure of Labor Requirements
on Minifundios

Actual Number of Workers on Minifundios	5,269,000
Computed Number of Workers on Minifundios[a]	1,079,000
Difference (Number of Excess Workers)	4,190,000

[a] Computed on basis of number of hectares per worker on family farms in each of the seven countries enumerated in the previous table.

[3] If even workers on family farms are not employed full time (as is shown for Chile in the text below), the computation becomes more complex; excess workers on family farms must then be added.

(Some of these workers may actually be employed part time on large farms.)

A more precise estimate of unemployment in agriculture was obtained for Chilean agriculture.[4] There, on the average, one third or more of the available labor supply was estimated to be unemployed in the sense that the same output could have been obtained with existing techniques and capital, but less labor, if work organization were changed slightly. Specifically, of about 536,000 active rural workers in Chilean agriculture in 1955, 173,000 were considered to be in excess of the number needed to produce the same output. It is interesting to note that in Chile there was an excess of workers in all classes of farms. Workers on minifundios worked on the average only five months out of the year; those on family farms, seven; on medium-sized multi-family farms, eight; and on latifundios, nine.

Evidence from other countries (including that provided by recent CIDA studies in Central America) is quite similar,[5] and a 30 to 40 per cent unemployment figure is now widely accepted. If one applied the ratios found in Chile to the other six countries for which data were given, agricultural output could be produced in the seven countries by approximately 14 million workers, or 7 million less than those actually employed. Widespread unemployment in Latin America has recently been demonstrated also for three Central American countries. For example, El Salvador had an estimated unem-

[4] CIDA, Chile Report, op. cit., pp. 515 ff, and Table XI–8.

[5] For example, in one area of the sierra in Ecuador, it was found that on three huasipungos the average number of days which an adult worker could potentially work was estimated at 212, 245 and 221 per year respectively, although it was not possible to ascertain how much work was actually performed on the plots. The work on the plots was supplemented by work on the estates, which appears, on the surface, to be a minor item, but was no doubt crucial for the total income. The ability of the huasipungueros and others living with them was above the actual work effort, hence additional work must be sought on the estates. Since there is often no additional work there, they see themselves obliged to work on the plots *although their participation there is not essential.* In other words, the work on the plots is partly contrived. CIDA, Ecuador Report, op. cit., pp. 215 ff. In Mexico, S. Eckstein, *El Marco Macroeconomico del Problema Agrario Mexicano* (Mexico: Centro de Investigaciones Agrarias, 1968), pp. 171 ff, estimated that unemployment is also very high, due to the continued existence of smallholdings.

ployment rate of 56.8 per cent; Nicaragua, of 29.6 per cent; and Costa Rica, of 3.2 per cent.

Of course rural unemployment must not be taken as evidence that Latin American agriculture cannot employ a much greater number of people on presently used farmland. Nor is it superfluous to note that excess labor does not imply a corresponding need for migration of workers out of agriculture, as some observers like to argue. There are many unutilized employment opportunities on existing farms, particularly on the large multi-family farms, and it is precisely the function of land tenure reforms to provide jobs for the workers who are now unemployed as well as for new generations of farm workers. In fact, given the high level of urban unemployment, one can no longer point to shifts of the labor force from primary occupations to the industrial and service sectors as signs of progress or economic development. It is true that during the last decades millions of farm people *have* migrated to the cities and villages and the proportion of the rural population has diminished. This has happened both in countries with incipient industrial development and those where industrial development has been practically nil. But many of these rural people living in urban slums are now unemployed or underemployed. Progress in the Latin American context can come about only after employment in agriculture has first been radically stepped up. So far, rural–urban migration has not eliminated rural unemployment.

It is reasonable to assume that, notwithstanding the constant migration of rural families to urban areas, unemployment in agriculture is increasing rather than decreasing, and that the factors which have contributed to bringing about unemployment also contribute to its intensification over time. Unfortunately, comparative statistics over a period of time are difficult to come by. But Brazil's recent censuses appear to confirm our assumption. In that country the number of farm workers increased from 12.6 million in 1950[6] to 15.4

[6] Actually the 1950 Census of Agriculture reported about 11 million farm workers; however CIDA, after careful examination of the available statistics, estimated that this census underreported the number of farm workers by about 1.6 million.

million in 1960, if one uses the preliminary census figures of 1960; or from 12.6 million to 15.6 million, if one uses the final census of 1960.[7] Either way, most of the added labor force was to be found on the smaller farms; *employment on the large multi-family farms decreased by 35 per cent*. (Even if, as we suspected earlier, the big estates had underreported their labor force, so that employment decreased less than the 35 per cent estimated from census data, it is still obvious that the owners failed to fulfill an important social function: to provide for new employment.) Thus the farms which control well over half of the farmland of Brazil reduced their labor force; and the proportion of the labor force on the smaller enterprises increased sharply, although they obtained only a tiny share of the additional farmland resulting from the geographic expansion of agriculture. For example, in 1950, the minifundios reported 11 per cent, in 1960, 20 per cent of the labor force.

There are three major factors which caused the sharp decrease of the labor force on the largest estates in Brazil. The first is the massive shift toward extensive livestock operations which occurred during the 1950's on the large farms both in traditional cropping areas and in newly opened frontier areas. Another factor is the larger proportion of permanent crops

[7] The Preliminary Census of Agriculture of 1960 was published in 1963, the final census in 1967, after the military coup of 1964. Normally final census data differ from preliminary data only slightly, after normal revisions of the computations and enumerations. But in the case of the final census of Brazil, a wholesale "adjustment" was made in the statistics which gave a radically different picture of Brazilian agriculture. The major difference consisted in the data on landholdings in large farms. Whereas the preliminary census had shown a huge increase in the holdings of the large estates (for example, the farms of 1,000 hectares and over had increased by 7.5 million hectares, with the result that the few additional farms in that group each accounted for an enormous additional amount of land), the final census now showed that these same farms had lost 7.8 million hectares. Total expansion of agriculture was over 33 million hectares according to preliminary figures; about 17 million according to the final census. In the classification used here (minifundios, family farms, medium-sized multi-family farms and large multi-family farms), the large multi-family farms lost about 5.4 million hectares, while the medium-sized multi-family farms gained about 14.7 million hectares, according to final figures. Those familiar with the development of Brazilian agriculture will find these final figures of doubtful value, but few people know of the existence of the preliminary census reports. Under the circumstances the preliminary census must be regarded as the more reliable one.

Shifts in Rural Employment in Brazil, 1950–60

Farm Class	Farmland (million ha)		Labor Force (million workers)	
	1950	1960	1950	1960
Minifundios	1.2	2.7 (2.7)	1.4	3.3 (3.2)
Family Farms	13.9	20.8 (20.8)	3.3	5.0 (5.0)
Medium-Sized Multi-Family Farms	78.9	93.6 (85.3)	5.2	5.4 (5.4)
Large Multi-Family Farms	138.2	132.8 (155.6)	2.7	1.9 (1.8)
TOTAL	232.2	249.9 (264.4)	12.6	15.6 (15.4)

NOTE: The 1960 data on farmland and labor force are based on the Final Census of Agriculture of 1960; the figures in parentheses are based on the Preliminary Census of Agriculture, the distribution of the labor force being an estimate.

requiring less labor. The third is the use of machinery; between 1950 and 1960 the number of tractors had risen nearly eight times, with an estimated four fifths of all the tractors being on the multi-family farms.

In conclusion, the contribution of the medium-sized and large multi-family farms to new rural employment in the face of a rapidly increasing rural labor force is at best disproportionately small.[8] As a general proposition it can be stated that in Brazil the contribution to new employment declines with the size of the farm. On balance it appears certain that no advances have been made toward fuller employment in agriculture during the decade, and it is apparent from the evidence that aggregate unemployment must in fact have risen. This must be regarded as a fateful trend from the point of view of the campesinos.

One of the telling manifestations of rural unemployment

[8] According to the final census, the medium-sized multi-family farms increased both their land and their labor (the latter slightly). The adjustments made in the census statistics (see footnote 7) make it appear as if the medium-sized farms, which controlled almost 40 per cent of the farmland, had now become nearly as important as the large estates. Nonetheless, the proportion of the labor force on the small farms (minifundios and family farms) rose significantly, although the land they controlled continued to be a tiny proportion of all farmland.

is the *forced geographic mobility of the peasantry*. This is the outward sign of a deep-seated malaise in rural Latin America, rather than evidence of a dynamic peasantry attempting to improve its economic and social status. By and large, farm people do not wander around in search of *better* jobs than the ones they have—they just look for *jobs*. Much of this migration proceeds in stages toward larger cities.[9] Its overall effect is to reduce the rate of increase of the rural population and labor force to between 1.5 and 2.5 per cent, but it is still not large enough to bring about an actual decline of the peasantry. The peasantry will, therefore, grow in absolute numbers through the 1970's and at least another decade thereafter. In fact, it may begin to increase at a higher rate again in the 1970's if, as is likely, employment in the non-rural sectors—industry, commerce and the services—grows at a reduced speed and if increasingly hostile slum conditions and unemployment in the cities discourage some rural–urban population shifts. The impact on the peasantry of reduced migration to the cities could be very serious.

Another shift of the rural labor force which has had some significance during the last decade was to non-rural occupations in the countryside. These occupations provide for better and usually much more effortless incomes. Wide business margins have provided incentives for many farm people to "get out of agriculture" into more remunerative and prestigious occupations, such as small store ownership, dealerships and trucking. However, without radical changes in the land tenure, production and marketing structure, these employment opportunities are now bound to become saturated and less remunerative.

The likelihood that non-agricultural employment in both rural and urban communities may increase at a considerably lower speed, thereby increasing still further the pressure of the peasantry on the land in the decade to come, cannot be entirely excluded.

Of considerably greater magnitude is the *seasonal or per-*

[9] Between 1950 and 1960, rural–urban migration in Argentina, Brazil, Colombia, Chile, Guatemala, Ecuador and Peru involved about 10.2 million people.

manent migration of farm people in search of jobs from one rural community to another. It is an impressive index of rural unemployment, although an aspect of rural life in Latin America for which there is still relatively little quantitative information. Most seasonal migration is in connection with the harvesting of export and industrial crops—coffee, cacao, sugar cane, cotton and others. Unemployed rural workers who migrate from their home communities in search of jobs in areas where the crops are grown, are never organized, although some of the hauling of workers is organized by labor contractors or the employers themselves—usually, of course, for a fee, which is then deducted from the workers' meager wages. The workers, who generally deal with the employers on an individual basis, must accept the wages offered them. Generally the supply of labor is much in excess of actual local needs, and employers encourage excessive migration by spreading rumors of labor shortages. Many workers remain empty-handed. From their low wages, migrants must frequently deduct the costs of transportation, and pay fees or bribes to labor contractors and farm managers. Seasonal employment is, from the point of view of the peasants, a degrading and unsatisfactory form of employment.

Large seasonal movements of labor are now a standard occurrence from Mexico to the southern tip of the continent. In Guatemala it was estimated that up to 200,000 persons from the altiplano yearly descend to the coastal regions to help in the coffee harvest there. According to other estimates, the total seasonal migration in Guatemala reaches as high as 300,000, practically all Indians, of which about one half migrate to the coffee harvest, the remainder to the cotton and sugar harvests. Using only the lower figure of 200,000, this represents about a third of the total rural labor force in Guatemala, or nearly one half of the labor on the minifundios. If the same shift were to occur in the other six Latin American countries for which we have given statistics in preceding tables, up to 2.5 million rural people—i.e., about 50 per cent of the labor force of 5.3 million on minifundios—would be traveling annually in search of seasonal employment alone. This may not be an unreasonable estimate, since most countries have important areas where export and in-dustrial crops are grown.

But not all migration within rural areas is seasonal. A good-sized proportion of the labor force is constantly moving from farm to farm, as "professional migrants." Their numbers are probably not even recorded in any census or other statistics. In Brazil's northeast, for example, it is reported that thou-sands of poor workers move around from place to place with their few belongings packed in a bundle (*bomba*).[10] This, too, is common throughout Latin America. Other migration may be longer-lasting when unemployed members of small-holders' families look for non-seasonal employment in other communities. A third type of rural migration occurs when farm people move spontaneously to unopened farm areas in search of land and a livelihood. In Brazil, as we have seen earlier, the settlement of such areas appears to have taken place on a large scale, but in most other countries this move-ment is only a trickle in comparison with other types of mi-gration.

All these population movements testify to a continuous, large-scale "milling around" of poor farm people in search of jobs or land, and involve annually several million people in the hemisphere—*no doubt the greatest migratory move-ment in all history*. Most people are unaware of this silent march of the poor.

The peasants' forced geographic mobility has, on balance, an increasingly damaging effect on the rural communities and probably on the uprooted peasants themselves, although this is apparently softened by short-run advantages. Seasonal mi-gration results in a geographic distribution of income. In a very few cases, however, it signifies a meaningful increase in the living standard in the place of origin of the migration, as with Mexico's "wetbacks," whose trips to the United States in the past allowed a few families to accumulate savings for reinvestment in their farm plots. Normally it is not sufficient to raise the status of the home communities above the level of poverty, although in Guatemala, for example, it serves the

[10] M. Correia de Andrade, *A Terra e o Homem no Nordeste* (São Paulo: Ed. Brasiliense, 1963), p. 116.

important function of preventing more starvation and misery. That migrants, notwithstanding low wages in the harvest areas, are able to bring home a portion of their earnings is testimony to their frugality and the real economizing of which poor people are capable. In communities that receive migrants, incomes of employers are higher to the extent that migrants' wages are lower than those paid to local workers. The latter lose out from the depressing effect on wage rates and greater unemployment.

Migratory labor is under prevailing conditions an almost unqualified advantage for rural employers, in that it keeps their local labor unemployed, submissive and cheap. The "beneficiaries" are, therefore, the migrants and the employers, although the benefits are obviously of a very different nature and are very unequally distributed. They are much more tangible for the latter.[11]

As to the social and political, as well as the psychological effects, the negative impact of migration on family life, community activities (including politics) and tenure status of the peasantry is serious. Migration is a heavy price to pay for "progress." Many migrants leave their families behind to take care of their homes or their land, at times for months on end. This disrupts family life, although some men are obliged to take their families along, depending upon the nature of the farm work to be engaged in—for example, in picking cotton, the able-bodied members of the families must also be put to work. This occurs in jobs paid "by the piece" (contract work), or when the men are hired only because of the "free" work of their sons and wives. The constant milling around prevents farm people from taking part in the activities of their home community and makes organized community life very difficult. Obviously migrants cannot share in the activities of the community to which they migrate, as they are considered

---

[11] There is now much talk about increasing the "mobility of labor" in connection with international regional integration schemes. Obviously there is no need to increase the geographic mobility of rural labor. But if conscious policies were to be established, as the result of international agreements, to allow the international movement of rural labor, this might have a depressing effect on wages under the conditions which prevail, and further impede the organization of the farm labor force.

unwelcomed outsiders. Most important, migration puts an end to the efforts of rural workers to organize into syndicates or leagues. Migrants are no doubt frustrated men without hope.[12]

All these consequences of migration are not lost on the landed elite. A shiftless, marginalized rural proletariat is their best ally in their campaign against organized labor, of which more will be said later. A decimated community from which many members migrate and where the men are gone most of the time, can easily be controlled. Migrants can be supervised by the police or the military in an area which is not their home. As proletarization of the peasantry expands, the marginalization of the peasantry will undoubtedly increase in the 1970's.

Another manifestation of unemployment and peasant restlessness is the large number of *invasions of land* owned or claimed by latifundistas, or of public land. Land invasions have been very frequent in the 1960's, particularly in the first half of the decade, and occur in all of Latin America from Mexico to the southern tip of the hemisphere. Their origin lies in the increasing lack of access to the land resource of a growing rural labor force, i.e., the increasingly tight control of a small landholding class over these resources, including those in the outlying areas not yet opened to farming. In some cases, land is invaded because of the peasants' historic claim on it. Much farmland has been—and is still being—acquired by estate owners through force or guile, by evicting indigenous communities or individual peasants and taking away, by force or fraud, land that belonged to them. In other cases, landless

---

[12] It is important to note, however, that many migrants who are able to work on farm enterprises using advanced farm and labor management methods, have acquired considerable skills. Some of the veteran cotton pickers, for example, are not only fast workers, but they also have learned from traveling. In a recent study in Mexico it was found that many migrant workers can intelligently discuss important political, economic and social issues and are much better informed than farm workers who do not leave their community. Of course this does not necessarily increase their economic status. In one cotton-picking area of Mexico (Apatzingán) the migrants are obliged to sleep on the public square and have no facilities whatever offered by employers. Although the heat in the area is intense, employers have no water facilities on their farms, and the workers are obliged to buy soft drinks at exorbitant prices.

peasants group together to take over idle land in areas of heavy population pressure because it does not "fulfill its social functions." Most invasions are on a small scale, involving isolated estates, but at times invasions are so numerous that they force the governments into significant land reform measures (as in Venezuela) or large-scale repressions (as in Peru in the early 1960's). Generally they are merely a passing phase in the generations-long fight of the peasantry for the acquisition of land.

Land invasions demonstrate that peasants can successfully carry out collective action to further their own welfare. Most invasions are carefully planned and executed. The participants are well integrated and aware that the "cards are stacked" against them from the very start: the law and law enforcement agencies protect owners or possessors of real estate property even if they hold the land illegally, and particularly if they own larger estates. The invaders often concentrate on properties where they can count on a maximum of public—although not necessarily government or police—support. The invasions of an estate in Algolán (Peru), for example, capitalized on the hostility engendered by the management of the enterprise in the region. In Colombia, the first land reform project was undertaken in an area where peasants had invaded land of owners who did not exploit and never visited their farms. The invading peasants usually make a careful study of the legal and factual status of the land and know its weaknesses. In some cases, invaded land is sold by willing estate owners to a land reform agency, as in Venezuela, where a large proportion of land reform beneficiaries were originally invaders and where the landowners were compensated by the government through high expropriation prices.

Invaders are at times prepared to regard their act as symbolic and to withdraw from the premises in order to avoid bloodshed if the police or the military arrive to remove them. They are "testing" the law and law enforcement and are prepared to act within the law in a non-violent manner. The real or symbolic redistribution of the land to peasants demonstrates good knowledge of ecological conditions and agricultural potentials, and the peasants' plans are often on a par with the much more elaborate and costly settlement schemes prepared by land reform or colonization agencies. This is not surprising, since peasants often know local agricultural conditions better than outsiders. There are also instances where the military does not care to oppose public opinion in favor of the landless, or even sides with them, in which cases the peasants remain on the land they invaded. But these are rare instances.

Few authors have dealt with the character and scope of peasant invasions, most of which are unknown to the general public.[13] In Mexico, for example, statistics on land invasions are kept confidential, but it is well known that they occur very frequently each year. It is reported that in Venezuela an estimated 500 invasions of expropriable land took place at the beginning of the reform process in the late 1950's and early 1960's. The lands invaded were frequently those taken away from peasants after 1948. Cases are known where the police helped the peasant leaders to give the occupation of lands an orderly course. In Colombia, the land reform institute helped legalize several invasions organized in lands which were disputed between peasants and landlords but which were basically public property. For example, along the Magdalena River on the Atlantic coast, several local priests and the Catholic workers' organization (FANAL) headed by Eugenio Colorado helped to organize the peaceful invasions of such lands. Such invasions were justified by FANAL on the condition that peasants who claim land are in real need.

The largest unsuccessful occupations of land took place in Peru in the early 1960's. They were unsuccessful in the sense that this movement was put down by military force and did not result in a nationwide land reform, or in a regional expropriation process of the landed elite. Since large military operations against the invaders were accompanied by a news blackout, few details are available and its history still remains

---

[13] For a recent account of several cases of invasions of estates, see Almino Affonso, et al., *Movimiento Campesino Chileno* (Santiago, Chile: ICIRA [Instituto de Capacitación e Investigación en Reforma Agraria], 1970), Vol. II, pp. 107 ff.

to be written. It began in a semi-tropical region in the state of Cuzco (Valle de la Convención) and spread over most of the Andean region, involving an estimated 300,000 peasants. It was therefore the largest peasant movement in this decade. The peasants claimed that they recovered lands of which they had been deprived and which were promised them again by the presidential candidate. The occupation of the huge Algolán estate, to which reference has already been made, took place after the owners prohibited the indigenous communities to graze their cattle, as they had been doing traditionally. Whole communities, including men, women, children and their cattle, passed the newly built fences and constructed symbolic living quarters on the invaded lands, where they settled until the police came to throw them out. This was repeated in various parts of the estate on such a large scale by a group of communities organized into a federation that there was no other solution than to come to an arrangement with the peasants. The estate was bought by the government and became one of the few projects of the Peruvian land reform. (An equally large invasion movement had taken place in Bolivia in the 1950's, resulting in a country-wide reform.) Invasions are also reported from Chile, Brazil and Central America. Normally only large invasions are publicized by the press and many go unnoticed, although they occur constantly.

Land invasions are here to stay. Many invasions have been repressed by police and military action throughout the 1960's, but it can be predicted that they will grow in scope and severity in the forthcoming decade if the peasants' hunger for land is not satisfied.

Finally we should add a few comments on *spontaneous colonization,* which was mentioned earlier in connection with the constant large-scale migration of farm people in search of employment and land. The spontaneous settlement by peasants of outlying regions has taken place, throughout Latin America, for generations; still, very little is known about its exact scope, the fate of the settlers, and its impact on their home communities or the new communities which they establish (if one can talk about "communities" there in the accepted sense). Spontaneous settlement is no doubt a relief valve for peasants living in overcrowded farming areas where unemployment is high. But its importance as a mechanism to relieve unemployment must not be overrated: it can take up only a very small proportion of the net increase in the rural population.

Some people have a rather idyllic view of this type of agricultural expansion which springs from an exaggerated opinion of the virtues of "free enterprise." They believe that the peasants move out to the wilderness, clear the ground of trees and rocks and within a few years become prosperous farmers. No doubt there are isolated cases of this type. But reality appears to be most often quite different. Only the most robust or adventurous, or the most desperate peasants, can migrate into virgin areas without roads, schools, hospitals, doctors and even neighbors. Although they presumably possess a few savings before they can undertake the voyage to areas distant from home, they usually begin their new life with next to nothing in terms of capital resources. Their fight against Nature is incessant. The plain truth is that most of the settlers begin and end their lives in these outposts in great poverty, because with their primitive methods of farming, quickly exhausted soils and distant markets, their ability to save is practically nil.

Although spontaneous colonization is minor in comparison to other forms of migration, it is widespread enough to cause considerable concern about wastes of important national resources of soils and forests. The necessarily primitive farming methods of the settlers have brought about continuing destruction of valuable forest areas and considerable soil erosion, the effects of which are felt far from the settlement areas. But as long as peasants remain unemployed in the traditional farming communities and as long as they are prevented from gaining access to land there, spontaneous colonization will continue. It is difficult to conceive of a realistic agricultural policy, other than a real land reform, giving land and employment to the peasants, which can put an end to this waste of human and physical resources.

The main beneficiaries of spontaneous settlement in the

long run are not the settlers but the landed elite and the real estate investors. From their point of view settlement was and remains a convenient tool to expand their landholdings, since they can buy, occupy or simply claim the cleared land (very often in connivance with local or state officials) and crop it or use it for pasture in extensive livestock operations. Then, unless the settlers have the stamina to move to new virgin areas and begin the same processes all over again, they become sharecroppers or hired workers of the new owners. Attempts of the new landlords' strong-arm men to dislocate the settlers have in some cases resulted in bloodshed. The fact is that spontaneous settlement has been a simple and cheap device to expand the latifundio system into new areas. Only with the disappearance of the system in the traditional farming communities can the virgin areas of Latin America be developed and settled for the long-run benefit of the peasantry.

B. THE LAND

When, as in Latin America, agriculture depends heavily on manual labor, of which there is an overabundant supply, the quantity of employment depends on how land is distributed among the farm people and on labor-intensive land uses. *New* employment depends on the redistribution of farmland and on the expansion of the labor-intensive land uses. We must therefore now take a look at the patterns of land distribution and land use and their relation to the employment of farm labor. Briefly, we wish to show that the peasants have access to land only under unfavorable conditions at best, and that the manner in which most of the farmland is being used is a strong impediment to raising employment.

CHAPTER 6

Is Land a Scarce Resource?

We must first briefly examine whether there is enough land to be made available to Latin America's poor peasants or whether land is a scarce resource, as some observers maintain. The "land" we are speaking about is above all farmland, now controlled by multi-family farms, on the assumption that in a land reform process it could be redistributed to the peasants, and land in virgin areas potentially suited for agriculture. Of course we should not wish to imply that the quantity of land is the sole determinant of the satisfaction of the peasantry. Much depends on the manner in which land is used and the capital invested in it. But as a rough approximation, let us assume that land is available for use at average levels of farm management and technology prevailing in the 1960's. The supply of land must be established in light of the potential need for it. For reasons of simplicity, we will assume that land is to be made available at a certain rate to all those peasants who now hold farmland in inadequate amounts as well as to the landless farm labor force.

The following table shows for ten Latin American countries the number of poor rural families without land or with inadequate amounts of land (8.7 million in 1960); their land needs, if each of these families were to be given the amount of land now in family farms; the average size of family farms in each country; and the total amount of land now in multi-family farms. It is apparent that for the ten countries as a whole, the amount of land in multi-family farms alone exceeds the land requirements of the potential land reform beneficiaries by about 120 million hectares. In some countries—Argentina, for example—there is apparently not enough land in the multi-family farms to distribute family farm units to the countries' potential land reform beneficiaries, and some of the families would have to be settled on the virgin areas, which, with the apparent exception of El Salvador, are plentiful. Hence it is almost absurd to speak of a scarcity of land resources in Latin America in an aggregate sense or for individual nations, now or in the foreseeable future.

Estimated Land Requirements and Availability of Farmland for 8.7 Million Potential Land Reform Beneficiaries in Ten Countries[a]:
A Rough Approximation

Country	Potential Land Reform Beneficiaries (thousand families)[b]	Average Size Family Farm (ha)	Land Needs (thousand ha)[e]	Land in Multi-Family Farms (thousand ha)[d]	Total Area in Country (thousand ha)
Argentina	467	343	154,166	90,360	277,666
Brazil[e]	4,525	16	71,535	240,900	851,197
Chile	244	32	7,779	25,668	75,695
Colombia	961	17	14,556	16,995	113,834
Ecuador	500	26	12,509	4,082	27,067
Guatemala	514	15	6,950	2,157	10,889
Peru	960	9	5,808	15,001	128,022
El Salvador	249	22	5,047	909	2,094
Honduras	183	14	2,280	1,454	11,209
Nicaragua	99	15	1,379	3,260	13,900
TOTAL	8,702	50	282,009	400,776	1,511,573

[a] As of 1960, approximately.
[b] Families on minifundios and of workers without land.
[e] Additional hectares needed by smallholders to increase their holdings to the size of a family farm and land needed by landless workers for the same amount.
[d] Medium-sized and large multi-family farms.
[e] Based on the 1960 Preliminary Census of Agriculture.

Actually, the statistics presented in the table are very much on the conservative side, for several reasons. There is in all likelihood more land in multi-family farms than reported. This implies that there are more hectares from land already in agricultural uses available for redistribution to the campesinos than is apparent from census data. For example, one Peruvian agency has claimed that in Peru's sierra there are eight million more hectares in pastureland than are reported by the census. This makes a total of seventeen million instead of the nine million hectares reported, and many additional thousands, or even tens of thousands, of campesinos could receive this land. A similar conclusion could be reached for a country like Guatemala, where, according to the 1964 Census of Agriculture, the area in farmland actually decreased since 1950. Farms or portions of farms have apparently been abandoned. But this land has not disappeared and it can be assumed to be potential farmland formerly in large estates available for distribution to peasants. Specifically the "abandoned" 632,000 hectares—representing the decline in land in farms of 450 hectares and over during the 14-year period—could benefit 28 per cent of the landless peasants at the rate of 15 hectares per family. (Of course in these cases the land should be deducted from the land not yet in agriculture but potentially suited for it.)

In some countries, like Argentina, where many family farms are located in the pampas region, ecological conditions have tended to raise the average size of the family farm for the country as a whole, resulting, in our simple calculation, in high average land requirements for reform and distorting the picture of land availabilities. A still more important factor is, of course, that the statistics reflect a static picture of agriculture. They are based on present patterns of land use, farm management and levels of technology. This applies both to the "model," the family farm, and to the multi-family farms which are to be, theoretically, turned over to the campesinos. With better land use and management and greater availabilities of production-increasing inputs to farm people, many more workers could find employment on the available farmland. In other words, the ratio of manpower resources to land is not merely a simple relation between the number of rural workers and the number of hectares in farmland or in virgin areas suitable for farming; it is also a function of the intensity and type of land use, farm management and the level of technology, all of which can be determined by appropriate agricultural policies. Better policies can hardly be expected as long as latifundismo continues to dominate Latin American agriculture.

Finally, we should briefly comment on our assumption that *all* poor families shall, as land reform beneficiaries, receive family-sized allotments. This does not necessarily imply that all poor families should actually "receive land" in the sense of a simple redistribution of farmland now in multi-family farms or, if necessary, in virgin areas. The formulation that all landless workers and smallholders should "receive land" is apt to be misleading, unless one conceives of land reform only in a simplistic way as a tool for the uniform establishment of family farms for all peasants. How many campesinos will actually "receive land" in the narrow sense of a redistribution in individual farm units and how many will receive other benefits (e.g., higher wages and social security) depends on the type or types of agriculture to be established and the tenure systems adopted. The use of the "family farm" in this context is only for convenience, on the assumption that, at present, labor on these farms is more fully employed than on other farms. (We are not advocating family farms for Latin America.) But it does not necessarily affect the availability of land for redistribution to the peasantry. Regardless of what "model" is to be used, the important point is the overall relation between the land resources and rural manpower, not necessarily under what new form of tenure the land is going to be held.

Apart from the fact that there appears to be more than ample land for securing full-time employment for every farm family in Latin America, another important conclusion emerges from the information provided here—namely that *there is by and large no need for large-scale transfers of peasants to outlying areas in order to provide them with land resources,* as some people have suggested. The colonization of virgin areas may become a necessity once the presently used farmland has been occupied and population pressures become very strong in future generations. But colonization at this time does not present a solution for the latifundio system and its land tenure problems. This is not to deny, of course, that there are regions in Latin America where the rural population is fairly dense, where local land may be scarce under existing conditions, and where farm people will have to be induced to seek land in other established rural communities or even in virgin areas if this would be more convenient. As a general rule, proposals for increased colonization are designed to bypass the land tenure problems posed by latifundismo.

CHAPTER 7

The Shrinking Land Base of the Campesinos

We now turn to another important question, which we must explore in some detail: control over land resources. In agrarian societies such as those of Latin America, land is traditionally the main source of wealth. "As a result, the control over land largely determines income, wealth and power. Income from land, however, cannot be realized without labor. Therefore, the distribution of property rights in land is necessarily accompanied by a system of interpersonal and intergroup relationships. In brief, landownership is closely associated with the power to make others do one's will."[1] This argument holds also in those Latin American countries with an incipient domestic industry, because of the close interrelation between the ownership of land and the ownership of industrial and commercial enterprises.

It is now amply demonstrated that in all countries the distribution of farmland is more unequal, and that a larger proportion of farm people live and work on an excessively small land base, than had been known prior to the beginning of the Alliance for Progress. Much additional information on the pattern of land distribution has come to light in recent years and we will not belabor this issue here, although it will be unavoidable to undertake some detailed analyses of census statistics. Less well known is the fact that the inequality in the distribution of the land resources seems to be increasing. The most complete information is available from ten Latin American nations with a total rural population of nearly 70 million in 1960, which represents about 70 per cent of the

[1] Solon Barraclough, "Why Land Reform?" in *Ceres* (FAO, Rome), November–December 1969, p. 22.

entire rural population of the hemisphere, excluding Cuba.

In these ten nations, according to official statistics, multi-family farms, that is all farms on which more than four people are actively engaged in farm work, controlled on the average about 76 per cent of the farmland. But these farms represented only about 17 per cent of all the individual farm units reported. The large multi-family farms alone—2 per cent of all farms—controlled about 46 per cent of all farmland. In the other nations of Latin America which are not included here, these inequalities are similar, although the situation in Bolivia and Mexico is somewhat more complex.

In reality the data underestimate—perhaps significantly—the true control over the land resources exercised by the small landed elite. As previously noted, there appears to be more land in the large estates than actually reported. In Peru, for example, it has been estimated by a government agency that the total amount of land in the sierra was seventeen million hectares, not nine million as claimed by the Census of Agriculture of 1960. Since most of the sierra farmland is in large landholdings, this enormous gap can best be explained by the owners' consistent underreporting.

Another source of inaccuracy is that many estate owners own not one, but several farms of various sizes. It is not possible to estimate multiple ownership accurately from available statistics. Cases where estate owners controlled dozens of large estates, as in pre-revolutionary Mexico, are probably rare today. But the ownership of two, three, six or eight large holdings is by no means rare. What is more, estate owners often own and buy up smaller holdings in their insatiable hunger for more land, and they have the material means to buy up small and large units alike. They buy up land for speculative reasons or to prevent the peasants from getting it, or because more land simply means more power.

Account must also be taken of the fact that in many cases farmland is owned not only by individual owners, but by *families* whose members each own several estates. This means that a large proportion of the farmland remains under control of a small number of estate-owning families whose combined social, economic and political power is enhanced, even on the assumption that some members of these families quarrel among each other.

In a sense, of course, the statistics on land distribution are grossly unfair to the rural population, because they leave out the large proportion of rural families who do not have any land. If farm families without land are included in the distribution of families with or without land, the proportion of families owning large multi-family farms declines to 1 per cent, and approximately 72 per cent of all families have no land, or not enough land to cultivate on their own. (Workers without any land represent about 40 per cent of all farm families.)

Statistics on land distribution alone are also inadequate, because they do not take into account the quality and location of land. Here quantitative information is sorely lacking, but field studies lead to the following conclusions. If the amount of land under cultivation is a high proportion of all farmland, as it is in the smallholdings, this cannot be taken as evidence that the land is on the average of high quality. On smallholdings, producers must cultivate all or most of their land, regardless of its quality, in order to make a living, within the limits of their labor and capital resources. Conversely, the high proportion of pastureland and fallow or unused land in large estates is not evidence of a low average quality of land, because much good, potentially cultivable land is used on these enterprises extensively or not at all. The use of the land is not merely a function of its quality; more important, it is institutionally determined. Even casual observation suffices to show that smallholdings are usually of inferior quality, as the best land is occupied by the estate owners. Most smallholdings are located on eroded hillsides and other poor soils, often of difficult access. Large estates usually have the bottom, or most fertile, soils. Small tenants and sharecroppers are systematically given the poorest portions of the estates (except when cultivating on shares commercial crops in which the estate owners have a direct interest)—for example, if the owners also produce these crops on their own account with the help of wage workers. Normally the best soils in estates are not "leased out" for cultivation by campesinos.

Where large estates and smallholdings share land in irrigation schemes (as in Mexico, for example), smallholders often receive excess water supplies only after the needs of the large estates have been filled. This is equivalent to saying that smallholders often do not obtain any water if water supplies are not abundant, and at times not even when they are. There are instances where smallholders are even forbidden to use water flowing in canals or ditches through or near their plots, under threat of punishment. In exceptional cases, smallholders may occupy good land. This occurs in the fruit and vegetable belts of large cities, in areas of alluvial soils subject to flooding and not occupied by anyone, in areas of invasions, or in areas of spontaneous colonization in outlying districts.

In summary, the inequality in the distribution of land resources appears to be significantly greater than is shown by available statistics. Multi-family farms probably control up to 80 or 90 per cent of all farmland, and the large multi-family farms alone probably control as much as 60 per cent. This inequality is compounded by the poorer quality of the land of smallholders.

Is the inequality declining or is it increasing? This crucial question has to be examined in two dimensions: in terms of changes in the distribution of land over time, and in terms of the increasing pressure of the rural population on the land.

The trends observed in Brazil and Guatemala may serve as an illustration, but an introductory comment is necessary. The average size of the larger farm enterprises is declining, at least in the older established agricultural communities. This has been taken by some observers as an indication that concentration of land ownership is declining. It is the result mainly of the inheritance process whereby large estates are subdivided among heirs. The phenomenon of subdivision is offset, wholly or partially, by multiple ownership; however, this does not appear in the available statistics. It is obviously not the consequence of the sale of farmland to campesinos, or of the redistribution of land through the land reform programs, as we shall show in detail in another chapter. A decline in the average size of larger farms could be indicative of less concentration of farm ownership only if part of the land previously controlled by the estates had shifted to the smaller farms, and if, at the same time, there does not occur a significant increase in the number of smaller farms. If the number of smaller farms increases sharply without much land being added over and beyond that which is added through the breakup of the larger units, then their average size is also bound to decrease and one could hardly speak of a decline in the concentration of land ownership. This has been demonstrated, for example, for a small area of the central part of Chile,[2] and Brazil and Guatemala seem to offer further evidence.

In Guatemala, the average medium-sized multi-family farm declined from 165 hectares in 1950 to 150 hectares in 1964, and the large multi-family farms from 2,944 to 2,303 hectares. At the same time, the total amount of land in the two groups declined by about 530,000 hectares.[3] In Brazil, the average size of all farms over 100 hectares declined from 644 hectares in 1950 to 609 in 1960 (or to 565 hectares if the final census figures are used). Farms exceeding 5,000 hectares, however, increased from an average of 15,116 hectares to 16,696 hectares (but decreased to 13,912 hectares in the final census). All farms over 10,000 hectares increased from an average of 28,125 to 31,000 (but declined according to the final census). An analysis of these figures shows that the increase in the average size of very large units was the result of the expansion of agriculture in Brazil's still largely unpopulated frontier areas. Therefore it can be assumed that in the countries with large unoccupied areas, into which agriculture moves slowly over time—and most Latin American countries still have areas of this type—the declining average size in the large estates in older farming communities is partly offset by the establishment of new large estates in the new agricultural communities.

To what extent the declining size of larger farms has been

[2] CIDA, Chile Report, op. cit., p. 10.

[3] Family farms, minifundios and microfincas gained 258,000. The total area in farmland declined, therefore, by 272,000 hectares. These figures are of course subject to the underreporting of landholdings in the large estates, described earlier, for other countries.

offset by rising multiple ownership during the last ten or fifteen years must of course remain speculation. Economic and political conditions for increased multiple ownership of large landholdings through repeated purchases of farm properties by rural and urban real estate owners certainly have not been unfavorable. Along with urban real estate, farm property is a preferred investment, as it can withstand (and even at times gain in the race against) the effects of inflation. Returns from rural property are not negligible, although they are lower than those from investments in other sectors of the economy. However, the difference is made up at least partly by the rise in rural real estate value resulting from the rapid increase in population, and by relatively profitable prices for agricultural commodities during the 1950's and 1960's.[4]

But regardless of multiple ownership, and without as yet taking into account the changing structure of smallholdings, the landed elite has definitely held its own between 1950 and 1960, and all indications are that it has done the same during the 1960's. According to the census, the multi-family farms in Brazil controlled about 93 per cent of all the farmland in 1950 and 91 per cent in 1960 (or 95 per cent if the final census data are used).

We must now take a closer look at trends affecting smaller farms in Brazil and Guatemala, because trends observed with respect to the large farms are meaningful only in comparison to the number of family farms, minifundios and microfincas and the land they control.[5] In both countries, the number of smaller farms has been rising dramatically. In Brazil, as we saw earlier, the number of farms of less than 5 hectares rose during the 1950's by about 575,000, and those between 5 and 10 hectares by about 214,000. All small farms up to 10 hectares increased by 110 per cent. The additional small farms accounted for 62 per cent of all new farm units. However, they increased their landholdings only by a total of about 2.9 million hectares, representing about 9 per cent of the farm-

[4] See in this connection R. H. Brannon, "Low Investment Levels in Uruguayan Agriculture," *Land Economics* (Madison, Wisc.), August 1969, pp. 304 ff.

[5] In Guatemala, microfincas have less than .7 hectares.

land added to agriculture during the decade. Of the 575,000 new farms of less than 5 hectares, each counted on 2.3 hectares of additional land, and the 214,000 units between 5 and 10 hectares on 7.2 hectares of additional land. In other words, each new farm unit counted on less additional land than the average unit in these two categories controlled in 1950. *As a result, the average farm size of the small units (up to 10 hectares) decreased from 4.3 to 3.9 hectares, with the relatively largest drop in the smallest units.*

A comparison between small and large farms shows, therefore, that each new producer on farm units between 100 and 1,000 hectares counted on 225 additional hectares (230, if the final census data are used); and each new producer on all farms exceeding 100 hectares counted on nearly 4,000 hectares if the data of the more plausible preliminary census of 1960 are used (only 58 hectares according to the final census). This high average is the result of the enormous area which each new producer added to the farmland in the categories of the largest farm units, which exceeded their average size in 1950.

In Guatemala, the census reported about 69,000 new farm units between 1950 and 1964, of which 57,000, or 83 per cent, were smallholdings not exceeding 7 hectares, and nearly 11,000, or 16 per cent, microfincas of less than .7 hectares. In most categories the average size of the small units declined also. As in Brazil, this is the result of the fact that the amount of land of each new producer was less than that of the average farm unit in 1950. But in Guatemala there is also the phenomenon of the total decline in agricultural land between 1950 and 1964. Did the land which the large farms abandoned actually benefit the small units? Did it result in less concentration of land ownership? Of the 632,000 hectares reported to be abandoned by farms of 450 hectares and over, at best only a small portion (i.e., about 108,000 hectares) could have benefited the 57,000 new farm families on farms up to 7 hectares, and about 253,000 hectares could have benefited the 12,000 new farm families on units between 7 and 450 hectares. The remaining 272,000 hectares abandoned apparently benefited no one. But the assumption that part of the abandoned land benefited smallholders is valid only if there was an actual transfer of this land to the smallholders, i.e., if the additional land in the new smallholdings did not stem from previously unoccupied areas, which Guatemala, like Brazil, disposes of in large quantities. Since the land distribution which took place on a large scale during the land reform of 1954 was later reversed and the land restituted to the estate owners, it is probable that the addition of the 108,000 hectares to the smallest holdings was not in fact an actual transfer. In any event it would have involved only a small quantity of land, insufficient to raise the level of living of the campesinos. Hence it is apparent that the reported decline in the amount of land controlled by the large estates did not consist of a large-scale transfer from the large to the small producers.

These tedious statistics point to an important fact: with the increasing pressure of the campesino population on the land resources, characterized by a progressively larger number of farm families forced to live in the aggregate on a relatively shrinking land base, *the degree of concentration of farm ownership remained at best the same but may have tended to increase.* According to calculations made by the Guatemalan census, for example, the index of concentration declined slightly from 96 to 94 per cent between 1950 and 1964.[6] This calculation, however, must be viewed with caution in light of the systematic underreporting of land by the large estates which we suspect is practiced in Guatemala and throughout Latin America.

From every point of view, the most serious development for the peasantry is the declining average size of their smallholdings. It is true, of course, that the average size of the larger holdings also declined. But obviously the problem is serious only for the smallholders whose land base is initially too small for more than subsistence living. In countries with enormous land resources, like Brazil, and with huge areas in estates, this has been an absurd development. It implies that smallholders on the average must become poorer. The output

[6] *Censo Agropecuario,* Tomo I, January 1968, pp. 65 ff; particularly Table 9, p. 71.

potential of their progressively deficient land base has not been offset by any significant or large-scale policies to secure greater access to production-increasing inputs or increase their bargaining power in the input and output markets.

CHAPTER 8

Land Use Patterns as a Source of Stagnation and Unemployment

We must now focus our attention on one of the basic reasons for unemployment of rural manpower: the manner in which the land in large estates is used by the landed elite, and trends observable in current land use practices.

Latin America's agricultural output has increased over the past thirty years, but per capita output has declined by 8 per cent. The hemisphere compares poorly with other parts of the world. In the last ten years agricultural output has lagged behind population growth in ten of the twenty Latin American countries, and has exceeded it in five countries by a margin of less than 1 per cent. Thus the whole region seems to be experiencing a performance crisis, with the livestock sector being its weakest link.[1] Since both the rural and the urban population already live on inadequate diets, food shortage may be possible with present rates of development. Many Latin countries are spending increasingly larger portions of their foreign exchange on food imports. Chile, for example, is now reported to spend one half of its foreign exchange earnings on food imports, most of which could be grown domestically. Without such supplemental imports—some of which are donated—severe food shortages could be imminent.

The observed absolute increase in total output is sharply affected by activities in the export sector, which consists principally of plantation crops. Output of plantation crops, for example, rose by 45 per cent over approximately one decade, whereas the combined product index increased by only 28

[1] ECLA/UN, *Economic Survey of Latin America, 1966, Part Four*, E/CN.12/767, Add. 3, 17 March 1967, pp. 6 ff.

per cent in seven of the most important nations of the hemisphere.[2] It has also been established that the increases in the output of food and fiber which did take place have been achieved primarily by increasing area rather than yields, reflecting extensive farm management practices. Over a period of approximately ten years, the area cultivated in twenty-four crops (including the most important staple foods, cotton and tobacco) increased in Latin America by 24 per cent, whereas yields increased by only 7 per cent. In contrast, in the world as a whole, the respective increases were 14 and 21 per cent. Of the twenty-four crops studied, only six, covering less than 14 per cent of the cultivated area, showed increases in yield exceeding 10 per cent, whereas in the world, fourteen crops showed strong yield increases and covered about 87 per cent of the cultivated area. The livestock position appears to be even worse. North America and Europe, with approximately 110 million head of stock each, produced more meat than Latin America, with nearly 200 million.[3]

There seems to be no obvious sign that past trends can be sharply reversed in the foreseeable future. A major reason for expecting no change is the structure of Latin American agriculture, i.e., of latifundismo and its concomitant minifundio sector. Since the estate sector occupies such a large proportion of the agricultural land, it follows that the poor performance of Latin America's agriculture is to a large extent a reflection of land use patterns and farm management practices in that sector. In the following pages, we shall analyze these patterns and practices and examine their impact on the employment of farm people.

It may come as a surprise to some that the big farm enterprises are generally poorly managed, and that the producers on smaller farm units are, within the limits of their labor and capital resources, quite efficient in the exploitation of their land. The belief that quality of management and efficiency of resource use increases with the size of the farm is based on the myth, propagated by the large landholders themselves,

---

[2] Argentina, Brazil, Chile, Colombia, Ecuador, Guatemala and Peru.

[3] ECLA/UN, *Agriculture in Latin America: Problems and Prospects*, E/CN.12/686, 6 April 1963, pp. 34–39.

that nature has endowed the wealthy with greater insights, resourcefulness and intelligence and therefore put them in a commanding position. It is true, of course, that by modern standards the producers on small units also utilize their land at low levels of management. But they are forced to do so by circumstances. They do not have easy access to land, credit, machinery, improved seeds, and fertilizers because they are excluded from the markets of these inputs through the action of the landed elite. Possibilities for better performance at the initiative of the peasants are systematically undermined by the landed elite and progressive peasants and peasant leaders are penalized. It should be kept in mind that one of the reasons for analyzing the performance of the latifundio sector is to demonstrate that the poor utilization of land and water resources is inherent in the latifundio system, and pursues in part political and social objectives such as the preservation of a cheap and obedient rural labor force.

An outstanding aspect of land utilization is the predominance of extensive land uses on large farms. As a general rule, farm size is inversely related to the proportion of land in intensive cultivation. In seven important countries, representing almost two thirds of Latin American agriculture, the combined amount of cultivated land (which includes annual and permanent cropland, artificial or improved pastures, and fallow or idle land) is 24 per cent of all land in farms, but only 16 per cent on large multi-family farms, which control about one half of the total farmland area. The percentage of cultivated land on the medium-sized multi-family farms is higher than on family farms (about 33 per cent). On minifundios 55 per cent of the land is cultivated. That the proportion of cultivated land tends to decline as farm size increases is a phenomenon found almost universally in all countries, both at the national and the local level. Although latifundios control nearly twenty-three times more land than minifundios, the amount of cultivated land on the former is only about six and a half times larger. Similarly, latifundios control two and a half times more land than family farms, but cultivate only about 40 per cent more land than the latter. In three of the seven countries (Argentina,

Colombia and Ecuador) the amount of cultivated land on family farms exceeded that on the latifundios, and in Brazil it about equaled it.

Nearly one half of the farmland in the combined seven-country area was in natural pastures and another 20 per cent in forest and bushes. The large amount of land in pastures—and to some extent also that in forest and bushes—is indicative of the importance of the livestock or cattle industries, particularly to the latifundios, which control about 55 per cent of all pastureland. Hence about 27 per cent of all the farmland is in pastures controlled by the latifundios. (See Appendix Tables II–III, pp. 105–6.)

Cultivated land is theoretically land which is now or had recently been seeded to some crops and pasture. For the seven countries combined, the area in permanent or annual crops (approximately 41.5 million hectares) is 36 per cent of the total cultivated area, but this represents only about 8 per cent of all farmland. About one fourth of the cultivated area (26 per cent) is in improved or artificial pasture and 38 per cent is idle or fallow. It is also evident that the proportion of land in crops alone is considerably higher on the smaller farms. On the latifundios, land in intensive crops is only about 4 per cent of all the land they control. In view of the enormous amount of land in large estates for the seven countries as a

Land in Annual and Permanent Crops as Per Cent
of All Farmland on Large Multi-Family
Farms in Ten Countries

Country	Per Cent in Annual and Permanent Crops
Argentina	2
Brazil	4
Chile	4
Colombia	3
Ecuador	6
Guatemala	15
Peru	4
All Seven	4
Honduras, El Salvador and Nicaragua	11

whole, it is significant that the total amount of hectares in annual and permanent crops on the latifundios is considerably
smaller than that on the family farms. This holds true also in
Argentina, Colombia and Ecuador, whereas in Brazil and
Guatemala the amount of cropland is about the same, and
in Peru and Chile it is higher on the latifundios although not
proportionally higher in view of the land they control. Recent studies in Central America show also conclusively that
extensive land uses on large farms are indeed a continent-
wide phenomenon. A summary picture of these discrepancies
is found in the following two tables.

Various Land Uses on Family Farms and Multi-
Family Farms as Multiple of Minifundios
in Seven Countries (A) and Three Central
American Countries (B)[a]

A.

Farm Class	Cultivated Land	Natural Pastures	Forest and Bushes	Other Uses Including Sterile Land	Total Land in Farms
Minifundios	1.0	1.0	1.0	1.0	1.0
Family	4.6	15.5	15.2	6.7	8.9
Medium Multi-Family	6.2	14.3	21.3	12.7	10.3
Large Multi-Family	6.4	38.8	62.6	33.6	22.6

B.

Farm Class	Cropland	All Other Uses	Total Land in Farms
Minifundios	1.0	1.0	1.0
Family	.8	4.0	1.8
Medium Multi-Family	.8	9.7	3.6
Large Multi-Family	.6	10.5	3.6

[a] Amount of land in each use as multiple of the amount of land in such uses
on minifundios. The countries included in A are: Argentina, Brazil, Chile, Colombia, Ecuador, Guatemala, Peru; in B: Honduras, El Salvador, Nicaragua.

There is apparently no uniform relationship between the amount of land in permanent crops and farm size. For the combined seven-country area, the importance of permanent crops tends to increase with the size of the farm, but this is principally accounted for by Brazil, which reported over one half of the 8.0 million hectares of permanent crops, with over 80 per cent being reported by multi-family farms. It is to be noted, however, that the total area planted in permanent crops is only a very small proportion of the total farmland, even in countries where they are an important source of foreign exchange earnings. For example, in Guatemala it is 4 per cent, and in Brazil only 2 per cent of the total land in farms.[4]

The predominantly extensive land uses on large estates could conceivably be explained on the grounds that the average quality of the land owned by hacendados is inferior to that owned by small producers. Reference to the comparative quality of land in small and large farms has already been made. It is difficult to prove or refute this argument with accuracy. If the argument were valid, it would imply that small peasants all over Latin America have succeeded in pushing estate owners out into marginal farming areas. Given the prevailing power structure in agriculture, this is not a very plausible explanation. Overall, good land in the hands of small producers appears to be the exception rather than the rule. Flat valley bottoms, irrigated land and fertile plains —whether intensively cultivated or not—are normally in the hands of the hacendados and eroded mountainsides are studded with minifundios and micro-plots.

The inverse relationship between the proportion of intensively used land and farm size seems to hold true, as noted earlier, in smaller geographic areas. But equally remarkable is that even in areas of intensive agriculture, such as those devoted to industrial or export crops, the proportion of the land in latifundios on which such crops are raised is small.

---

[4] It is interesting to note that, in contrast, resources other than land going into the production and marketing of these crops (government subsidies, price supports, priority access to fertilizers and credit, institutional organizations, etc.) are greatly in excess of resources of this type going to all other products.

To give a few examples, in Itabuna (Bahia, Brazil), the center of Brazil's cacao area, which earns substantial foreign exchange for the country, the large estates which control 50 per cent of the farmland have less than .5 per cent in annual crops, 13 per cent in permanent crops (cacao) and 62 per cent in natural and artificial pasture for their growing livestock herds. In Ecuador, a foreign-owned estate of about 12,700 hectares located in the fertile coastal area typically had 5,150 hectares in bananas, cacao or coffee, but 6,060 hectares entirely unused. Sugar plantations throughout Latin America have areas devoted to pasture which exceed by a multiple the area in sugar cane—allegedly to raise oxen for the transportation of the cane, although it is never clear why this has to be pure-bred cattle. Obviously the owners hold this extra land not so much because it is needed for the production of sugar, but because it affords them a greater control over the land resource. *Hence, intensive cropping is not synonymous with intensive land use.*

One point must here be clarified: a small *proportion* of land in crops still implies, because of the large size of the estates, many *hectares* in crops. Large producers each have seven times more total cropland than producers on family farms, and forty times more than producers on minifundios. With or without livestock enterprises on the extensively used land, crops can yield good economic returns for their owners, the members of the landed elite. From the point of view of the peasants and the economy as a whole, however, the present underutilization of the land implies less food and less rural employment.

Improved or artificial pastures as well as idle or fallow land occupy an important share of the farmland. With some exceptions, like the growing of alfalfa in irrigated zones, artificial pasture is the least intensive of the intensive land uses. (In fact, the terms have several meanings, ranging from land seeded in high-protein grasses or legumes for hay or silage for livestock, to unimproved but fenced-in pastures.) If the 30.6 million hectares of artificial pastures are added to the 239 million hectares of natural pastures, then at least 55 per cent of the agricultural land, or close to 60 per cent of

Average Amount of Cropland per Producer in Seven Countries, around 1960[a]

Farm Class	Annual Crops	Hectares per Producer Permanent Crops	Total Cropland
Minifundios	1.3	.3	1.6
Family	7.9	1.2	9.1
Medium Multi-Family	12.3	3.5	15.8
Large Multi-Family	48.5	16.9	65.4

[a] Argentina, Brazil, Chile, Colombia, Ecuador, Guatemala, Peru.

the land controlled by the latifundios alone, is used for live-stock (mostly cattle).

We must now comment briefly on another aspect of land use, namely field rotations or shifting agriculture. Nearly two fifths of the cultivated area, or 9 per cent of the total farm-land, is idle (fallow), i.e., land formerly cultivated, but now resting or recovering for future cultivation. And 43 per cent of all idle land is in latifundios. On the small farms the amount of cropland exceeds idle land by a large margin, but on the latifundios, the reverse is true. In fact, on latifundios, idle land comprises more than twice the amount of cropland for the combined seven-country area of Argentina, Brazil, Chile, Colombia, Ecuador, Guatemala and Peru. The trend toward a higher proportion of idle land on the estates is observable in each of these countries, as well as in El Salvador and Nicaragua, although in El Salvador the family farms had, on the average, the highest proportion of idle land.

Leaving land idle and holding land "in reserve" is in many parts of Latin America evidence of a shifting agriculture in which there is no crop rotation, but land or field rotation. (This includes the primitive "slash and burn" method, which is still widely used on all types of farms). The fact that large estates have relatively more idle land cannot be taken as evidence of better land use practices. Enormous areas are left fallow or idle because, for the Latin American estate owner, land is not a scarce resource, and improved land management methods just are not in his scheme. It is one of the methods whereby the landed elite maintain their control over the land. Small producers who may wish to let their normally overutilized soils recover find that their limited land and financial resources do not allow this practice.

When soils become exhausted by continuous faulty cultivation and poor management, estate owners often convert their farms into livestock (cattle) enterprises or shift to new land in relatively unsettled and uncultivated frontier areas. This is another aspect of shifting or "migrating" agriculture which occurs in several countries, particularly in Brazil, on a very large scale. There is still an immense frontier in Latin America; the total land area, as we have seen earlier, exceeds the land in farms by about 230 per cent in the ten countries which we have used repeatedly as examples (the total area being 1.5 billion hectares, while the total agricultural area is only 498 million hectares), and the existence of additional land has been historically conducive to extensive land uses even where economic and physical conditions justify more intensive uses. Unless the access to unused land is better controlled, it will be difficult to convince large producers that soils have to be managed with greater care.

The expansion of agriculture into new areas might be taken as an indication that in the older farming communities there is not enough more good land available for cultivation. But this is an argument which is not supported by any evidence. The amount of "cultivated" land (or cropland) is not a good index of potentially cultivable land *now in farms,* except perhaps for the smallest units. There are untold millions of hectares now in extensive use which could be used more intensively from both the agro-technical and economic views. Examples are numerous. A typical case is the valley of the Cauca in Colombia, where in one proposed irrigation district, a flat and fertile area with a highly favorable climate, a substantial proportion of the land in the large estates was in pastures, although it was perfectly suitable for intensive cropping. In Colombia 635 estate owners of farms of over 2,000 hectares (averaging about 11,000 hectares) reported in their declarations made to the Institute of Land Reform (INCORA) that two thirds of the land controlled by them was unutilized and obviously a good proportion of their holding could be cultivated. A similar significant case is the Central Valley of Chile, where on the latifundios, which controlled 81 per cent of the farmland and 78 per cent of the irrigated land in 1955, about 51 per cent of the irrigated land was in natural or improved pastures destined for livestock, and 28 per cent was in natural pastures alone. Although this part of Chile has undergone important changes, the situation still holds. Even in the highlands of Peru, now mostly devoted to raising sheep, competent agronomists hold that crops, adapted to the altitude and the short growing season, could be raised in many areas. There is widespread evidence that in the past, crops were in fact raised in these areas, but in their hunger for land, the estate owners deprived the Indian population of their holdings and incorporated them into their more convenient and lucrative sheep-production enterprises.

There is, therefore, no doubt that much more land in the estates controlled by the landed elite could be used for crops. But the expansion of the cultivated areas and better land management cannot now be expected from the latifundio sector, because it would require their undivided attention, the reinvestment of their farm earnings in improvements (which would allow an increase in the cultivated area), and their much fuller identification with the interests of the farming communities. And since this would also imply much fuller employment of the labor force, at higher wages and under better working conditions, it would run counter to their strategy of maintaining a cheap and obedient, partly unemployed labor force.

Since 1950 the fundamental patterns of land use do not appear to have undergone significant changes, with the exception of a few qualifications made below. If land use has been intensified in some instances—for example, on modern enterprises producing export or industrial crops or on modern dairy farms—it appears definitely to have been offset by less intensive land uses elsewhere. This development has escaped many observers of Latin American agriculture. As a general phenomenon, the intensification of land use seems to have taken place on individual farm enterprises, operated by profit minded entrepreneurs, rather than on an area basis, while the opposite appears to have occurred with respect to shifts from intensive to extensive uses, such as those involved in shifting from cropping to livestock. A detailed study of these trends cannot be undertaken in this context, but Brazil may serve as an example.

Brazilian agriculture expanded by about 33 million hectares or about 14 per cent according to the more plausible Preliminary Census of Agriculture of 1960 (or by about 18 million according to the final census). Cropland increased by 10.5 million hectares, or by about 15 per cent. According to reliable estimates, about 4.6 million hectares of the new cropland, or nearly 45 per cent, is accounted for by the minifundios and family farms, although these two farm classes accounted for only about 9 per cent of all farmland in 1960. The remaining 5.9 million hectares represent the increase in cropland in all multi-family farms, which controlled about 91 per cent of the farmland. Hence the smaller farms contributed more than their share to cropping. During the 1950's, the large multi-family farms increased their cropland less than family farms, so that in 1960 the latter had about as much land in permanent and annual crops as the former, although they controlled only about one seventh the farmland. That land use is increasingly intensive on the smaller farms is evidenced by the fact that of the 1.5 million hectares of farmland added to the minifundios during the 1950's, 1.2 million (80 per cent) were cropland. On the latifundios, only 2.5 million (14 per cent) of the additional 17.6 million hectares of land were in crops. Hence the importance of the large estates in the growing of crops tended to diminish slightly; in 1950 their cropland was 28 per cent of all cropland on Brazilian farms, but in 1960 it was 27 per cent. (A similar conclusion can be reached using even the final census data.) This is significant in view of the fact that the large multi-family farms captured about 54 per cent of all new farmland added during the decade. A further implication of these trends is that the cattle industry appears to play an increasingly larger role on the estates, because of the enormous increase in the area in pasture.

Developments in Brazil are not unrepresentative for the Latin American hemisphere.[5] Extensive land uses, particularly on the largest landholdings, have not been replaced by radically expanded cropping; in other words, traditional patterns of land use have by and large been maintained. What is significant, however, is that the contribution of the smaller farms to the cultivation of crops in general and domestic consumption in particular has tended to increase, notwithstanding their lack of access to land and capital resources.

Another characteristic of land use also appears to have undergone little change: namely, the traditional separation of cropping ("agricultura") and livestock ("ganaderia"). There are few signs that pressures to maintain this separation are abating. The traditional split between "agriculture" and livestock farming implies that livestock enterprises are managed on an extensive basis and that extensive management of livestock compounds the extensive use of land. Although serious efforts have been made in some countries to improve the livestock industry, intensified operations on a few progressive cattle ranches or dairy farms are offset by the type of livestock enterprises which develop in newly opened farming regions, or on estates which shift from "agriculture" to cattle. There, poor cultivating practices are simply carried over to the new livestock business. The role of the smaller farms in intensifying the livestock industry in Latin America is not significant, because most of the cattle are owned by large landowners. Usually only sheep, goats or swine are found on small plots, and in small numbers. The smallholders' land base is inadequate for larger animals and they receive neither credit nor technical assistance for buying or improving their livestock. In addition, the landlords do not allow their tenants or sharecroppers to keep any animals without their express permission. But permission is usually given only if part or all of the offspring of the livestock is turned over to the land lord. In fact, the attitude of the landed elite vis-à-vis livestock production by small producers is entirely negative. It can therefore be concluded that the performance of Latin Amer

[5] In some countries, the area in crops has even decreased over the decade, although for a given census year, this could be attributable to climatic factors.

ica's cattle industry is shaped predominantly by the estate sector. The impact of the traditional separation between "agriculture" and livestock has not yet been explored systematically, although its negative effects on land and soil management, agricultural output and rural employment must be taken for granted. But characteristically it seems to be intimately related to the monopolization of the livestock industry by the landed elite, in connection with their underutilization of the land.

It cannot be overlooked that a small but growing number of Latin American farms are operated with modern methods. The landed elite and those who are allied with it use the few examples of progressive farming as constant reminders of the progressiveness of latifundismo itself, and its advantages for the economy in general and the peasants in particular. The modernization of agriculture affects principally the technological and financial aspects of farm management: mechanization, the use of improved seed and fertilizers, irrigation, and rational bookkeeping and profit-calculating methods. It does not affect the basic social structure and human relations in agriculture, except in isolated instances. Modernized farms can be found among small enterprises (for example, fruit, vegetable or dairy farms), as well as among large properties, such as intensive cattle operations, enterprises specializing in the production of rice, cotton and sugar, or modern plantations. (Plantations are by no means synonymous with modernized agriculture, as later examples demonstrate.)

It is very important to realize, therefore, that the blessings of a small modern sector in the midst of a latifundio system are entirely mixed. The progressive sector makes an important contribution to total agricultural output, although it occupies only a tiny fraction of the total land resources; but it also makes a disproportionate demand on other resources, such as credit, farm machinery and equipment, and receives innumerable government services and subsidies. No wonder, then, that during the past decade efforts made by governments and individual producers to modernize farm enterprise have resulted in benefits for the economy as a whole, in the form of larger supplies of agricultural products, including foods for domestic production. But few benefits for the campesinos have resulted from these changes. In some respects the development has been decidedly unfavorable to them. This stems from the fact that the growth of the commercial sector takes place within the framework of the traditional latifundio agriculture. While commercial agriculture still remains a relatively minor sector, it benefits from some of the important elements which give strength to latifundismo, and sees no need to change them: the existence of a cheap, unorganized and obedient labor force and general agricultural policies and institutions, the benefits of which are reaped principally by the estate sector. For that reason, in the progressive commercial sector, wages and living conditions of the campesinos are generally no better than they are in the remainder of agriculture. At times commercial agriculture is accompanied by some of the most abusive labor management practices known. More often than not, the development of commercial agriculture in a latifundio agriculture is accompanied by a sharp increase in migratory labor, with all its disadvantages for the campesinos and the communities from or to which they migrate. On the other hand, a few plantations which employ large amounts of labor have been the seats of pioneering labor organizations which have succeeded in wresting from management concessions for their members in terms of better wages and employment conditions.

To the extent that this small commercial, modernized sector draws on an increasing proportion of the nation's resources other than land, the campesino sector—smallholders, sharecroppers, tenants and laborers—remains at an increasingly larger disadvantage if there are no countervailing government policies. We shall return to this subject in the last chapter.

Before we turn to the implications on employment of continued extensive land uses in the face of a rapidly growing farm labor force, we must first make a few comments on some little-known farm management practices which are found to exist on the estates, because they are closely related to land use and agricultural performance. In drawing attention again to the estate sector, we do not wish to imply that poor farm management practices are not to be found also on the smaller farms. They are. But they are much more significant for Latin America when they occur on the former, not only because the estate sector owns most of the land, but also because the owners have easy access to all the inputs which enable them to operate their land along the highest levels of management and technology. But the estate owners do not make use of these possibilities, and cannot do so, because this would mark the beginning of the end of the latifundio system. For this reason it is not uncommon to find, for example, that the members of the landed elite subscribe to domestic and foreign farm journals, and are acquainted with the contents of recent publications on modern farming practices and technological advances, but rarely apply their newly acquired knowledge to their properties.

There is widespread belief that the quality of farm operations increases with farm size. This erroneous belief is based on two grounds which are themselves founded on a superficial evaluation of facts. Technological improvements, when adopted, are used almost exclusively by a few large farms. This gives the impression that the estate sector as such is progressive. But the adoption of technological improvements is not necessarily synonymous with improved management. Secondly, the enterprises which produce industrial or export crops have expanded output more rapidly than other sectors; but this does not take into account the facts that their owners receive strong public and private support and much publicity, that they are the beneficiaries of the general tendency to starve that portion of agriculture which is devoted to domestic food crop production, and that many institutional arrangements are entirely geared to the welfare of the estate sector.

It has previously been pointed out that the increase in agricultural production in Latin America was chiefly attributable to an extension of the cultivated area, since average unit yields had improved little. In other words, production would fall were it not for the continuous incorporation of new, still unexhausted lands. The average yield per hectare of nineteen important staple crops, for example, expressed in physical terms, increased by only 5 per cent over a twenty-year period.

Even some important export crops show similar trends, and the available information on livestock production reveals totally inadequate management practices.

The low yields of crop and livestock can be attributed to a number of factors which are often closely interrelated.[6] There are, for instance, the primitive systems of cultivation, the scant use made of fertilizers or improved seeds, deficiencies in water utilization, the poor livestock feeding (mainly because of seasonal shortages of food and inefficient pasture management), the generally low standards of animal health and genetics, and the lack of integration between livestock and crops. All of these are closely related to the low educational level of the rural worker, the system of land tenure in force, and, in general, the lack of an agrarian policy that would stimulate the application of modern technical methods on a broad scale. All this is intended to bring out one fundamental point: the gradual destruction of the land's productive capacity that can be observed in many agricultural areas of Latin America. Even when trustworthy data on soil destruction in Latin America are not available, there are manifest signs of it in most countries—dune formation and advance, marginal areas of cultivation, impoverished pastureland, etc. This process has assumed alarming proportions, owing to the lack of soil conservation practices and, to a large extent, the lack or insufficient use of fertilizers to replace the nourishment that the crops extract from the soil. Even though fertilizer consumption increased more than fivefold in Latin America during the last fifteen years, it is still very low in absolute terms, especially in comparison with levels in other regions of the world. In fact, in the 1959/60 crop year, the total amount of fertilizers consumed in Latin America (in terms of nutrients per hectare) was equivalent to only 10 per cent of the total in Europe, and little more than a quarter of the consumption in Oceania and North America. Chile, for example, which is a major producer of sodium nitrate, does not use more than 7 per cent of the total amount consumed by Japan, with an arable area of about the same size. In many

---

[6] For the following observations I am indebted to ECLA/UN, *Agriculture in Latin America: Problems and Prospects.*

parts of Latin America the arable area was enlarged at the expense of the forests, without a proper conservation policy. This has meant that, with the passage of time, large tracts of land have become useless for both timber and crops, since most deforested land is unsuitable for permanent crop or stock farming.

These general remarks from United Nations studies can be substantiated by a few examples from the recent land tenure studies of CIDA. These examples reflect not only prevailing farm management practices, but also the attitudes of the landed elite toward various aspects of the operations of their holdings. In Guatemala, for example, both traditional and "modernizing" estate owners were encountered. Members of the conservative group regard the advent of changes in the *status quo* (regarding the use of their land) with disfavor, and prefer to maintain the traditions and customs existing in agriculture. Among them is a large number of coffee growers. Members of this group are not interested in improving their plantations, but in continuing the monoculture without technological changes. They are openly opposed to social progress for the workers, which would be the inevitable consequence of technological progress. On two estates visited on the Pacific coast, for example, the owners did not allow agricultural extension agents to enter the premises. According to the agents, this is not a rare attitude. These operators are highly suspicious and believe that extension agents or other experts come to their farms for reasons not related to agriculture. On the other hand, there is a group of estate owners with advanced ideas who accept technical and social changes and seek to diversify agriculture, although it was not possible to determine how numerous this group is.[7] The negative attitude of many estate owners toward technical experts is not peculiar to Guatemalan estates or plantation owners. Only in rare instances do large producers seek the advice of, or employ technically trained people, whom they could afford to hire; nor do they give their own workers a chance to acquire training and skills in various fields, except at times in the

[7] CIDA, Guatemala Report, op. cit., pp. 81 ff.

handling of motorized equipment. In the latter case, they usually take advantage of free facilities offered by machinery and equipment dealers. This negative attitude on training is particularly significant as far as their farm managers are concerned, about whom a few comments will be made later.

In Brazil, the operation of large crop and livestock enterprises, including the coffee, sugar and cacao plantations, is generally at a low level, with the exception of the newer agricultural enterprises of southern Brazil. To a large extent, methods of farming are no better than those of the Indians generations ago. Only the simplest farm tools operated by hand are in use in large sections of the country. For example, in the cattle zone of Santarém (Pará) in the Amazon River Valley, livestock production is carried on under the most primitive conditions: the farms are located near the river and cattle production is affected by periodic swelling and receding of the water, as well as by the pattern of land distribution. Producers who have no land in the higher areas leave their cattle on wooden constructions surrounded by water and the cattle are fed grass swimming on top of the water, which may be up to two feet deep. Those who have land higher up transport their cattle by boat or walk them. During the winter, the cattle become "walking skeletons," which implies a long delay in reaching adequate weights for marketing. There are very large losses during the transport back and forth from the higher areas to the lowlands. It has been reported that if the recession of the water in the river is delayed by one month, it is possible to lose up to 30 or 40 per cent of the livestock maintained in the higher land.[8] One cattle disease causes large losses although it can be cured by relatively simple treatment. In the case of one producer who had 970 head of cattle, death losses amounted to 130 head (apparently none of the cattle were lost in other ways). Similar losses were experienced by other producers.

It might be argued that this is an extreme example, because it is reported from a rather distant community. But it has been noted that Brazil's cattle industry has generally low pro-

8 CIDA, Brazil Report, op. cit., pp. 488 ff.

ductivity and output because of a number of management factors. This fact is significant in the light of the high concentration of cattle on large farms. According to the Preliminary Agricultural Census of 1960, about 104,000 farms with over 100 head of cattle reported nearly 34 million (61 per cent) out of a total of 55.7 million head of cattle, but 13,600 farms with herds over 500 head reported about 30 per cent of all the cattle. Cattle are practically unknown on the small farms. Inadequate feeding, animal diseases and pests, problems regarding breeding techniques, the type of land tenure systems, and inefficient farm management are the main obstacles to the development of Brazil's livestock industry. One typical management factor is the seasonal forage shortage causing severe losses. It has been reported that up to the time of slaughtering for beef cattle, the seasonal pasture shortage amounts to four three-monthly periods of under-nourishment for each animal, making a total of twelve months, which means that for six to eight of these months the cattle are living off their own fat. Consequently it takes four to five years to condition cattle for slaughtering. Regional losses can be illustrated by the case of Rio Grande do Sul, where the recorded deaths from starvation during the winter forage amount to almost a quarter of a million cattle, the equivalent in value of one ninth of the total budget for the state. Lack of subdivision, overgrazing, and uninterrupted grazing of pastures lead to their rapid deterioration. The burning of weeds leads to further losses of forage. Annual losses from parasitic infestations alone (ticks and hematozoa), not including mortality and the costs of building dipping vats and spraying pens, must be in the neighborhood of 2,800 million cruzeiros just in the state of Rio Grande do Sul, an area "specializing" in livestock or cattle production. In Brazil as a whole, breeders of cattle, pigs, sheep and goats who run their own farms at a high level of administrative efficiency are still few in number, the general rule being routine management with inadequate farming methods. There are several reasons for this state of backwardness, the more salient being the difficulty of investing in improvements; the lack of incentives, particularly under the tenant farming system; absenteeism on the part of owners of large properties and their failure to introduce modern practices into stock administration; ignorance of such practices on the part of many small producers; and certain limitations in the national agency responsible for extension services and vocational training in the field.[9]

It was also reported from Minas Gerais, the heart of Brazil's livestock industry, that farms were not organized along rational (i.e., planned) management and production methods, and that they do not have a systematic and full account of their activities. The accounting practices are rudimentary, empirical and often based simply on memory, so that the very owners have difficulty in furnishing, even if they were inclined to do so, the most elementary information on their undertakings. The livestock industry in this state is obviously exclusively for the large estate. Cattle are kept on pastures without any special care and for this reason the average productivity of pasture is one head of cattle for 1.78 hectares of pasture.[10]

It would seem to be obvious that with the enormous extensions of pastureland devoted to cattle, but operated at very low levels of efficiency, the owners of livestock farms are completely successful in keeping the peasants off the land. In truth, the livestock industry is an effective mechanism to monopolize the land resources. This would hold true also in areas such as the heart of the cacao production region of Itabuna (Bahia, Brazil), where many producers have shifted from cacao to the raising of cattle because of the steadily declining cacao yields. As a result, Itabuna is now one of the state's most important cattle regions. One observer reported that the development and expansion of livestock (cattle) is very similar to that observed in other parts of the country. Although it is as lucrative as cacao, cattle raising and marketing does not require great efforts or large investments and

[9] These observations are taken from United Nations/FAO, *Livestock in Latin America, Status, Problems and Prospects*, II, Brazil, E/CN.12/636 (New York: 1964), pp. 30 ff. See also Report I, on Colombia, Mexico, Uruguay and Venezuela, E/CN.12.620 (New York: 1962), about low levels of management of livestock enterprises in these countries. See also CIDA, Colombia Report, op. cit., pp. 260 ff, pp. 142 f.

[10] CIDA, Brazil Report, op. cit., p. 526.

assures possession and use of large extensions of land. It represents simply another phase of the economics of the area, not a different system of exploitation of the soil. It is probable that the tendency of the cattleman to maintain the same extensive methods which he employed previously in the cacao plantations is a function of the availability of land which he controls for livestock. The adoption of intensive methods and a high level of technology is a change which is extremely difficult for the cacao grower in his double function as livestock grower, in view of the fact that as cacao producer he always obtained high incomes and fabulous profits, *always playing with the land and the human labor and never with the employment of specialized techniques of cultivation, systematic and uniform shading and more adequate installations.*[11]

It is highly significant that the rapid decline of the cacao plantation area, controlled by a few large growers, is due to an extremely low level of management, which is an inherent part of the estate system. It is of significance because it shows how *even an "intensive" agriculture can be carried out "extensively" and at a low level of efficiency.* The impoverishment of the soil, the old age of the trees, the diseases, assume today extraordinary proportions in the eyes of the cacao producer and the technicians; this is due particularly to the system of exploitation which is responsible for the behavior and relations among men and between land and men. The system itself, with its orientation toward exterior markets, has created problems of enormous scope and complexity which escape solutions of a purely agro-technical nature.[12] And it goes without saying that as long as the system continues, there will be little hope that the management of the plantations will improve radically or at all. Average production of cacao in Itabuna was 780 kilos per hectare in 1945, but only 430 in 1960. The experience of Itabuna is characteristic for the entire cacao zone. According to official statistics, average Bahia yields dropped from 637 kilos for a 1931–40 average to 355 kilos, the 1952–60 average. Total production increased by 40 per cent, but the area cultivated in cacao has increased

[11] Ibid., pp. 508 ff.
[12] Ibid., p. 498.

two and a half times, as the growers of cacao attempted to offset declining yields by expanding the area planted in cacao —including into soils not too well suited to this crop.[13]

Cacao growers have repeatedly received large subsidies from the federal government of Brazil, the latest being a special organization (CEPLAC), which gave loans to 574 "distressed" but mostly large-scale cacao growers to adjust their debt situation at the rate of 354.2 million cruzeiros between 1957 and 1960. In addition, over 600 million cruzeiros were lent for improvements through 1962. An examination of these improvements shows that they went primarily for capital investments (buildings and processing facilities) and that *growers generally failed to use them for the improvements of their plantations.*[14] In fact, the growers were aggressively hostile to CEPLAC until they had made its principal function— the improvement of the management of the plantations— inoperative.

Striking evidence of poor management on the cacao plantations is the failure to replace old trees. On one typical large plantation, 45,000 out of 83,700 trees were between twenty-six and fifty years old. The statistics, however, do not entirely reveal the seriousness of the problem of old age of the plantations, since other factors which aggravate the problem, such as diseases and plagues, the drought and the impoverishment of the soils must also be taken into account. Hence there is no systematic management policy to renovate the cacao stands. On the contrary, as one large producer said: "If the soil is exhausted and used up, the best solution is to transform the area into pasture." This statement came from a producer who theoretically admits the need for gradual replacement, but also believes that when an old tree falls, the branches which penetrate the ground make spontaneous renovation possible.[15] He also stated that he did not need any agronomists to assist him. Similar lack of good management is found with respect to the pruning of cacao trees, an important step in the care of the plantations. One of the pro-

[13] Ibid., p. 499.
[14] Ibid.
[15] Ibid., pp. 504 ff.

ducers, for example, declared that if the pruning is done well, it is not necessary to do it again for five years although yearly prunings are recommended as a basic minimum. To this must be added that until the workers who do the pruning have adequate experience in this operation, they often damage the bark of the trees. This is of course prejudicial to the producers. Even the administrator is not always capable of requesting a better job, since often he was previously a worker or contract worker and therefore is without much training himself.[16]

The northeastern region of Brazil is only one of the areas where poor estate management is the norm. Even in São Paulo, Brazil's most technologically advanced agricultural state (the state reported nearly 45 per cent of all tractors in 1960), management is still at a low level. Monocultures—coffee, sugar, etc.—have dotted its history. The heavily subsidized sugar industry, which now occupies a small fraction of the state's agricultural land, and a few other estates are well managed. But in the aggregate, the amounts of wasted land, capital and human resources have been extraordinarily high. The production of coffee, for example, which originates in southern Brazil to a large extent, rose 90 per cent between the five-year period 1958–62, following an increment of 61 per cent in the cultivated area, but only 18 per cent in average yield; the fact that the new land brought into cultivation was more fertile, especially in the state of Paraná, helped to raise yields.[17] In a fertile area like Sertãozinho (São Paulo), coffee trees were almost entirely eliminated between 1926 and 1956, and the area was planted in sugar cane—a shift from one monoculture to another in an exceedingly short space of time. In neighboring Jardinópolis (São Paulo), the home of coffee kings, coffee is now practically extinct. Such radical changes are sometimes initiated by the large and well-financed owners because yields of the first monoculture have declined as a consequence of inadequate farming practices—as in the case of the cacao plantations of Bahia—and also because they wish to reap the benefits or subsidies from better markets for

[16] Ibid., p. 506.
[17] ECLA/UN, *Agriculture in Latin America, Problems and Prospects*, p. 37.

the second monoculture. Given the low wages of labor, such transformations can be undertaken with relatively low costs to the plantation owners. But in some cases, the economic and social costs to the local communities and even the economy as a whole can be exceedingly high.[18]

According to one competent agronomist, improved planting materials, better farm and soil management, control of diseases and other improvements could raise in Brazil the output of cane sugar, peanuts and rice by roughly 20 per cent; soya beans by 25 per cent; citrus, yucca, long-fibered cotton, peppermint and pork by 50 per cent; and cacao and coffee by 100 per cent *in areas where they are presently grown.*[19]

In Chile's livestock industry, breeds are often unsatisfactory for the purpose for which they are used. Vast areas of land are covered by blackberries (*zarzamora*), and in the southern provinces alone it is estimated that this tough weed covers one million hectares. The use of water for irrigation is inadequate and some observers speak of enormous losses in the use of water and irrigated land. 18.8 million hectares of farmland suffer from light to severe erosion. Of this, about 700,000 hectares have been overrun by dunes. Erosion on small plots is significant because of the intensity with which their holders must farm them; it is significant on the large farms because of poor management practices. According to a study undertaken by a government agency, part of the erosion comes from the allotment of small plots on submarginal land in the hills—land which the owner himself has no interest in cultivating—to inquilinos, who use the slash-and-burn technique, which destroys the soils completely.

These are a few of the many available examples of poor farm management on land owned by the landed elite, which is part and parcel of the latifundio system throughout Latin America. The very organization of large estates is, by and large, a serious impediment to progress and improvements. We must now refer briefly to absentee ownership or management, an institution prevalent throughout Latin America, and

[18] CIDA, Brazil Report, op. cit., pp. 518 ff. See also pp. 510 ff.
[19] Ibid., p. 44.

its implications for the productive processes in agriculture. (Later we shall examine its sociopolitical implications for the peasantry.) It is curious that the abundant literature on Latin American agriculture contains few references to the existence and functions of so important an institution as the administrators, who symbolize, from the point of view of the peasantry and agricultural production, estate management and absentee landlordism. Not all estate owners are absentee owners, but all of them have administrators on their properties. (Some administrators are even absentee managers.) The presence of administrators means that the daily work routine, and in the case of owners living elsewhere, farm management as such, are carried out by remote control. Whether or not the estate owner lives on his property, his relationship to his labor force is like that of a general to his soldiers: he is largely invisible, although his existence is always felt as his "orders" are being executed.

It is widely known that absentee ownership in Latin America is very widespread and that the larger the enterprise, the greater the probability that the owner lives off the farm in some distant city. For example, in Brazil in 1960, half of the owners of large multi-family farms in eleven municípios did not reside on their property, and of those, 85 per cent lived in some city outside the immediate zone of their property.[20] In Uruguay, absentee landlordism also increases significantly with the size of the farm and is highest on livestock farms. According to a recent study, it reaches 100 per cent on the largest estates.[21] In Ecuador, on nine large typical haciendas studied, the owners either did not reside there or resided there only temporarily.

[20] Ibid., pp. 158 ff. There is also some absenteeism on smaller farms, a phenomenon which needs some investigation, but it can be assumed that it is to some extent due to the multiple ownership of land by large landlords, and the leasing out of land to smallholders. However, there is also some degree of "multiple ownership" of small plots by smallholders. The reasons for absentee ownership on small farms on the part of smallholders may, however, be different from those prevailing on large enterprises. For an interesting note on *absentee producers* (rather than owners) see ibid., pp. 162 ff.

[21] "Situacion Economica y Social del Uruguay Rural," Ministerio de Ganaderia y Agricultura, Comisión Honoraria del Plan de Desarrollo Agropecuario, October 1963, p. 108.

Residence of Owners (or Administrators) on Nine Typical Large Haciendas, Ecuador

Size of Hacienda (hectares)	Comments
610	Owner, a foreigner, lives in Paris. Present administrator distant relative of owner; lives eleven months on farm. The mayordomo lives in nearest town.
2,955	Owner resides there eight months with his family, is important politician.
690	Lady owner, lives outside of Ecuador, owns other farms. Son is administrator, lives eight months on farm and is only white person.
2,441	Owner is government (Asistencia Social). The administrator has little contact with local community.
1,298	Owned by church, rented to Jesuit Foundation. Administrator is owner of neighboring farm who is replaced by a mayordomo in his absence.
264	Livestock enterprise near Quito, operated by tenant with a "co-administrator," brother of tenant. Residence not given.
12,000	Owner stays two weeks every month and lives in Quito. One administrator.
444	Owner lives 36 kilometers away in provincial capital. Has only a mayordomo, but does not delegate authority. Mayordomo only follows instructions and has same pay as common workers.
12,711	Owned by Swedish corporation, located in Stockholm. Operated by a *"gerente."*

NOTE: The first eight haciendas are located in the sierra, the ninth is on the coast.

What is less widely known is that administrators are not normally well qualified for their jobs in terms of modern farm management, although there are of course exceptions. By and large, they represent a very conservative element in the management of estates.[22] This means also that it is much less significant for management whether the landlord lives on

[22] See also below, Chapter 12, on the managers' social function.

the farm or in some distant city. Contrary to a common belief, most of the administrators have only rudimentary knowledge of agriculture and do not possess specialized skills in
the growing of crops, the handling of the soil and water, or
the production of livestock.

The reason for this state of affairs lies in the estate owners'
need to put a person in charge of the immediate operations
on the farm who can be trusted to continue to operate the
farm along traditional, well-established lines. Therefore, administrators are usually workers who have worked for the
landlord for a number of years and are well acquainted with
these "lines." An administrator is most effective for the landlord, particularly for the absentee owner, when he faithfully
follows a pattern of cropping and livestock farming which
prevails on the estate and on other estates in the community
—a pattern which may have been established by the owners'
fathers or grandfathers. In general, this does not have to be
spelled out for him in great detail, because he is already acquainted with it. For the owners, therefore, the administrators' ability to "develop" the enterprise is in most cases im-
material. In fact, he has no authority to use any initiative,
but is merely a worker with a slightly higher wage and a few
extra privileges who must follow explicit or implicit orders. It
is therefore no accident that few estate owners allow their
administrators an opportunity to improve their knowledge at
the owners' expense.

The quality of farm management, then, depends almost entirely on the interest, the effort and the time which the estate
owner can devote to his farm enterprise. But two important
characteristics of a traditional agriculture like the latifundio
system must be noted in this context. The first is the close
relationship which exists between raising the level of farm
management and improving standards of work and living conditions of the farm workers. Although there are some owners
who have a keen interest in improving the use of their soils
and the operation of their enterprise, any improvement which
they introduce must not sap the basis of the traditional economic, social and political relationships prevailing between
the landed elite and the peasantry. Hence the close relation-

ship between farm management and the sociopolitical and economic structure is a severe deterrent to most changes. *New farming techniques are likely to be adopted only if they do not disturb in any fundamental manner the rural social stratification and traditional labor relations.* This is the beauty of adopting modern motorized farm machinery, from the landed elite's point of view: it allows them to replace man by machine, maintaining thereby the traditional excess labor supply, and it avoids the necessity of incentives for higher performance of labor, which would imply higher wages and incomes and allow more independent workers the exercise of greater initiative. Above all it avoids the necessity of recognizing farm labor unions or peasant leagues and having to bargain with them collectively. The payment of a higher wage for tractor drivers to allow for their higher skills does not break this rule, and in fact falls squarely into the customary existence of "pet workers." It must also be remembered that there is a strong social pressure on the members of the landed elite to adhere to the "rules of the game" of latifundismo. Few estate owners would wish to antagonize their peers by introducing on their properties practices considered inimical to the foundation of latifundismo. If they tried, they would probably not be successful for long.

So far we have been talking about those farm owners who might have an interest in improving their farm operations. But by and large, such owners are not numerous. This brings us to another characteristic of Latin America's agriculture: the "divided interests" of estate owners. Although the economic, social and above all the political power of the landed elite is land-based, their major interests are not necessarily agricultural. A high proportion of politicians, lawyers, doctors, merchants, farm equipment dealers, owners of transportation (trucking) businesses, exporters, importers and even industrialists are also owners of large sections of farmland. Thus an enormous proportion of the total national resources is in the hands of a small landed elite which has branched out into the various sectors of the nations' economies, and which is strongly motivated to maintain latifundismo. Agriculture is often a sideline for them, from an economic viewpoint. Major attention does not have to be paid to it by the estate owners if outside, non-agricultural incomes are derived from the other professions. Management of estates through administrators by remote control is a convenient mechanism for the landed elite to pursue and even enlarge non-agricultural activities.

Hence for a large number of estate owners there is little economic incentive to improve traditional land uses and farm management methods when returns on rural investments can be maintained for the landlords with prevailing methods of absentee operation. Traditional economic incentives, of which the economists like to speak—prices, credit or subsidies—just do not work in the case of estate owners, or their impact is minimal when other factors governing farm management and production strategies are much more important. The best guarantee for maintaining such returns, which may be entirely adequate for the owners, is the mere control of large extensions of farmland (although this may conflict with the interests of the economies as a whole). Total returns can remain quite substantial even if per hectare yields are very low and declining, if much land is being farmed.

A Brazilian sociologist, Geraldo Semenzato, described brilliantly the typically divided interests of the landed elite in his comments on Bahia's (Brazil) cacao industry. He stated that in Itabuna, Bahia's most important cacao production center, the upper class is composed of families of the large estate owners who produce cacao, big merchants, bankers and livestock farmers. Its members are defined by the number and the value of their patrimony, the size of their bank accounts, the monopoly of the factors of production, the control of the market, the volume and value of the production of cacao, the loans in cash which they grant and the votes which they obtain in case they devote themselves to politics. On the whole these privileged classes make up no more than 10 per cent of the population. They are, however, the members who retain the economic power, as they are part of the directorates of export firms, co-operatives and banks. They have political power as the most influential members within their parties, and at the same time enjoy extraordinary social prestige, generally as members of the local clubs, the Rotary, Lions and the Free Masons. In the privileged classes there is a constant preoccupation with finding formulas to keep their positions from being disturbed. And thus the privileged classes become more and more aggressive and, in a certain sense, innovators. There is among the members of these classes a continuous effort to justify their position, including the constant reminder of the difficulties which they and their forefathers (in the words of the descendants: "real heroes") had to face in settling the forests and starting the first cacao plantations.

It is interesting to note, Semenzato says, that "it is invariably the same men who are in the cacao production, who are in the directorates of the banks, in the top organs of the cooperatives and at times in the export houses. On the other side, these very firms are also owners of the cacao plantations. There are banker-cacao farmers and livestock farmers. There are members of the directorate of cooperatives who are influential politicians, large cacao growers, livestock men and great merchants. Besides, these are the same men who are tied, directly or indirectly, by reason of their prestige and social position, to the industry of cacao by-products. And so forth. The greatest portion of the economic sectors is in the hands of the large producers." And one must add that the cacao producer is a member of the Rural Association, a landlords' association which is represented in the Institute of Cacao of Bahia, an organization which wields a strong influence upon the central government of the country.[23]

Remote control of management remains the ideal of those who have capital resources to invest, and, as a result of the transfusion of values from the rich to the poor, even of those who aim to enrich themselves by investing in the labor of others. This ideal shapes private and public policies. For example, a survey of officials of an autonomous public agency in Ecuador showed that over 80 per cent of the officials or members of their close families owned or had owned rural property, although only 11 per cent were presently owners

[23] CIDA, Brazil Report, op. cit., pp. 170 ff.

or tenants of land. But 75 per cent of the officials aspired to acquire land or a parcel in a colonization scheme, or to use their savings in the acquisition of land or suburban lots. Of those who stated that they or their families wished to own a farm, only 31 per cent wanted to operate it themselves. Land as capital investment rather than as a basis for a profession or a way of life is part of Latin America's value scheme among the rich. This attitude permeates public policy and from a social viewpoint it is particularly obnoxious where public agencies have allowed it to occur in colonization projects. Lots are often assigned to persons with little farm background or to professionals or politicians. In the settlement project of Santo Domingo de los Colorados in western Ecuador, to name one typical example, only nine out of thirty-three initial settlers who received lots in 1959 were farmers or administrators, the latter on the assumption that they are better potential farmers than the peasants.[24] The remainder were ex-employees (seven), military personnel, including one wife of a military official (seven), businessmen (two), chauffeurs (two), an electrician, mechanic, circus artist, dentist, jeweler and telegram operator. Thirteen of the thirty-three, however, abandoned their parcels and in the subsequent assignment only two farmers were selected. The remainder were again mostly ex-employees and military personnel. In 1960, twenty-three more lots were assigned, nine to military men or ex-employees, three to farmers, and the rest to a factory owner, lawyer, dentist, etc. Seven of these gave up their lots and were all replaced by non-farmers. The performance of the experienced farmers sharply exceeded that of the non-farmers, but of course performance was not an essential criterion for obtaining or keeping a plot of land.[25] In a colonization project near the city of Rio de Janeiro (Itaguaí, state of Rio de Janeiro), with over 1,000 lots of ten hectares each,

---

[24] This is of course not true. Administrators bring with their equipment a healthy contempt for working the plots themselves and are prone to establish on their assigned land a latifundio system in miniature.

[25] CIDA, Ecuador Report, op. cit., pp. 355 ff. For a further penetrating criticism of Ecuador's colonization schemes see Edda Eisenlohr, "Agrarreform in Ecuador im entwicklungspolitischen Kraeftespiel," *Sozialforschungsstelle* (Universitaet Muenster, Dortmund), September 1969, particularly pp. 145 ff.

about 10 per cent of the parcels were not in production and many lots were operated by sharecroppers or "administrators." Some of the lots had apparently been assigned for political or speculative reasons.[26]

A typical custom of the landed elite which characterizes their "long-distance approach" to agriculture is visiting the farm enterprises only at harvest time, when the productive processes have all been terminated, but not during the remainder of the year, or of sending some agent to supervise the harvest. This again is closely related to one of the outstanding attitudes of the "agriculturists" of Latin America who form the landed elite (and who are fond of speaking on behalf of the rural people of their community): namely, their proverbial contempt for manual labor in general and farm work in particular, regardless of whether or not they live on their estates. As a result, the principle of "the land to the tillers" has always operated in reverse in the hemisphere. Most of the land belongs to the non-tillers, who regard actual farm labor as dishonorable. They have come to consider themselves as called upon—in view of their wealth and their social and political status—to direct the labor of others and to reap its fruits. To become rich by exploiting the work of the peasants is one of the most important credos of the landed elite. Occasional visits, farm management by remote control, and contempt of actual farm work in general qualifies no estate owner as farmer in the proper sense of the word.

In this section an attempt was made to show that rural poverty is caused by the peasants' inability to gain access to adequate plots of land; that their land base is shrinking; that poverty is strongly related to unemployment and underemployment; and that farm employment on the estates either is not increasing as fast as the labor force, or may even tend to decrease in absolute terms (as happened in Brazil), thereby shifting the burden of "employment" to the smaller farm units, including the minifundios. It is evident that quite apart from any conscious or unconscious policy of the landed elite to restrict employment opportunities on their estates—evidenced by such methods as extensive land uses in livestock enterprises which can be operated with a handful of cowboys or the use of motorized equipment to replace labor, and others, all of which result in maintaining an excess supply of labor—*traditional farming practices carry with them the seed of lessened rural employment and greater poverty, because poor management and the resulting exhaustion and destruction of the soils affect the number of workers hired and the returns from the land in which sharecroppers and small tenants share.* Not a few estate owners have declared openly that they shift to livestock in order to "solve their labor problems." While this may in some cases only be a pretext to hide the more obvious reasons—e.g., the exhaustion of their soils or the greater convenience with which the land can be operated—this policy only enhances aggregate unemployment for the nations as a whole.

It is clear, then, that employment on the multi-family farms could be raised if the land were used more intensively. Unfortunately it is not easy to estimate in precise terms the gap between the existing and the potential employment of farm labor. Accurate estimates should be based on much fuller knowledge of the physical resources in agriculture, and particularly of the land resources controlled by the landed elite. Such information is not available. We must therefore content ourselves with simple calculations, using simple assumptions, in order to evaluate this gap in an approximate manner. Such a calculation reveals that in seven countries for which adequate information is available it would appear that about fifty million more workers could find rural employment on existing multi-family farms.[27] This estimate uses as a

[27] The largest number of additional farm workers is shown for Brazil (about forty-four million), computed from the 1950 census. As we showed earlier, the number of workers on all multi-family farms declined between 1950 and 1960. Farmland in all multi-family farms increased. This means that at the rate of ten hectares per farm worker (which is twice the ratio of farmland to worker on family farms in 1950, and therefore yields a conservative estimate), there could have been an additional employment of between one and almost two and a half million workers on the additional farmland in the multi-family farms alone, without counting the possibility of increased employment on the already existing farmland in 1950. In other words, Brazil's ability to absorb additional farm workers on multi-family farms has increased since 1950.

Measures of Potential Labor
Absorption on Large and Medium-Sized
Multi-Family Farms in Seven Countries
(1950–60)

Country and Multi-Family Farm Class	Number of Workers			No. of Under-privileged Families in 1960
	Actual	Computed	Difference	
		(in thousands)		
Argentina				
Medium	212	240	27	
Large	94	587	493	467
Brazil				
Medium	5,222	18,792	13,571	
Large	2,679	32,907	30,227	4,525
Chile				
Medium	142	294	153	
Large	256	2,104	1,849	244
Colombia				
Medium	189	838	649	
Large	112	1,781	1,669	961
Ecuador				
Medium	83	83	1[a]	
Large	138	195	57	500
Guatemala				
Medium	75	195	120	
Large	41	253	212	514
Peru				
Medium	58	113	55	
Large	397	1,572	1,175	960
All seven				
Medium	5,981	20,556	14,575	
Large	3,717	39,400	35,683	—
TOTAL	9,698	59,956	50,258	

[a] About 565 in total.

NOTE: The above estimates are not indicative of actually available job opportunities. See text.

"model" the relationship between land and labor which exists on family farms,[28] on the assumption that labor there is more fully employed, and that with the resources available to producers on family farms, at existing levels of farm management and technology, their land is used with reasonable intensity. It also assumes that the average quality of the land in the multi-family farms is about the same as that in family farms. Potential total employment on multi-family farms is then calculated by applying the land–worker relations existing on the family farms to the estates, so that their land would now be theoretically capable of supporting farm workers at the same rate as that of family farms. It is obvious that the largest gap between existing and potential employment, as calculated on the basis of these assumptions, prevails on the latifundios, because of their now predominantly extensive land uses. The largest expansion numerically could take place in Brazil.

It can be observed, by comparing these estimates with the number of poor or underprivileged farm families, that an expansion of employment as envisaged here would either do away with existing unemployment or reduce it considerably, if unemployment is estimated at about 30 or 40 per cent. Of course such statistics must be used with caution. They are only a rough index of the possibilities of expanding employment in the estate sector without improving farm management methods or levels of technology. They are not indicative of actually available job opportunities now. It is almost certain, however, that these estimates are on the conservative side. A real land reform would simultaneously modify the land tenure structure and improve resource use patterns, farm management methods, and technology, all without sacrificing the goal of full employment. Thus, employment in agriculture might go well beyond the estimates presented for the seven countries (and it can even be increased on family farms).

We shall conclude this section by commenting on two other aspects of Latin American agriculture, one being the landed

[28] This, however, is not to imply that the family farm is necessarily the ideal farm type.

elite's low propensity to invest, and the other, the disproportionately large contribution made by the small producers to total agricultural production.

Among the factors which affect the growth of the agricultural sector, capital investments in agriculture are the least known and explored, although they are crucial. There are no adequate statistics on public and private investments on a regional or national scale. It is widely estimated that both public and private total investments in the sector are low. One author estimated that only around 10 per cent of the total annual investment in Latin America has been in the agricultural sector, notwithstanding its significantly larger participation in the national product and its share of the total population. Policies regarding the annual public investments are influenced to a large extent by the estate sector through the political and economic power it exercises on all levels, and, as can be expected, public investments are undertaken mainly (and sometimes only) when they are of benefit to the landed elite—whether they stem from domestic resources or are financed by international loans. A good working hypothesis is that Latin American agriculture is starved of capital funds.

If we turn our attention to private investments, it is obvious that holders of small plots and many producers on family farms earn incomes which preclude savings and, therefore, investments, or they earn their incomes under conditions in which such investments are not allowed by their landlords. Hence their capital resources are low, as we have pointed out earlier. However, although the total fixed and working capital on the large farms is considerably larger, it is not necessarily adequate. In fact, one of the reasons for agricultural stagnation is the lack of private investments and the tendency of estate owners to spend their agricultural earnings on consumption goods or in other ways not related to agriculture. Inasmuch as estate owners control most of the farmland and earn the bulk of the income generated in the sector, their spending habits have a crucial bearing on agricultural growth.

By and large, the big landowners keep little of their income for reinvestment in their farm properties. We can gain some insight into the level and pattern of investment in the traditional agricultures of Latin America from an analysis of recent census statistics on "capital outlays" in eleven municípios in Brazil, two of which were relatively progressive areas of colonization, the remaining nine being typical traditional areas with most of the land controlled by large estate owners. Total investment was low, regardless of the type of farm, but nearly one half of the investment (47 per cent) was reported from the two colonization areas, despite the fact that the other nine municípios had seven times more farmland and three times more farms. The total investment per farm on the minifundios was insignificant. However, in several municípios investment per hectare on the latifundios was even smaller than on the minifundios, and in all municípios it was always smaller than on family farms and the medium-sized multi-family farms. In general, total investment per farm increased more rapidly than the average size of farm up to the medium-sized multi-family farms, but decreased for the latifundios. Thus, total investment per farm on the medium-sized multi-family farms was fifty-eight times larger than on the minifundios, though their average size was only twenty-nine times larger; investment per latifundio was 153 times larger than investment per minifundio, but the average size of the latifundios was 316 times larger. The lack of effort needed to improve agricultural output also becomes apparent when investment in machinery and improvements (excluding livestock) is related to cropland. It appears that such capital outlays per latifundio were 175 times larger than per minifundio. Investment per hectare in cropland rose considerably less than the amount of land sown to crops, since latifundios had on the average forty-six times more land under crops than minifundios, but their investment per hectare in crops was only four times higher than on minifundios and no larger than on family farms.

Although this evidence is not conclusive, since census statistics are not the best basis on which to judge the financial practices of producers, it supports the well-known fact that the financial efforts of the large *fazendeiros* of Brazil to improve their agricultural enterprises are insignificant in comparison with their resources, and inferior to the efforts made by the other producers, some of whom are financially much less able to make substantial improvements on their land. There is little doubt that if the large estate owners had a lower propensity to consume, there would be far more funds available each year for productive investments. But a high propensity to consume is an inherent, institutionalized aspect of the latifundio system which has a significant cumulative (negative) effect on economic growth over the longer term.[29]

Another important aspect is that when investments are actually made by estate owners, by their very nature they must yield lower returns, in terms of increased production, than they would in a more dynamic agriculture.[30] The pattern pursued by the landed elite accords high priority to *conspicuous investments*, i.e., investments which do not improve the quality of the soil or the productive capacity of the farm enterprise, but which simply tend to raise the capital value of the farm. In other words, the penchant for conspicuous consumption expenditures of the wealthy is paralleled by a penchant for showy structures and the like. An interesting

[29] The economist Nicholas Kaldor, in "Problemas Economicos de Chile," *El Trimestre Economico*, April–June 1959, concluded from an analysis of the Chilean economy as a whole that if the ratio of consumption to gross income from property were reduced to levels found in Great Britain, the personal consumption expenditures of this group would fall sharply and the resources released would be sufficient to double investment in fixed capital. This means that net investment would increase from 2 to 14 per cent of net national income. Chilean landlords have as high a propensity to consume as property owners in general, according to another study. In a sample of twenty large farm operations, approximately only 11 per cent of their total gross farm income was reinvested in agriculture and a high proportion of consumption expenditures went for the purchase of luxury and imported items.

Some estate owners argue that as long as there is a threat of land reform, they will abstain from investing in their farms. But this argument has no merit. The threat of land reform exists because of the landed elite's use of the agricultural resources, the cause of the social conflicts. With existing land reform laws, estate owners are in fact encouraged to invest in order to be exempt from expropriation. See Part III.

[30] In a recent article on Uruguay, R. H. Brannon (op. cit.) tried to show that estate owners invest their savings in land rather than in the intensification of production practices on current holdings. He maintains that much of this investment has sought land purchase opportunities in areas requiring minimal input of managerial time and production-increasing technology.

case is the previously mentioned cacao plantation area of Bahia, where the Brazilian federal government inaugurated a plan to improve the management of the plantations. Heavy subsidies were being paid to the growers. But the majority of the large producers showed little interest in a systematic renovation of the old cacao stands, good tree-trimming practices, disease eradication and fertilization. Instead, they used the subsidies to invest heavily in warehousing or drying facilities, which increased the capital value of the plantations but were clearly a loss for the economy as a whole in view of the steady decline in the quantity and quality of production. This is by no means an isolated case. Many estate owners are fond of building modern barns and stables—usually with considerable excess capacity—and warehouses or private dwellings which must be considered extravagant and are often unnecessary, except if the purpose is to *épater le bourgeois*.

Estate owners tend to use credit for these investments (and even for operational expenditures) rather than their own capital, and in countries where the rate of inflation is higher than the rate of interest, this is good business. But borrowing is good business anyway, because of the preferential access of estate owners to the loanable funds, and because the estate owners' own capital can be used in more profitable enterprises, where rates of returns exceed the interest paid on agricultural loans. Obviously estate owners are given the highest priority by the private lending agencies, who lend them funds on the basis of their social and political status, often without investigating whether or not these funds are actually used for agricultural purposes. But even public credit agencies whose specific function is, theoretically, to promote agriculture, and which are organized with the express purpose of assisting the small producers, have adopted lending policies geared to the large borrowers' farm management practices and propensities to consume and invest, rather than to the needs of the economy as a whole. In Chile, for example, the largest portion of loan funds for agricultural purposes drawn from the Banco del Estado went to finance the operations and current expenditures of large farm owners. Borrowers who reported substantial capital assets requested even small loans. Since the loans are usually short-term and the wealthy borrowers kept renewing their requests, they were in fact obtaining long-term credit to finance short-term operations.[31] The political, economic and social influence of the landed elite is so strong that it is able to bend institutions, established especially to assist the peasants, to its own advantage.

Because agricultural investments are so inadequate, it is often recommended that policies and programs be adopted to increase their present rate, perhaps double it, in order to provide sufficient impetus to expand output at a much faster rate. Often this takes the form of suggestions to increase the availability of credit funds. Such recommendations do not take into account the realities of a latifundio agriculture. Beyond the inherent institutional obstacles to increasing private investment, the present structure of agriculture as a whole makes it very difficult for the agricultural sector to benefit *pari passu* from increases in public and private investments. New investments do not yield sufficient returns, because they are poorly executed by the estate owners, who are the primary beneficiaries of credit and the major owners of capital. Within the present structure of agriculture, it would appear that growth can be achieved only at an increasing cost.

Finally we must again draw attention to the fact that the contribution made by small farmers to the countries' total agricultural output is generally beyond the resources to which they have access. In five countries for which data are available, the minifundios controlled between .2 and 17 per cent of the farmland, but contributed between 3 and 30 per cent of the total agricultural product. In contrast, the latifundios controlled between 37 and 81 per cent of the land and their contribution varied between 15 and 57 per cent. These figures do not fully reflect the importance of small producers for the production of domestic consumption foods other than beef (since cattle come almost exclusively from large farms).

---

[31] E. Feder, *El Credito Agricola en Chile* (Santiago, Chile: Instituto de Economia, Universidad de Chile, Monograph No. 29, 1960). Recent research in the field of credit for agriculture in Chile reveals that the findings of this study were on the conservative side.

Many important staple foods, such as corn, yucca and vegetables, are supplied principally by the small plot holders. In fact, the contribution of the latter is still larger if one includes all the laborers who work the land on behalf of the owners, such as Chile's inquilinos. In Chile, for example, the smaller producers' contribution to total output rises from 4 to 9 per cent, and that of the largest producers declines from 57 to 54 per cent, if this adjustment is made in the statistics. These figures also demonstrate how intensive cropping by workers with land benefits the large landlords.

As in most underdeveloped agricultures, production per hectare on large properties in Latin America is generally inferior to that on smaller units, whereas the value of production per worker is, on the average, less than on smaller farms. Higher average productivity of land on the smaller enterprises is the result of more intensive land use. Small producers concentrate on intensive food production, including garden crops. Production value per hectare is smaller on the larger farms even if one considers only cultivated land, which (except in Colombia) includes artificial pasture and fallow land. In other words, the value of production per hectare of cultivated land, which includes returns from *all* products (including livestock), is still smallest on the largest farms after natural pasture and other land uses have been excluded. *The intensity of land use is, in fact, so much greater on the small farms that it outweighs all their disadvantages in terms of poorer soils and lack of capital and other resources.*

Such wide discrepancies in the average productivity of the land, which result from wide differences in intensity of land use, reveal a grave shortcoming of the land tenure structure. They imply that there is less total product for the economies as a whole or a composition of the output which is unsatisfactory for the nations in terms of an adequate diet. They also imply a clear predisposition of small producers and workers with land to use their land effectively. From the point of view of the peasants themselves, and for the long-term development of Latin American agriculture, this is a very hopeful phenomenon.

Distribution of Land and of Agricultural Production by Farm Classes in Five Countries

Country and Farm Class	Percentage of Land in Farms	Percentage Agricultural Output Supplied
Argentina		
I	3	12
II	45	47
III	15	26
IV	37	15
Brazil		
I	1[a]	3
II	6	18
III	34	43
IV	60	36
Chile		
I	—[b]	4
II	7	16
III	11	23
IV	81	57
Ecuador		
I	17	26
II	19	33
III	19	22
IV	45	19
Guatemala		
I	14	30
II	13	13
III	32	36
IV	41	21

I—Minifundios; II—Family Farms; III—Medium-Sized Multi-Family Farms; IV—Large Multi-Family Farms.

[a] .5 per cent.
[b] .2 per cent.

Another important aspect is labor productivity. The increase in output per worker, measured in monetary terms, which usually accompanies an increase in farm size is often regarded as evidence that large enterprises are more efficient.[32] This is, however, highly debatable. The discrepancy between small and large farms is caused largely by the very same factors which explain the difference in the productivity of land. In part it is also due to smallholders' lack of access to resources and to their being prevented from working their inadequate parcels full time. Furthermore, some large land-holders tend to invest in labor-saving machinery in order to be more independent of human labor. On the other hand, the average value of production per worker on large farms is affected by extensive uses of land, such as for livestock or permanent crops. Both can be operated with relatively low labor inputs. In fact, output per farm rises with increase in farm size, but faster than the number of workers per farm. In the context of Latin American agriculture differential productivity per worker can therefore be taken as indicative of a defective land tenure structure and land use pattern.

[32] This assumption was made recently by W. H. Nicholls and R. Miller Paiva in a study of Brazilian agriculture. Partly on the basis of higher labor productivity, the authors concluded that Brazil owes a substantial debt to the large landowners and underwrote feudalistic traditions. Both the economics and politics of the argument are valid only if one assumes that it is best to leave the present-day structure of agriculture untouched. Such an assumption is clearly outdated. See Carlos Alberto de Medina, "Agricultural Productivity and Political Innocence," in *America Latina* (Rio de Janeiro), July–September 1968.

APPENDIX TABLE I

Distribution of Farms and Farmland in Ten Countries, around 1960
(in per cent)

A. Farms

Country	No. of Farms (thousands)	Minifundios	Family	Medium Multi-Family	Large Multi-Family
Argentina	446	43	49	7	1
Brazil	3,334	31	39	27	3
Chile	151	37	40	16	7
Colombia	1,194	64	30	5	1
Ecuador	344	84	13	3	—a
Guatemala	417	87	11	2	—a
Peru	852	85	11	3	1
El Salvador	227	91	7	1	1
Honduras	178	67	26	6	1
Nicaragua	102	51	27	21	1

B. Farmland

Country	Farmland (thousand hectares)	Minifundios	Family	Medium Multi-Family	Large Multi-Family
Argentina	173,948	3	45	34	18
Brazil	249,862	1	8	38	53
Chile	27,712	—a	7	12	81
Colombia	24,264	5	25	25	45
Ecuador	6,000	12	20	23	45
Guatemala	3,449	19	19	36	26
Peru	18,605	15	5	5	75
El Salvador	1,581	22	21	20	37
Honduras	2,417	12	27	33	28
Nicaragua	3,823	4	11	44	41

a Less than .5 per cent.

NOTE: Minifundios include so-called microfincas in Guatemala, El Salvador and Nicaragua, and 808 indigenous communities in Peru, with its numerous smallholdings.

APPENDIX TABLE II

Land Use by Farm Class in Seven Countries,[a] 1950–60
(million hectares and per cent)

Land Use	Sub-Family (Minifundios)	Family	Medium Multi-Family	Large Multi-Family	Total
Cultivated Land[b]					
Hectares	6.3	29.4	39.5	40.7	115.9
Per Cent	55	29	33	16	24
Natural Pastures					
Hectares	3.4	53.3	49.0	133.2	239.0
Per Cent	30	52	42	52	49
Forest and Bushes					
Hectares	1.0	14.7	20.8	60.9	97.5
Per Cent	9	14	18	23	20
Other Uses, Including Sterile Land					
Hectares	0.7	4.6	8.7	23.1	37.1
Per Cent	6	5	7	8	7
Total Land in Farms					
Hectares	11.4	102.1	118.1	257.9	489.5
Per Cent	100	100	100	100	100

[a] Argentina, Brazil, Chile, Colombia, Ecuador, Guatemala, Peru.
[b] Cropland, artificial or improved pastures, and fallow or idle land.

APPENDIX TABLE III

Various Land Uses on Family Farms and Multi-Family Farms as Multiple of Sub-Family Farms in Seven Countries (1950–60)

Land Use	Sub-Family	Family	Medium Multi-Family	Large Multi-Family
Cultivated Land	1.0	4.6	6.2	6.4
Natural Pastures	1.0	15.5	14.3	38.8
Forest and Bushes	1.0	15.2	21.3	62.6
Other Uses, Including Sterile Land	1.0	6.7	12.7	33.6
Total Land in Farms	1.0	8.9	10.3	22.6

PART II

AN ARBITRARY SYSTEM OF AGRICULTURE

Under the system of manorial justice, the proprietors had such wide powers to judge and to punish their serfs, that they could enforce compliance with almost any kind of extortionate demand. According to the Code of 1833, the proprietor was free to employ, for the maintenance of order and authority, any domestic means of correction which would not endanger life, or result in mutilation. . . . A devilish cunning had been employed in perfecting a whole arsenal of flogging instruments: rods, staffs, whips, bundles of leather thongs twisted with wire—sometimes, though certainly rarely, so zealously employed that the serf was beaten to death. The punishments permitted by the law of 1845 were still severe enough . . . but laxity in enforcement competed with laxity in the law itself, in contributing to peasant misery . . . the enforcement of the law against a given proprietor depended so largely upon other members of the proprietorial class and upon officials under their political control or secretly in their pay.

> G. Tanquary Robinson, *Rural Russia under the Old Regime,* Chapter III, "The Peasants in the Last Decades of Serfdom," pp. 42 ff.

If by any chance the agricultural workers thought of trying to improve their conditions by a strike, they found themselves faced with numerous perils. An individual laborer who quit work before the expiration of his contract was liable to a month's imprisonment. If a group of laborers stopped work in this way, and by means of force, threats, or "exclusion from intercourse" (personal boycott) compelled other workers to do the same, the offenders were liable to imprisonment for from six to twelve months. Still more severe was the punishment provided for the members of any organization which incited agricultural laborers to stop work in violation of contract; the penalty here was imprisonment in a fortress for from one year and four months to four years, with a permanent loss of the right to vote or to hold office. The government was apparently determined not to tolerate any foolishness among the agricultural laborers, and in particular it aimed to check the activities of individual agitators and of radical organizations. In part, no doubt, as a result of this policy of repression, the farmworkers remained almost entirely unorganized (except for the many small and primitive artels), and the number of strikes between 1907 and 1914 was inconsequential.

Ibid., Chapter XII, "On the Eve," pp. 248 ff.

CHAPTER 9

Individual and Institutional Harshness

The flagrant inequalities in the distribution of resources and income by themselves cause serious dissatisfaction among rural people. In addition, Latin America's peasants find another cause for discontent, resentment and even rebellion, in the humiliating treatment they have received from the landed elite for generations. Latifundismo has been and still is an agriculture of oppression and arbitrariness. We must now turn our attention to the human relationships between the small oligarchy of estate owners and the peasant masses.

If one judges progress by the adoption of institutions which will permit access to income and wealth-producing resources for those who work for others, as well as the self-employed, then Latin America's peasantry has progressed very little. Progress, however, can also be measured in terms of peasant participation in the social and political activities of their country, and in terms of their ability to contribute to decisions on matters which affect their own status. From this point of view, there has been even less improvement.

Latin America's peasants have been in an extremely weak bargaining position for generations. This has been the by-product of a permanent and growing rural labor surplus. By this we mean that their working and living conditions—wages, hours of work, housing, health and sanitary facilities, education, community life, etc.—are determined almost exclusively by the landed elite. The small rural elite obviously has a vested interest in keeping the peasantry in a subordinate status, even at the risk of constantly increasing conflicts, such as land invasions or peasant uprisings. Until now it has maintained a totally inflexible and uncompromising attitude. A whole set of institutions, mechanisms and strategies has been developed to serve its ends. It seems as if the entire economic, social and political structure of Latin American society is turned against the peasants when they seek to gain increased bargaining power, political participation and greater prestige.

There is, of course, a wide range in the attitude of estate owners toward the peasants. But the issue at stake is not whether there are decent landlords or employers, in addition to the harsh ones, who permit one to claim that latifundismo is perhaps "not as bad as all that." The crucial issue is that any decent estate owner can reverse his attitude and become a harsh landlord without risking punishment or damage to his economic, social and political status. This is because latifundismo condones harsh landlords and indeed considers them essential elements for safeguarding the foundation of the system. Thus a hacendado might punish a shepherd who lost one of his sheep to a fox, by deducting three days' instead of the traditional one day's wages. Or he might dismiss without pay a group of workers to whom he promised work and who waited idly on his premises for a couple of days. In neither case would he be considered anti-social or immoral by his peers.[1] In fact, it is the decent landlord who is likely to be scrutinized and criticized if his behavior appears to threaten the foundations of the system and upset the traditional relations between estate owners and peasants. It is therefore the harsh landlord who sets the ultimate tone in landlord-peasant relationships by adhering faithfully and perhaps even excessively to the "rules of the game." This explains why the landed elite's reaction to even the mildest questioning of their superiority is generally violent and entirely disproportionate to the actual challenge of their authority, and usually contrary to the laws and morals of advanced societies. It explains why peasants are generally unable to obtain any kind of redress if they are being defrauded, mistreated or humiliated. In latifundio agriculture, landlord harshness is institutionalized

[1] For a description of such a case see CIDA, Brazil Report, op. cit., pp. 293 ff. The case quoted there is unusual because it took place in an area near a large town where unions were strong and which is the seat of a labor court. In addition, a labor contractor was involved who lost his fees and sided with the workers.

In a sense, the landed elite is prisoner of its own harsh system, which it has fashioned because it cannot relax the rules regulating peasant treatment without sapping the foundation of the system. But the peasants too are prisoners of the system, because their attitudes and values have themselves become institutionalized over time and represent a significant internal obstacle to the process of self-liberation. They are part of the total cultural pattern of Latin American rural life. Their fear of the landlords or their agents, the administrators (farm managers), and in fact all agents of authority associated with the elite, is a difficult obstacle for them to overcome in their search for greater freedoms and greater welfare. This fear manifests itself in submissiveness, evasiveness, distrust and a sense of frustration. In this manner, the peasants have become their own enemies.

CHAPTER 10

The Composition of the Rural Labor Force

Before entering into a fuller analysis of the human relation in a latifundio agriculture, we must first understand the people who comprise the rural labor force in a managerial dependent status, i.e., the people who are actively engaged agricultural work, be they producers or hired or family workers (but excluding non-working family members). We shall also describe the trends affecting the composition of the work force.

Unfortunately, the available statistics are not always very reliable, nor are they adequate for classification of the workers in a manner which would give full justice to the realities of rural society. The most detailed, but still far from complete information is available for the seven countries (Argentina, Brazil, Chile, Colombia, Ecuador, Guatemala and Peru) which repeated references have been made earlier. In the seven countries, the rural labor force consisted of 23.2 million members in the beginning of the 1960's. To repeat, this excludes by definition the non-working men, women and children in the families of the rural workers. These number around thirty million in the seven states and are obviously also affected by the terms of employment of the active labor force, since they are dependent upon them.

Hired farm workers (as opposed to independent producers who work for rural employers under one of several possible contractual arrangements can be classified in several ways by residence (on farms, in villages or in towns); the type remuneration they received; and their access to land. A classification by one criterion alone, e.g., type of remuneration,

Approximate Distribution of the Rural Labor Force
in Seven Latin American Countries
(around 1960)

Class of Farm	Total Labor Force (in millions)	Family Labor (in millions)	Hired Labor (in millions)	Per Cent Hired Labor
Sub-Family	7.2	6.1	1.1	15
Family	6.9	4.8	2.1	30
Medium Multi-Family	6.2	2.5	3.7	60
Large Multi-Family	2.9	.3	2.6	90
TOTAL	23.2	13.7	9.5	41

NOTE: Data based on CIDA statistics, adjusted for more recent censuses.

impractical, because in many cases the total remuneration of farm workers consists of a combination of cash wages (a modern form of remuneration), the products of the land (the traditional form), and perquisites offered by the employers a hut, a portion of the milk, etc.). The following classification, which differs from that adopted by the censuses, would include most hired workers in Latin American agriculture: (1) workers with small, usually inadequate amounts of land and workers who cultivate land under the landlords' orders. In this group we include producers on minifundios who work full time or part time for others; sharecroppers, tenants and similar workers; resident workers on farms with garden plots; and workers living in or near small towns or villages with small plots of land, but hiring out on farms. And (2) workers without any land. In this group we include hired workers living on farms in huts or barracks; workers living in villages who hire out on farms; and workers without any firm attachment or residence who wander from place to place in search of farm work.

The available statistics permit only an approximate breakdown into workers with the right to cultivate a plot and the landless workers. They seem to show that workers without land outnumber sharecroppers and similar farm workers with

land by about three to one. Certain adjustments in the c
sus data, however, made on the basis of the apparent sta
of the campesinos, allow us to conclude that in reality in
early 1960's there had still been just about as many work
without land as those workers with some access to land. T
would confirm field observations about the continued e
nomical importance of traditional forms of employment
campesinos whose remuneration consists wholly or in part
the right to the use and produce of a plot of land. Paym
or part payment in terms of some right to the use of land s
has considerable advantage for rural employers in most ar
of Latin America. It attaches the workers to the land a
guarantees the employers a more than adequate supply
labor at all times. It reduces the employers' need for cash a
allows control over their workers' activities. Contrary to w
one might expect, the type of employment is not necessar
a function of the type of land use. Livestock enterprises m
employ salaried workers or sharecroppers; plantations m
employ sharecroppers, tenants, or workers with or with
plots of land. Employment is actually influenced by ma
factors: tradition, the owners' participation in the mana
ment of the farm, and institutional arrangements, such
labor laws, credit and banking facilities, and even the politi
situation.

We must not overlook the fact that in recent years
proportion of hired landless workers who work only for ca
wages has increased. The rural labor force grows more rapi
than their access to land, which automatically tends to
crease the number of the landless. The increasing proport
of the landless is also a function of both the "pull" of
workers who abandon onerous working conditions in ru
communities to seek the greater freedoms of the villages a
towns (although they continue to depend on agriculture
a living), and the "push" of the employers who replace th
workers by motorized equipment or shift to pure wage e
ployment, both of which simplify their labor problems. I
the shift to cash wage workers is still only partial in m
areas. In São Paulo, for example, one of the most advance
agricultural states of Brazil, the number of sharecroppers a

colonos on coffee plantations increased between 1955 and 1960 from 514,000 to 527,000, although at a slower rate than daily workers and piece workers, whose numbers rose from 222,000 to 281,000. The former, therefore, still outnumbered the latter by almost two to one in 1960.

The long-run decline of traditional resident rural workers is due to a number of socioeconomic and political factors. The right to the use of land is becoming an increasingly unsatisfactory basis for securing an income. The workers and their families need cash to acquire necessities of life, even in the most remote rural communities of the hemisphere. On the other hand, the traditional terms under which workers are hired and work their plots allow them increasingly fewer opportunities to grow enough food or provide for their own clothes and other material items. As a result, many workers seem to be paid now both in kind (i.e., through the proceeds of their produce) *and* in cash, usually as wage workers. To a large extent, the need for more cash arises out of the fact that the plots of land to which campesinos have access deteriorate in quality as the soils become exhausted, because the campesinos do not obtain the benefits of technical assistance, and because they do not have easy access to credit for improved farm inputs. Very often, too, the landlords' requirements for labor are such that they are in conflict with the campesinos' needs for time to tend their plots.

It is noteworthy that the campesinos' demands for cash have accompanied many conflicts between estate owners and workers when the latter request better terms of employment and easier access to the land resource. These demands are one of the ways in which these conflicts come out into the open. Since there is practically no access to more land, demands for better terms of employment normally imply more cash earnings, and they are usually opposed by the rural employers.

In Brazil, the slow shift from one type of labor use to another has been and still is exceptionally violent. In the Northeast's marginal sugar cane areas, for example, absentee landlords had rented their land to small tenants during the period of low sugar prices. The tenants planted fruits and vegetables, with which they supplied Recife and other cities, paid annual rentals, and provided some free labor for the landlord under feudal arrangements. When prices of sugar rose after World War II, the owners evicted workers or forced them to destroy their permanent crops. Sometimes the owners paid a compensation, but more often they did not. The conflicts that arose out of the tenants' treatment gave rise to the *ligas camponêses*. Now these conflicts continue as large landowners seek to reduce the number of their resident workers who live on the estates and are usually allotted a tiny garden plot. The owners normally refuse to build new houses or huts for the workers when the old ones become uninhabitable, or do not allow new workers to enter the houses when they become vacant, or they tear them down. All this has led to violent, even armed clashes between rural workers and organized "vigilantes" in this region.[1] The expulsion of workers is practiced in many parts of Brazil. It does not always have dramatic consequences, since open clashes occur only when workers are organized and can resist the landlords.

In Ecuador's sierra, numerous conflicts have arisen from the hacienda owners' attempts to reduce the number of huasipungos and restrict the workers' or small owners' access to the land, and the subsequent subdivision of the minifundios. Farm workers' demands for better wages and their aspirations toward better living conditions are looked upon by hacendados as subversive. Since they are accustomed to request and receive free or nearly free labor services from their workers and to allow only changes which originate from their own initiative, they see in these wage demands an attack against their status and prerogatives.[2] It might seem that the hacendados' strategy is self-defeating, but on closer analysis it is fundamentally designed to preserve excess labor forces who are obliged to work at or below subsistence wages. On one large typical hacienda of twelve thousand hectares, for example, the landlord had adopted a strict policy of limiting and even decreasing the area of the huasipungos, which caused increased deterioration and erosion of

---

[1] CIDA, Brazil Report, op. cit., pp. 230 ff.
[2] CIDA, Ecuador Report, op. cit., p. 97.

their land. Yields became successively smaller since the workers could not shift their cultivation to other parts of their farm, as the owner could. Furthermore, the landlord reclaimed the huasipungo land for his own use when the head of the huasipungo family died. This represented a definite break with tradition and obliged the remaining family members to live on other huasipungos without obtaining new living quarters. The result was great overcrowding on the remaining huasipungos. Although the majority of huasipungos had existed on the farm for a long time, new land had been allotted to only a few, and there were more non-huasipunguero families (*allegados*) than there were huasipungueros. The conflict was of such magnitude that a solution through mutual concessions appeared to be impossible.[3] Another process that occurs throughout the area of the sierra is the landlords' declining ability to meet the workers' refusal to work without remuneration and demand for cash wages, in view of the low productivity of their own estates. This is of particular interest because it demonstrates that the landlords' traditional and inadequate management of their haciendas contributes, as we have mentioned elsewhere, to the impoverishment of the workers and becomes at the same time a basis for the hacendado to use increasingly repressive measures against his workers. The Indian population, which for centuries was attached to particular plots of land, has lost this security and is presently migrating in search of some means of livelihood. Human settlements are being destroyed; everywhere there are abandoned huts, stables without animals, and huasipungos cultivated by the landlords. Conflicts are also reported in other areas, for example, the demands of the so-called *arrimados* in Loja (southern sierra). According to a lengthy newspaper report appearing in the respectable *El Comercio* (Quito), an open rebellion occurred in 1962 on at least one hacienda. According to this report, the hacendados violently expelled their workers, allegedly because they were afraid of land reform.[4] Another change in the traditional employer-worker relationship in Ecuador is

[3] Ibid., pp. 280 ff.
[4] Ibid., pp. 162 ff.

occurring through the transformation of huasipungueros into simple "tenants" who have relatively less secure tenure. These "tenants" actually have a status similar to that of common hired workers. It is also noteworthy that in areas of minifundios completely encircled by large estates, the process of subdivision and the increase of the population causes tremendous pressure on the land and forces migration to other parts of the country.

During the latter part of the 1960's, there was an increase in evictions of workers with land from the estates on which they had been living. This was the direct result of land reform laws that attempted to protect sharecroppers and small tenants. But it is doubtful whether any census statistics will ever reveal the full extent of the landed elite strategies.

The shift toward cash wages is not likely to alleviate the financial hardships facing most of the workers, since it does not solve the basic problem of unemployment in agriculture. Hence it will not prevent new conflicts as the oversupply of labor—now partly available from "urban" areas to which many displaced workers migrate—continues to allow landlords to determine unilaterally the terms of employment, including wages. This means that workers are mistaken in their expectation that remuneration through cash wages necessarily implies an improvement in their economic status. In fact, it can bring about a decline in their yearly incomes, as the amount of work they perform is reduced and the security of employment is eliminated, although access to cash may imply a certain independence. Thus in Ecuador the wage worker in the sierra is, according to Rafael Baraona,

> the most obvious product of the advanced and dramatic process of expulsion of workers in the sierra . . . a group of human beings is eliminated from the traditional social scheme and prevented from incorporating itself in the emerging modern scheme of things. . . . Perhaps there is no more severe criticism and condemnation of the predominant process of change in Ecuador's agriculture as that which refers to the situation of free or wage workers. . . . In the absence of general economic development in the country as a whole and the lack of pos-

sibilities of absorbing the new rural wage workers (in productive employment) the situation would tend toward further cheapening labor, perhaps even toward an incredible proliferation of underemployment for the aggregate labor force in the sierra . . .[5]

This observer concludes that the misery of the farm workers in Ecuador is tied to a process of spoliation which, though it may be indirect, "generates an outcast in the full meaning of the word, a miserable being whose outlook for a better material and spiritual life can be changed only by a radically different process of change." But in other countries, of course, the displaced workers' situation is no better.

Finally, we must point out that the landed elite is able to control the workers' terms of employment and living conditions simply because it has at its service, directly or indirectly, a very large proportion of the rural labor force. In the seven countries listed in most of our tables, about one fourth of the hired workers were employed on the latifundios alone. All multi-family farms employed approximately 75 per cent of all the hired workers. But it is very doubtful that these statistics fully describe the control which the landed elite exercises over the labor market. In addition to the "hired workers" on the estates enumerated by the censuses, at least part of the family labor force on the minifundios must be considered an actual and potential source of (hired) labor for the estates, because of the large number of excess laborers there. The total labor pool upon which the landed elite can draw is therefore probably larger than statistics reveal. A conservative assumption is that about one fourth of the family labor on minifundios was actually employed on the large multi-family farms in addition to the hired labor they report. This means that over 40 per cent of the hired labor force is available full or part time to the latifundios alone.

But a complete view of the estate owners' control over employment opportunities in agriculture can only be obtained from a more detailed analysis of the employer-worker (or campesino) relationships, and the institutions which shape these relationships.

[5] Ibid., pp. 155 ff.

CHAPTER 11

The Social Organization of Latifundios

Autocracy is a fundamental aspect of Latin America's lati-fundismo. It affects all phases of the relations between employers and workers, and the large landowners and the small-holders. An estate is normally an autocratic enterprise, regardless of the number of people working on it, or whether the owner lives on it or not. The power of the estate owners influences the entire community in which the latifundios are located. The owner may not be directly responsible for the day-to-day operation of the farm—normally he is not—and the operation may be left to a tenant or an administrator (farm manager); but the final decisions on all important issues, such as the labor force, what and how much to plant, or what, when and where to sell, or even on any "minor" issues, rest with him. Minor matters may be those regarding the life and welfare of his workers which in advanced societies have been taken over by public authorities or are resolved through co-operative and collective action. The power of the landlord extends, therefore, over the farming activities as well as over the "private lives" of the individuals who participate in these activities, and very often he also wields power over people who are only indirectly involved with his farm operation, such as his nearby neighbors, who may furnish part-time or full-time labor. It is common for communities where latifundios predominate to see all their activities regulated and controlled by the local landed elite.

What makes this power distinctive is that there is no external check on its exercise. If there is any "check" at all, it stems from the estate owners and their peers. The estate owner retains on his estate the exclusive privilege of making the final decisions. Any other power which may be granted gives those to whom it is delegated only limited authority, and they remain subject to intervention, even arbitrarily. Subordinates' decisions on minor issues are always subject to explicit or implicit sanctions by the hacendado. Since most of the farming activities are routine, there is usually no need for the exercise of explicit orders and sanctions, and the workers of the estate at various levels of responsibility do not constantly have to be reminded of where the authority lies. The same is true for community life at large.

Large estates, except for those which are left unused or devoted exclusively to livestock, normally employ many workers. On most estates, therefore, the social organization is rather complex. Usually the labor force on individual estates includes several types of supervisory workers, each type being hierarchically endowed with a specific set of functions and range of activities on which to make decisions. The lowest class of workers—those who do the actual farm work—cannot make any decisions. They simply obey orders. A typical traditional hacienda of 630 hectares in the sierra of Ecuador, with a dairy enterprise and cultivated crops, may have, for example, the following clearly defined hierarchy in approximate order of decision-making power: the top command is retained by the absentee owner, who may live outside the country; next in command is the administrator, who may be his son, living part of the year on the estate; then there may be several accountants or clerks and other persons charged with service (including domestic) functions; as the enterprise is diversified, there will be a manager-supervisor, and under him there may be several supervisors for each of the enterprises (e.g., one for livestock and one for the crops). The productive work force is also subdivided into several groups, ranging from a practicing veterinarian and the working members of the resident campesino families (huasipungueros)—the women doing the milking and the men the heavier farm work—to the temporary workers without land. When the campesinos are working in the field or in the stables, they are usually supervised by foremen and their assistants, who are part of the "administration" and do not perform any actual work. A similar hierarchy can be found on estates in any Latin American country.

It is noteworthy that the proportion of administrative or supervisory employees, of the total work force on a hacienda, is normally very high. In some cases, it may be almost a third of the work force.[1]

The need for supervision and administration arises out of the fact that the productive work force has no decision-making power and therefore cannot take any initiative in executing its work. For example, if the workers have to weed a field, they are assigned a certain amount of work by their foreman, and when they have terminated, they are assigned another plot. But since the decision-making power of the foremen is also very limited, they in turn must be controlled and supervised, and so forth. Hence, besides being complex, the social structure of the estate tends to be rigid in terms of both economic development and satisfying the campesinos' demands, should they deviate from the norm. The efficiency of use and distribution of power is highest when affairs remain routine. It can, however, be quickly diluted when emergency situations arise or major changes occur. Since there is normally no direct contact between the productive work force and the top command, demands of the unorganized workers have little chance of being heard by the estate owners, so that the total organization of a latifundio is clumsy and inflexible from the point of view of the low-level workers. The hierarchy, therefore, tends to aggravate discontent and even precipitate conflicts. Since administrators can solve conflicts only within a framework narrowly defined by tradition and owners' orders—which are in most cases synonymous—they cannot solve problems on the spot, or can handle them only by exceeding their own power, which may result in further heightening of tension. The most important point is that the rigidity of the social organization of the estates rarely allows even a gradual improvement in the living conditions of the peasants.

[1] For example, on one Chilean hacienda, eleven of the thirty-six people employed on the farm belonged to administration. CIDA, Chile Report, op. cit., p. 51.

In terms of economic development, the social organization of the estates has two further drawbacks. The complex and autocratic nature of the estates just does not allow the farm workers, no matter what their status, to improve the cultivation of the land or the care of the livestock, even in the many cases where those who actually do the farm work would be able and willing to exercise the initiative. Changes in technology and management can be introduced only by the "patron." And as we have seen, most estate owners see no economic need to improve farm management and do not see any connection between the practices they follow and national welfare. For them, changes in the management of their enterprises are always risky, because they may involve changes in the labor relations existing on their estates. If a worker were to go beyond the pattern set by his employer, as transmitted to him through the various layers of the hierarchy, he would be accused of attempting to upset the "rules of the game," and his employment on the estate would be of short duration. For that reason, few workers dare to propose changes in the traditional ways of doing things.

One Brazilian sociologist described this characteristic of latifundismo in the following brilliant analysis of the status of sharecroppers in northeast Brazil, on the assumption that the sharecroppers would want to use their own seed rather than the seed furnished by the employer—a very small demand indeed.

> Nothing would be more logical than for the owner of the enterprise or his agent to conclude that this sharecropper wishes to obtain in the future some additional right beyond those commonly established by the contract of sharecropping. If such a proposal would come from the worker not yet admitted to the farm, but candidate to a parcel of land, it would be only with difficulty that he would become a sharecropper. If he is already a sharecropper on half shares on the enterprise, he would not receive another parcel to begin his plantings. If he were to insist, he would be dismissed from the farm for breach of the original contract and without receiving any indemnification—that is (in the words of the owner), "since he left of his own will, that is, he created the situation to leave." And the cotton which he had was al-

ready in the soil and came from the owner's seed. This problem can only arise in the realm of hypothesis since the producer who is well integrated in the social organization of the community . . . makes a careful selection [of his sharecroppers] before admitting any workers, with a view of avoiding conflicts and tensions on his property.[2]

Estate owners do not allow their workers to use any initiative, partially because of the low opinion they hold of their workers' ability to work on their own. This opinion has little merit in many cases, since the workers have been doing the farm work for generations. Experience throughout Latin America as well as in other continents has shown that once the campesinos are given responsibility and are allowed to use their own initiative, their performance rises spectacularly. If after generations the campesinos were indeed unable to perform better than assumed by the landed elite, it would be greatly to the discredit of the latifundio system, rather than the campesinos.

No less important for development is the fact that the landed elite's heavy investment in administrative personnel represents for the economy as a whole a considerable social cost and a waste of human resources. The major function of the administration is to keep the productive workers in line and to exercise an internal control over the farm operations. The benefits of the administrative work force accrue solely to the large estate owners, as it assists them in maintaining the status quo, rather than improving the working or living conditions of the campesinos or their farming practices. The energies of the "administration" of the estates could, theoretically, be used more profitably if they were marshaled for the benefit of the campesinos in terms of assisting them to obtain greater productivity and better living standards. Under the conditions which prevail, it is doubtful that the present-day members of the administrative work force would be inclined to exert themselves for the benefit of the campesinos, because their authority over the workers—little as it may be—makes them allies of the landed elite.

[2] José Ferreira de Alencar, quoted in CIDA, Brazil Report, op. cit., pp. 573 ff.

CHAPTER 12

The Social and Political Function of Administrators

The overwhelming majority of estates are operated with the aid of administrators. The administrators are the most visible symbol of absentee landlordism and absentee management. As we explained earlier, absentee landlordism is too narrowly defined if mere residence is used as a criterion. Even if an owner or producer resides on the estate, his administrator provides for a certain degree of absentee or indirect management. In fact, for the rural worker almost every estate owner is an absenteeist.

With few exceptions, an administrator is not skilled and experienced, nor is he knowledgeable about the latest farming methods. As we explained earlier, he is in general merely a worker who has been on the landlord's payroll for some years and has distinguished himself by his thorough knowledge of local customs, which he respects, and by his loyalty to his employer. He supervises the farm operation under orders of the landlord within a strictly limited sphere of action. He makes no major decisions with respect to the use of the land, the number and kind of livestock to be raised or fed, or what to buy and sell. His powers over operational expenditures are normally limited to small cash transactions or charge accounts with merchants. From the point of view of the landlord, the administrator is merely another worker, although he receives higher wages—usually not much higher —and certain minor privileges not accorded other workers. But the administrator is the patron's "man of trust."

For the worker, the administrator personifies "management." He represents in nearly all respects the nearest authority, because his most decisive function lies in the day-today handling of the farm workers. He assigns the daily work, pays wages, punishes, fires a farm worker and hires a replacement—within the framework set by the landlord. This implies that decisions regarding the number or type of workers to be hired and their remuneration are exclusively with the owner. The owner may receive a request for more workers from his administrator and dispose of it as he sees fit, and he may consult his fellow landlords in setting the terms of employment without resorting to his administrator's advice.

Farm workers rarely enter into direct contact with the employer, and any sentiments the workers may harbor with respect to the treatment received or the "system" as such are first directed against the administrator. The administrator is, then, their first object of respect, or (more frequently) of resentment. He also represents the worker's main contact with the outside world. He is the delegated judge and jury in most routine matters regarding the work and the life of the worker and his family. In practical terms, this implies that there is no fair mechanism which can insure that justified claims of the productive work force can be vented. It is rare that such claims are heard at all, and when they are, they are almost never decided in favor of the worker. Workers simply have nowhere to turn, unless there is a workers' syndicate or a labor court. But these are extremely scarce throughout Latin America, and many of them take the attitude that employers cannot be wrong.

Given this power, the administrator can treat the men severely, and arbitrarily, without disapproval, because the landlord needs his administrator more than he does the workers. Since he is by far the workers' most powerful superior, he is usually distinguished, like an officer in the army, by some symbol of authority, such as a horse, a pickup truck, almost always a whip or a stick, and very often a gun.

The administrator is therefore a sort of "sponge" who absorbs the immediate reactions of farm people. This fulfills the important function of contributing to the stabilization and fortification of the existing power structure. The aloofness of members of the landed elite allows them to appear innocent to the workers and small producers. They are actual or potential conciliators when conflicts come to their personal attention directly or via the administrator, who, in turn, absorbs the blame for any harsh treatment. Thus absentee management in the wider sense (i.e., management through administrators) is both a convenience for the landlord (whose main interests normally lie outside agriculture and whose incomes from non-farm sources often exceed his farm income), and a method to maintain the existing power structure, since the landlords' political power is derived from ownership of land. Only when conflicts become very intense will the campesinos take the estate owners directly to task. To a large extent, the relationship existing between the administrator and the farm workers—or between the estate owner, via his administrator, and his workers—also prevails between the estate owner and the campesinos living in the neighborhood.

The "ephemeral" presence of the estate owners is used daily on the estates as a screen to exonerate the owners for measures taken against the campesinos. A typical case, which occurred in Brazil in 1962, illustrates the characteristic behavior of the landed elite. A farm worker, having resided on an estate for eleven years, had requested permission from the landlord seven years earlier to replace the leaky hut in which he lived with his family. The landlord had finally allowed its construction, but had asked the worker to sign a paper according to which he (the worker) would pay for the building material while the property of the building would remain with the estate owner. According to the worker's wife, who was interviewed in 1963 after a bloody incident in which the worker was apparently killed, the owner then became sick and left for the capital of the state. The administrator and the owner's son came to her and said that the new house could not be built because the owner had not given the order. Subsequently the administrator, the son of the owner and his friends tore down the framework of the new house.[1]

Obviously, then, social conflicts often materialize at a level well below that of the power elite and serve either to strengthen it or leave it unmolested. The administrator is an

[1] CIDA, Brazil Report, op. cit., pp. 230 ff. See also ibid., pp. 142 ff, for another example.

important strategic element in the maintenance of the system.

Nothing characterizes the autocratic nature of a latifundio agriculture better than the fact that on many large estates and plantations the authority of the landlords and the administrators is reinforced by strong-arm men—a private police force. They make the workers "toe the line" through intimidation, terrorization and corporal punishment. At times they kill. These "policemen" prevent workers from joining syndicates or peasant leagues by threatening those who become active union leaders. They contribute a great deal to the violent conflicts between workers and administration, and cases of brutality arise frequently. We ourselves saw, on the northern coast of Peru, that a powerful landlord had burned down homes of his resident workers and had used caterpillars to shut irrigation canals bringing water to the workers' garden plots. Armed guards were posted at night to prevent the workers from opening the ditches. This forced the families to abandon their plots and houses. In Ecuador, complaints of the altiplano campesinos addressed to the leaders of workers' organizations testify to some of the physical violence and punishments they received. Here are two examples: burning down the huts of the workers; giving an Indian worker on domestic duties ten blows and putting him in jail after accusing him of having taken some clothes.[2] Manoel Correia de Andrade reports from Brazil's poor Northeast that workers who are in debt are kept in private prisons on the estates until they have worked off their debt.[3] As late as 1968, the manager of a land reform project in the Northeast beat up campesinos because they had joined a co-operative!

[2] CIDA, Ecuador Report, op. cit., pp. 87 ff.
[3] *A Terra e o Homem no Nordeste,* pp. 116 ff.

CHAPTER 13

Rural Employment at Subsistence Levels

Rural workers, including smallholders on "leased" plots and the working members of their families, earn lower incomes than any other significant sector in the society. In Part I we made reference to the income level of campesinos. Here we shall examine the conditions under which wages and incomes are earned, and particularly the mechanisms by which incomes are maintained at subsistence levels. Indeed, a low-cost and obedient labor force is the cornerstone of latifundismo. It is therefore in the continuing interest of the large estate owners to have an adequate supply of cheap labor on call at all times. In fact, it is apparent that farm people are confronted with a conscious wage-income policy on the part of the landed elite which we might call *the iron law of subsistence wages and incomes.* Upon closer analysis, the landed elite reveals greater ingenuity and imagination in finding ways to shortchange the peasants and keep their earnings low than in employing methods to put the many physical and human resources which they control to better and more productive uses. Subsistence wages and incomes are not "natural." They are the result of the lack of bargaining power of farm people which the landed elite now has no difficulty in fostering. This means that the iron law of subsistence wages and incomes is promulgated and enforced by the rural power elite, not by Nature.

We should first explain briefly why smallholders and other resident workers with "leased" plots of land are included as "hired workers" and are therefore in a sense earning wages, although their returns may be "in kind" from the produce they raise on their plots. These smallholders—principally sharecroppers or small tenants—are not agricultural producers in the sense that they can freely determine what to grow, how to grow it and what and how to sell. They work under strict orders and under the control of the landlords. Most countries regulate sharecropping and tenancy in some detail by law and guarantee sharecroppers and tenants a considerable degree of freedom in the use of their plots and produce. But there is a wide gap between the law and the realities of rural life. Theoretically, sharecroppers and small tenants obtain possession of the land for a specified period—usually until after the harvest, unless their contract is renewed. But in practice, the hold of the campesinos over the "leased" plot is most tenuous and they can be removed at any time. The law entitles them to reimbursement for the labor they have put into the plots and for improvements (including the planting of permanent crops), but in reality landlords hardly ever reimburse them when they are forced to leave. Theoretically also, the campesinos are free to dispose of their share of the produce as they see fit, but in practice, they must often sell it to their landlord or to a merchant of the landlord's choice as a matter of tradition or agreement, although this may be in violation of the law. But the landed elite, in its overall relation with the peasants, does not easily distinguish between the sharecroppers, small tenants or resident workers with garden plots and ordinary cash wage workers—although we do not wish to minimize the significant differences in the status of the workers.

Sharecroppers and small tenants are a great convenience for the estate owners because they are thereby assured of an inexpensive and effortless way to secure an income from the "rented" plots. Also, free labor services are provided for the crops or livestock that the owners raise on other parts of their enterprise "for their own account." *But although the landed elite wishes to tie its workers to the farm enterprise, it does not wish to tie them to the land*—particularly not through the possessory rights granted them by law, because the law obviously limits the owner's rights to act as he pleases. Therefore the landlords use various methods to make it perfectly clear to the campesinos that they have no right whatever to their land on which they work. They forbid them to plant permanent crops or keep livestock in any significant numbers. They retain ownership of a hut or house the campesino may build at his own expense, and they often shift their men around by assigning them a different plot every season, which results in a small but forced internal migration on the enterprises. To this should be added that the landed elite can tie workers to the farm enterprise not only by "leasing" them a plot of land, but also by keeping them indebted by advancing small loans at exorbitant rates of interest for their farming activities and living expenditures, or through the sale of merchandise in "company stores" on the estates. Workers without land who live on the estates, and even workers who do not live on the premises can be tied to the farm enterprise in this manner. It is apparent that indebtedness is "planned" to tie workers to the farm, from the very system that exists for keeping the accounts, since normally the landlord alone keeps a record of the advances he makes. Here are two interesting, typical cases involving one male and one female worker in Ecuador:

Antonio S.	Debt (sucres)	Mariana Y.	Debt (sucres)
Previous year's unpaid debt	237	Deceased father's debt	108
Febr. 22: barrel of ocas	25	Febr. 23: cash advance	23
July 16: barley	40	Febr. 28: barley	40
Note: for stealing potatoes	50	May 5: cash advance	5
		July 16: one barrel of ocas	25
TOTAL Debt	352	Dec. 9: cash advance	10
		Dec. 22: cash advance	80
		TOTAL Debt	291

At the going wage rate, the yearly earnings would have been insufficient for the worker ever to pay off the debts, even working full time, and the debts would be carried over to the next year to be worked off.[1] In a sense, the campesinos are tied to the latifundios even if they are indebted to the village merchants rather than the estate owners, because the mer-

[1] CIDA, Ecuador Report, op. cit., pp. 143 ff.

chants often act as agents of the landlords and are their close allies when it comes to robbing the campesinos of their potential savings. We shall return to these subjects later.

The economic situation of the campesinos is so precarious that statistics cannot adequately reflect the squalor in which they live. Obviously one finds certain variations in wages or incomes received, with some workers or families earning more, others less. In terms of percentages, these variations might be significant, but the range within which campesino wages or incomes move appears to be rather narrow in absolute terms. It provides only for variations in poverty levels, not for any differences between poverty and well-being, although we do not wish to imply that a campesino and his family would not wish to fall within the upper "poverty bracket" rather than the lower.[2] Actually, information on the various "poverty brackets" is sorely lacking. For example, some campesinos receive larger plots, or plots with better soil, than others for reasons that no one has as yet investigated. Perhaps the plots with better soil are smaller because they are calculated to give about the same income as larger plots with proportionally poorer soil. But this would not account for differences in incomes. A good hypothesis is that, given the makeup of latifundismo, the landed elite prefers, and remunerates slightly better, a passive and obedient campesino who has a large family, all willing to work without or at nominal wages, to a hard-working and resourceful one who grumbles about conditions in the community and is likely to join a peasant league at the first opportunity. Some workers earn slightly higher wages than others for the same job (except where hired "in bulk" through labor contractors). It is likely, therefore, that employers discriminate among their workers on the basis of loyalty and obedience, length of employment, size of family, age and other factors, although it is not clear in what proportion. This does not mean that employers ignore the iron law of subsistence wages or incomes. On the contrary, it seems to show that employers calculate carefully

[2] See, for example, Andrew Pearse, "Agrarian Change Trends in Latin America," op. cit., p. 26 ff.

in each case the quantity (but not necessarily the quality) of work which can be extracted from a given wage. This calculation is made with respect to the wage level and the type or form of wage payment, in such a manner that the final "take-home pay" of the campesinos remains just about the same, subject of course to the small variations to which we have referred.

Some income and wage differentials also result from the employers' apparent intention to provide "incentives" or "disincentives" for other workers. Some employers select "pet" workers, who receive higher remuneration or are granted special privileges. For example, in Ecuador, a young member of an Indian community was made *veterinario* (practicing veterinarian) although all other workers were serfs. In Brazil, in the township of Matosinhos in Minas Gerais a father and son cut wood in a little community, earning significantly more than their fellow workers. Or a small producer may be singled out for privileged treatment as the recipient of credit and other advantages denied his neighbors. The selection of "pets" is no doubt often carefully made by the landed elite in an attempt to raise in other farm people greater hopes for the possibilities of advancement. This is a useful maneuver in the face of the stark reality, which implies little if any hope for improvement in the status of the campesino.

In contrast to urban workers, the campesinos usually secure incomes from a variety of sources, some of which can only be imputed at arbitrary values. This complicates the analysis of their economic situation. Their incomes are derived from wages, from the sale of commercial or food crops, from home-produced and -consumed foods, and from perquisites furnished by the landlords, or a combination of these. The imputed incomes, if there are any, raise the total earnings to a higher level, but normally they do not raise them significantly. It is found that in many campesino families, *it is only the cash income from the sale of crops or from wages that really counts.* Cash is the bond between the campesinos and the outside world. What is most significant, however, is that the combined income from all the various sources is usually not sufficient to put the farm families beyond a subsistence level. Furthermore, most rural families are large, so that even if family incomes appear at first sight to be more adequate, per capita incomes are still very low. The solution to this problem is not necessarily population control, but better terms of employment, brought about by massive tenure reforms. Under several types of work contracts a peasant family *must* be large if it is to have any employment at all. The sharecropping arrangement is such a contract, because with existing levels of technology and the demands of the employers for free or near free labor services, a large family is a prerequisite for holding onto a plot of land. The same is true for work which is paid by the piece. Usually the work assigned a pieceworker is too big for one man to handle and he must use the able members of his family or hire additional men at his own expense.

The fact that the campesinos obtain their incomes from a variety of sources arises from what the Brazilian sociologist Julio Barbosa referred to as *polyvalency of employment,* a phenomenon not mirrored in statistics and to which little attention has been paid until now by observers of Latin American agriculture. Polyvalency, one of the more effective mechanisms to keep campesinos in a state of imbalance, comes about in part from the initiative of the campesinos, who, underemployed and faced with the impossibility of making an adequate living under one contract, are obliged to seek other types of work. Viewed in this manner, polyvalency is a byproduct of the excess supply of manpower in all of Latin America. On the other hand, polyvalency may have some economic implications for the employers when they shift their workers from one contract to another in order to reduce the costs of labor, in search of that combination of contracts which will result in a minimum wage bill and still have the workers at subsistence incomes. Obviously in this respect the shifting of workers from one mode of employment to another does not necessarily imply for the workers an increase in alternative job opportunities or a greater quantity of employment. It may merely imply that for a given quantity of work they are remunerated in various ways.[3] But on the whole, the more important consequences for the employers seem to lie in the scattering of the laborers' efforts, which leaves the men in suspense and uncertainty, as none of the contracts imply any security of tenure. Landlords benefit from this insecurity and encourage polyvalency through their employment practices, at times even to the extent of forcing the workers or members of their family to seek work outside of the estates.[4] Polyvalency of employment prevents the campesinos from resorting to collective action to protect their self-interests. It implies that the peasants are never sure whether they wish to improve their situation with respect to the share of crops to which they are entitled, the daily wage, housing or any other employment conditions which need improvement. Polyvalency, then, enhances restlessness and social tension in the rural community to the extent that farm workers try to get into the various job markets and compete with each other for the sparse job opportunities.

To illustrate: one type of case arises when a small owner, tenant or sharecropper seeks additional work as day laborer or seasonal worker, at times leaving his plot in care of his family. Or he may seek employment as a farm manager or sharecropper on another farm. He may fill as many as three or four functions. In other cases, sharecroppers, huasipungueros, inquilinos or the like are obliged to work certain days for wages on their landlord's crops, or work one or more days free of charge as "homage" to the landlord, on the farm or in some domestic tasks. Or a sharecropper may work one plot of land on half shares, another plot of land on thirds or fourths. Or a resident worker receiving daily wages may work on a piecework basis part of the time. Thus the "employment" pattern of the rural workers presents a complex picture.

Polyvalency is a distinct characteristic of much of Latin

[3] For individual workers, the shifting may imply a greater quantity of employment and income, e.g., if resident workers are requested to do the work formerly done by outsiders, in addition to their regular duties. Normally, however, the work duties are fairly rigidly laid down. The flexibility introduced by employers when they pay the workers in various ways for various duties performed is of benefit principally for the employers.

[4] However, many estate owners forbid their workers to work off the estate.

America's poor farm labor with an insecure land tenure status and very low levels of living, and in fact it contributes to both. It is most common on farms that produce crops, and least common on livestock enterprises or on enterprises with an advanced division of labor. Where it exists, it makes collective action of the workers almost impossible. Barbosa concluded that "the parcelization of the supply of work benefits the employers, and with this reduces to almost nothing the bargaining power of labor."[5]

In Latin America's market for "unskilled" rural labor, the terms of employment are determined unilaterally by employers.[6] Only skilled workers, such as tractor drivers and mechanics, can command better terms. In essence, each contract of employment is an individual arrangement between an employer with overwhelming bargaining power and the rural worker whose bargaining power is nil, except in rare cases of collective bargaining with labor unions. Another exception exists when labor contractors hire workers "in bulk," on similar terms. However, this does not increase the bargaining power of the workers. On the contrary, the use of labor contractors is only a convenience for the employer and is itself evidence of the workers' lack of bargaining power. A labor contractor is an agent and hires workers at a wage rate set by the employer, less a fee payable by the workers, and at times less transportation cost. The use of labor contractors increases still further the social distance between employers and workers, diffuses responsibilities and may make the liabilities of employers toward the workers even less enforceable than when workers are hired directly by the employer through his administrator. It also increases the insecurity of tenure.

Generally the character of the landlord, his sense of social responsibility, his interest in the farming operation and in

---

[5] CIDA, Brazil Report, op. cit., p. 189.

[6] The term "unskilled" is used here principally with reference to workers' skill in the use of modern equipment. In reality, most farm jobs require certain skills, although these skills do not have much prestige. The landed elite thinks of the campesinos as an unskilled labor force, but it is not always consistent in its thinking. For a large number of duties—handling irrigation facilities, pruning cacao or coffee trees, picking cotton—it relies on "skilled" men to do the job, although it does not pay them accordingly.

creating incentives so that his men will perform and live well, are important elements in establishing working conditions on individual enterprises. This explains a certain amount of variation in working conditions on the estates, and the workers have an uncanny knowledge of good *patrónes* and of bad ones. However, for reasons explained in the beginning of the chapter, differences in the working conditions from farm to farm or within farms are of a very minor nature, since landlords must act within a traditional framework beyond which they cannot step without incurring the hostility of their fellow employers and to the formation of which they have contributed. Because of their lack of bargaining power, the workers always accept the terms offered, since under conditions of excess labor supplies their only alternative is a job with similar terms or no job whatever. Again, differences in working conditions reflect variations in employment at subsistence levels, not differences between poverty and well-being.

From the very start, contracts of employment are fashioned so as to make tenure, i.e., the probable length of employment, highly uncertain. The uncertainties of tenure therefore become a device of repression. Uncertainty is derived not only from the nature of the agreement, but also from the inferior bargaining power of the workers. In societies with high labor mobility and an active demand for labor services, flexible labor contracts are of advantage to both workers and employers, because the former can shift to other jobs promising better returns and the latter can hire better services. In a buyers' market for labor, uncertainty of tenure favors only the employers, as the workers, faced with dismissal at any time, are bound to bow to even excessive maltreatment or face forced unemployment.

Rural workers are practically always hired informally by oral agreement. Only exceptionally does one find written contracts in Latin America. Given the workers' lack of education and resources, written agreements are more in the nature of a "protection" for the employer. Normally such agreements are made out in only a single copy, which is then retained by the employer so that the worker cannot refer to its "fine points" or present it to legal authorities as evidence. But whether oral or written, the precise conditions of the agreement are not always spelled out when the worker enters the establishment, but are often determined during the course, or at the end, of the work period. Given the overwhelming bargaining power of the patrón, *open-ended contracts* allow the subsequent imposition of terms more unfavorable for the worker than expected. This contributes sharply to the uncertainty and suspense under which most rural workers live. Lack of precision does not imply greater freedom of action for the workers, but on the contrary facilitates arbitrary decisions, punishments and evasions of the laws by the employers.

As we have noted briefly with respect to "leasing" arrangements, the contracts under which rural workers are employed are normally well covered by the countries' civil codes or by special labor legislation. The provisions of the law may not in all cases fit the realities of rural life and the law may be incomplete. But this is much less significant than the consistent and conscious evasion or violation of the law by rural employers, such as the widespread failure to pay legal wages as established by minimum wage legislation. An interesting example comes from Brazil, which is typical for Latin American agriculture. It shows not only how minimum wage legislation is only partly adapted to the needs of the campesinos but also the widespread, systematic violations of the law. Numerous recent case studies demonstrate that the employers frequently pay a wage rate inferior to that established by the law. In 1957 this was demonstrated indirectly by a rural wage survey undertaken by an agency of Brazil's federal government. (See table, page 139.) In the table, the gap between the legal and real wages has been computed conservatively. Wage legislation is better adapted to the needs of urban than agricultural workers. This arises out of the fact that the law sets minimum *monthly* wages which are presumed to give the urban and rural wage earners a bare subsistence income.[7] Daily wages are computed by dividing the monthly figures by thirty. Agricultural workers, who normally receive wages on a *daily* basis, do not work thirty days. A worker who earns only cash wages

[7] Legal minimum wages are lower in rural areas.

is therefore disadvantaged in two ways: first, because he is not paid the legal daily rate, and second, because he only works part of the month. It might be claimed that it is, after all, not the employers' fault if the legislation is not adequate. Such an argument has a certain amount of validity, but only if one overlooks the fact that the landed elite is strongly represented in Parliament and effectively opposes legislation favorable to the rural workers.[8]

Gap Between Wages Paid Various Types of Workers and Legal Minimum Wages for Specified States in Brazil, 1957

State	Percentage Deviation of Actual Wages from Legal Wages		Deductions for Male Field Workers' Housing as Per Cent of Wages	
	Male Field Workers	Cane Cutters	Authorized by Law	Actual Deductions
Ceará	−31	−29	30	48
Paraíba	−31	−26	27	42
Pernambuco	−36	−27	27	43
Minas Gerais	−42	−41	28	51
Espírto Santo	−31	−26	31	44
São Paulo	−23	−18	33	37
Paraná	+ 6	+ 9	24	16
Rio Grande do Sul	− 8	− 5	24	36

NOTE: The estimates were prepared on the basis of the lowest prevailing wage rate in each state. Hence the extent of wage violations is underestimated or the payment in excess of the legal rate overestimated (e.g., in Paraná, where agriculture expanded very rapidly during the period). Hoe workers and cane cutters are relatively uncommon in Rio Grande do Sul.

[8] For example, for workers who are permanently or semipermanently employed on farms, the daily wage rates could be computed by dividing the monthly minimum wage rate by the number of days effectively worked. This would in effect resemble a guaranteed monthly minimum income equal to the monthly minimum wage rate established by law. Unemployment insurance could be financed out of estate owners' contributions to a national compensation fund. But the argument that the law is inadequate does not explain why the employers do not pay the existing legal minimum daily wages. It is likely that under prevailing circumstances, no matter how the laws read, employers would still violate them systematically.

There is also another source of disadvantage for the campesinos, closely connected with the previous two. In countries where the cost of food and other essential items increases in absolute or relative terms—which is the case in most of Latin America—cash wages rise usually only as a result of increases in the legal minimum wage rates. Here rural workers often lose out on two accounts: the legal increases are promulgated a long time after real wages have declined significantly, and rural employers violate the laws by adjusting their wage payments only some time after the new legal minimum rates have gone into effect. Thus there is a constant downward pressure on real wages in agriculture.

Finally, it must be noted that another abuse exists with respect to overtime. Although the legal minimum wages refer to an eight-hour day, overtime is almost never paid. During the planting or harvesting seasons, workers normally put in a ten- to twelve-hour day. If this overtime were included in the calculation of the wage law violations, the difference between legal and effective wages would increase astronomically.

We shall briefly explore the economic implications of these and other exploitative methods for the landed elite in the following chapter.

These phenomena of vague contracts and violations of the law have been and continue to be the source of serious conflicts. In the absence of unions, violations of the law and obscure agreements are possible because there are not enough courts; because the authorities are biased in favor of large landlords, to whom they usually owe their appointment; because workers have no money to hire lawyers to represent them in court; and because many lawyers do not care to accept cases involving conflicts between workers and estate owners. The fact that the benefits of the laws are rarely available to the workers results in the governing of the patron-worker relationship by power, not by law. Such a relationship is intrinsically one of uncertainty for the weaker partner.

Contracts may be open-ended with respect to the wage rate, the share of the crop or the length of employment. The latter is obviously most relevant to the worker's tenure. However, there are even cases where the plot, which is the object of a rental agreement, may remain undefined. In this way the land-lord can prevent his "tenant" from entertaining any thoughts that he has some rights to the land he cultivates, although the law provides for the tenant's acquisition of possessory or other rights. In Brazil, for example, the well-known historian Clovis Caldeira found in a study of written contracts in the state of São Paulo that the size of the plot was not mentioned and concluded that "the omission of the mention of the size of the area ceded the cropper, and even the failure to be more specific in some cases, enable one to have only a partial insight into this phase of the arrangement. The fact that the 'rent' paid to the landlord has no relation to the area explains the indeterminateness of many contracts. In such cases, it is usual to declare only that the landlord cedes 'a site' or a piece of land."[9] This omission has a direct bearing on the security of tenure of the tenant and hence on the length of his employment.

It is not easy to find general clues which indicate the length of the period covered by a work contract. The method of payment could be taken as a rough index. For example, a daily wage could indicate that the contract is renewable from day to day. However, most arrangements are more complex. In fact, one of the difficulties arises precisely from the polyvalency of employment to which reference was made earlier. The variety of arrangements under which many workers are employed makes the issue of the length of employment very nebulous.

What is clear, however, is the fact that since work contracts are concluded informally and length of employment in most instances is not specified, rural workers depend entirely on the unilateral decisions of their employers as to how long they will work for them. Normally law or custom dictates the length of a contract in the absence of a specific agreement, but the workers cannot rely on this. Although a daily non-resident worker's dismissal customarily comes at the end of a work day, and a tenant's at the end of the harvest, there is nothing to prevent an employer from firing a worker "on the

[9] Cited in CIDA, Brazil Report, op. cit., pp. 197 ff.

spot" for an alleged misdeed, lack of obedience or other reason. Even if a worker is hired for a specified period of time,
the employer can—and often does—break the agreement. Since
employers often make use of their right to dismiss workers at
any time, this partly accounts for the enormous turnover of
labor on the estates. This turnover appears to prevail on most
latifundios but increases in areas where workers are conscious of their dependent status, where they attempt to organize into labor unions or peasant leagues, or where there are
already conflicts. A high labor turnover is, as the employers
know, an important weapon in fighting labor unions.

The daily workers have the least security of tenure, while
the tenants' and sharecroppers' tenure is somewhat more secure, at least during the crop season. The sharecroppers' fears
arise with respect to their ability to stay on their plots or to
find other ones. In recent years, their fears have increased
whenever landlords have threatened to dismiss workers with
plots or have in fact dismissed them, for a variety of reasons,
two of which are land reform and peasant unrest. Sometimes
threats are vague or dismissals temporary, but this makes the
workers feel still more dependent upon the estate owners. For
example, in Sapé, northeastern Brazil, the wife of a small
tenant reported that "almost all the people here have a plot.
Last year, there was the greatest amount of hunger because
the latifundistas did not wish to cede land to anyone. But
this year things improved. . . ."[10] When large estates monopolize the land and campesinos crowd on tiny plots, this
implies that tenants not only face the insecurity of their particular arrangement, but the landlords withhold the land to
impose their terms of employment. One campesino said: "The
day he sends me off, I will have to go without raising any
questions, because it is his land and it is his house . . . My
own land will only have six feet when I die some day."[11]

The aggregate income of the rural labor force is affected to
a certain extent by climatic conditions (good harvests may require a slightly larger labor force), and general economic
trends, such as inflation. But for a variety of reasons indi-

vidual workers are not in a position to benefit from better harvests, prosperity or improvements in productivity. As one sociologist, Carlos Alberto de Medina, said of the peasant workers in the drought-ridden Northeast of Brazil: "Their income is always low, regardless of whether or not there is a drought." The conditions of employment are such that the patrón can determine the total amount of returns going to the workers, keep them indebted and hence dependent, and prevent them from accumulating savings. It is not possible to describe here the many widespread devices which can deprive workers of the ability to make more money. The few examples given below are indicative of general "labor management" practices in Latin American agriculture.

There are four major types of arrangements which keep workers' returns low: (1) setting wages (including shares of crops raised by tenants, croppers or plot holders) at a low level; (2) modifying the general terms under which workers are hired by shifting from one type of employment to another, less favorable, one; (3) violating or modifying the terms of individual work agreements; and (4) defrauding the workers. The examples which follow may fall into one or more of these categories. We have already made reference to some of these arrangements, but we wish now to explore more specifically their impact on the incomes and savings of the campesinos. We shall first deal with those arrangements which keep the incomes of workers with land at subsistence levels, and subsequently with those involving the landless workers, although there is obviously some overlapping.

Some workers are ceded plots *only for their own use*—e.g., huasipungueros and resident workers with garden plots—in payment or part payment of their labor services. In many cases workers are not ceded a specific piece of land, but they are permitted to grow subsistence foods between rows of permanent crops such as coffee or coconuts, and in turn must care for the commercial crops until they have matured. These workers are then dismissed, but they can be shifted to other new planting areas or to pure wage employment on the plantation. Ideally the plots should furnish food for the workers and their families and any surplus could be sold for cash. In practice, however, the conditions under which the plots can be exploited are usually adverse to the adequate utilization of the land. Normally the plots are too small, of inferior quality, in eroded and exhausted soils, often on hillsides, so that yields are low and declining. The workers obtain no financial or technical assistance to improve the management of their land. If they obtain a small loan or seed from the employer, this can be deducted from the wages at exorbitant rates of interest or call forth additional labor services. Such "assistance," therefore, puts the workers under further obligation to the landlord. Nor can the workers grow what they please or keep livestock, except a few chickens or a hog. The plantings are limited normally to traditional subsistence crops. The raising of the same crops grown by the landlord, which may command good returns in well-organized markets, is usually forbidden. In this manner, the campesinos are prevented from gaining access to these markets and from earning larger incomes. To keep livestock, they must obtain permission from the owner, who usually demands that any increase in the stock be turned over to him in compensation for this authorization. This again makes it impossible for the campesinos to build up capital assets for improved incomes and savings.

Management of the campesinos' land is further complicated by the priority which is always assigned the landlord's own farm work. In case of conflict—e.g., the worker needs to cultivate his garden plot, while the employer wants to irrigate his fields—the worker's plot suffers the consequences. The landlords argue that the worker's family can do the work, or that the worker himself can manage his plot after hours or on weekends, and in fact it is very common to hear the estate owners criticize their workers for not managing their plots well. The truth is that under the arrangements which exist between the landlords and their workers, better management of the plots would require more physical and mental stamina than most workers or their wives and children can display, but the estate owners would be the last to admit that they practically prevent their workers from doing a better job. Thus the management of the subsistence plots is entirely under the landlords' control, and they cannot be used to increase earnings above subsistence.

Given the workers' extremely low incomes and near total lack of resources, sales of produce from the plot are most often not from "surplus" production, but are emergency sales to provide cash for current, urgent needs. These sales are made even though the balance of the produce may be insufficient to provide food for the remainder of the year. Hence it is customary for campesinos to have to purchase the same foods at higher prices on the market or in farm stores operated by the estate owners, when they run out of food at home. Often, they repurchase the same food they sold previously to their landlord, and the difference in the sale and purchase prices is pocketed by the landlord.

Garden plots, then, are managed under the least advantageous circumstances for the workers. As a result, although the garden plots are supposed to furnish workers with sufficient food, cash wages earned by the workers are spent mostly on food. If cash wages are inadequate, they go hungry. A typical case is that of resident cacao workers in Bahia (Brazil). Their average cash income, almost totally from wages, amounted to about 67,000 cruzeiros in 1962, but expenditures for food, tobacco and drinks alone—not luxury expenditures, but necessities of life—were about 93,000 cruzeiros. As a result, they entered the new year with a large deficit. The plot is not a profitable business for the workers because the food produced does not compensate them for the efforts they invest in the land. Again, this is not because the campesinos are poor managers, but because they are prevented from being better producers. But under the conditions which prevail, to deprive the workers of these plots without giving them some other compensation would obviously result in worsening their status still further. On the other hand, the allotment of subsistence plots is a lucrative business for the landlords.

In contrast to workers with garden or subsistence plots, sharecroppers or small tenants cultivate land *essentially on behalf of their landlords* and receive a portion of the crop, or the proceeds from its sale, as remuneration. Sharecropping occurs also in livestock enterprises. Many of the characteristics of the arrangements for garden plots also apply to those with sharecroppers or tenants, but the latter generally give the estate owners more frequent occasion to shortchange the campesinos. Whether landlords employ resident wage workers or cultivate their land indirectly by leasing it out under traditional forms of labor use, it is common practice to lease only the poorest land to the workers. Sharecroppers and tenants, like other rural workers, have no savings and are normally out of food and money at the beginning of the agricultural season. Since they receive their incomes only at harvest, they require financial "assistance" from their landlords or merchants by the time the planting begins, even in those cases where the landlord furnishes all the inputs needed to start the farm work. The financial "assistance" is always an expensive business arrangement for peasants—and a lucrative one for the landlords or dealers—because of the usurious terms of the loans. It was found, for example, that in one community in Ecuador, the peasants' scarcity of capital resulted in an onerous credit system through local moneylenders on whom the workers had become very dependent; seed and money is lent against 50 per cent of the harvest and the remainder of the output is purchased at prices well below the prevailing zonal market prices. As a result, the lenders' returns are significantly larger in relation to their inputs than the workers' returns. In another community, usurious moneylenders use fraudulent methods by advancing funds and seed, and at harvesttime take 50 per cent of the total production *after taking out first the amount of the seed lent*. Or when the worker furnishes the seed, the lender just shares the harvest as if it were a sharecropping agreement. For the money lent, the interest rate is 10 per cent per month plus a security, which may be the production or the plot of land itself, and "at times this results in cases of pure and simple robbery."[12]

Only in relatively few cases can a campesino obtain credit directly from an institutional lender at reasonable interest rates. At times, the landlords obtain funds from an institu-

12 CIDA, Ecuador Report, op. cit., pp. 254 ff, 305.

tional lender for the express purpose of distributing it to their men (as happens frequently in Brazil), but lend it to them at a higher rate. The difference becomes a profit for the landlord, allegedly for the risk of lending the funds. In reality, of course, these risks are minimal, because under the conditions which prevail the campesinos must always pay or work off the money owed before they can leave the premises.

Landlords' or merchants' interest rates are not normally advertised as such, but if they are computed they customarily vary anywhere from 50 to several hundred per cent. There are many different "assistance" methods, some resembling outright theft. One common procedure is to lend money or seed on the condition that the worker return one and a half times the amount lent at harvest. If the harvest comes after six months, the annual interest rate is 100 per cent; after three months, 200 per cent. High interest rates sharply reduce the workers' returns to a point where they remain in debt at the end of the year, particularly when the harvest is poor. An interesting case also arises when a small tenant has to pay all or part of his rent in advance, as happens frequently in Brazil. Theoretically, this should free him from the control of his landlord for the season. However, since the payment of the rent leaves him without resources to begin the cultivation of the land, he has to request financial assistance from the landlord, and thus finds himself in the position of dependence described for other sharecroppers or small tenants. Advance payment of rent is requested by the landlord in those cases where the campesinos' demand for land exceeds the supply. This is an artificial situation, brought about by the estate owners' control over the land resources.

Indebtedness, a widespread phenomenon, not only ties the workers to the farm, but also is economically lucrative for the employer-lender. If a worker is indebted, he must turn over (i.e., sell) his share of the crop to the landlord at the prevailing market price, which is always lowest at harvesttime, or even below that, depending on the landlord's whims, and the landlord can sell both his and the worker's share when prices have again risen. The difference is pocketed by the landlord. The same occurs with merchant-lenders. For example, in studies of the Várzea do Açu (Brazil), the merchant financed the planting on the condition that the sorghum be sold to him *in advance* at 600 cruzeiros per unit, when the current price of the product varied between 1,000 and 1,200 cruzeiros.[13] Thus the dependence of the workers prevents them from taking advantage of price fluctuations, as they are forcefully shut off from the market mechanism. The point is not that the campesinos are too uneducated to participate in the modern economy, as the members of the landed elite are fond of declaring, but that they are prevented by violent means from becoming part of the economy. In many instances, however, sharecroppers or tenants have to turn over their share of the crop under the original contract regardless of any indebtedness. They are obliged to agree to these terms in order to avoid losing the plots of land which the landlord ceded them.

A similar situation arises with respect to the management of the land and the selection of the crops. Both are controlled by the landlord, with the result that his workers seldom benefit from favorable market situations which might put them above the subsistence level. The share (income) of the worker is also at a low level not only because it is lower than his and his family's contribution to output, but also because of the quality of the land, which is normally low and declining, or extra-contractual arrangements initiated by his landlord. Both may deprive him of any additional returns, or, in fact, of his due. One serious instance arises when the share of the crop going to the worker is formally determined only prior to or at harvest. In Brazil, for example, instances have been found where the share is determined only after the condition of the harvest is known by the landlord. If the harvest is good, the share going to the landlord increases. This means that the income of the campesino does not rise with yields. In some cases even a specified agreement may be violated by the landlord. The sociologist Maria Brandão stated that in Camaçari, a municipio in Bahia (Brazil), "as a rule the worker begins his work and only afterwards ascertains the system of payment. At times the system is tacitly decided upon by custom so that the worker without land knows at any moment how each owner proceeds with respect to any type of land he has. Occasionally there are surprises, mainly when, after a superficial agreement on the payment of the rental in cash, the owner requests payment in kind after inspecting the condition of the plot."[14]

Other devices fall into the category of frauds or near-frauds perpetrated against the workers. One of the most widespread practices is the use of false weights to shortchange the sharecroppers or small tenants when the crop is divided. False weights are also commonly used by the administrators or other employees to weigh the cash wage workers' harvest, e.g., in the cotton harvest. Or the foremen or administrators may cheat the workers by assigning them a plot of land to cultivate but measuring it incorrectly and paying them for a smaller quantity of land than that cultivated. Of course there are also instances where the workers attempt to defraud the employers, particularly the absentee landlords. For example, cotton pickers, who know which estates have false scales, add a few stones to the cotton at the bottom of their bags. But the presence of the administrators makes this very hazardous for the campesinos. A worker found to defraud his landlord would be summarily punished, but a defrauded worker has no way of obtaining redress.

All these examples show that the workers' returns are geared not to the productivity of land or labor, but more nearly to wage policies and practices of the employers which effectively limit these returns to the subsistence level. A wage theory which claims that wages are a function of productivity is based on ignorance of the conditions which prevail in agriculture.

A few comments on free or almost free labor services are needed to complete the picture of the employment conditions of workers with land. The right to use and cultivate land, whether on behalf of the landlord or for the workers' own benefit, is, as we have repeatedly mentioned, accompanied by

[14] Ibid., p. 211.

obligations to work for the owner for a number of days free of charge or at lower than the prevailing wage rates. The services may consist of extra farm work on the landlord's other farm enterprises or in domestic duties. These semi-feudal services are among the reasons why workers' incomes cannot rise above the subsistence level.

In Ecuador, for example, on one large hacienda of 690 hectares, forty-five yanaperos residing in a small nearby community completely surrounded by large estates are obliged to work on the estate in return for the right to use its roads and other facilities.[15] They form the estate's largest labor force. Circumstances force them to use the estate's land to collect firewood and its water and the grass growing along the roads for their animals. In return, they are obliged to work two days per week without pay, furnishing the estate annually with a minimum of about 4,700 days of free labor. However, since the overseer assigns the workers more land than they can handle by themselves, they must call on the able-bodied members of their families to assist them. Thus the total free labor supplied exceeds 5,000 days.

In the province of Cotopaxi the inhabitants of one indigenous community have to pay with three days of labor per year for the right to use the roads of the estates (*pago de los pasos*). In addition they must turn over their sheep to the land-owner for a week to help fertilize his land (*majadeo*). Without previous notice, the employees of the landlord collect the workers' animals by going from house to house, and round up about three to four thousand animals without cost to the landlord, and at times with considerable cost to the owners if the animals are returned damaged or poorly fed.[16] On another hacienda of 444 hectares the workers must furnish six days of labor per month for each unit of land allotted to them, as well as performing other tasks, including domestic work when the owner is on the farm, although these are discounted from the obligatory workdays. For the right to collect

[15] In another community surrounded by estates, the campesinos must pay four sucres per person and one sucre per animal to gain access to outside roads.

[16] This contrasts sharply with the severe sanctions levied against workers for real or alleged damages to the landlord's livestock.

firewood and use pastures in the dry hills they must furnish work which is not discountable. Half of the workers contract other workers at fourteen sucres per day to replace them at times during the obligatory workdays if there are no members of the family to do so. Similar examples can be found in Peru. In Brazil semi-feudal obligations are still widespread. In the municipio of Quixada (Ceará), on one typical large farm, the payment for the use of the land is one half for the cotton. However, the cropper is also obliged to give one day of work per week on the basis of a daily wage well below the prevailing rate. Thus sharecropping and bondage (*sujeição*) are associated.

On another farm in the Northeast bonded workers obligate themselves to work three consecutive days per week for one half the wage prevailing in the area, although in this case there is no formal sharing agreement. However, the employer retains the right to request which major product is to be planted, as well as the right to buy the whole salable output. The sale of the cropper's share to the owner was the norm.[17] In Paraíba (as in other states) workers are obliged to give one day per week of free work to the owner. This feudal practice, the *cambão*, was one of the reasons for the growth of the ligas camponêses and other farm workers' organizations. One observer reported that the cambão:

> . . . is a personal obligation as a "homage" to the owner, which implies that in some areas it is not allowed that the tenant pay someone else to undertake this task. If we compute one day of work on the basis of 150 cruzeiros . . . one can observe that the tenant works every year for the landlord for 7,800 cruzeiros free of charge, which represents a really exorbitant rent for the little plot he cultivates and the hut he lives in. [These rates probably refer to 1960.] Thus one can see that in the work relations described, there is a great harm which befalls the worker who does not possess land when he is obliged to subject himself to conditions of contracts which are truly treacherous.[18]

[17] Many estate owners in the area have livestock and cotton. It was found that on the farms studied, income per hectare farmed by sharecroppers was higher than on the land operated by the owner. This demonstrates the valuable contribution which sharecropping makes to the owner.

[18] M. Correia de Andrade, op. cit., p. 200.

It is to be noted that beyond the cited obligations, estate owners customarily charge heavy fees for minor services performed for the peasants. A typical example is the peasants' use of the landlord's mill to grind yucca or corn for home consumption. Normally the landlord receives for this service a share (e.g., one fourth) of the meal, and the peasants must furnish the labor for the grinding.

A few additional comments are now needed on employment practices regarding landless workers. The highly uncertain tenure of wage workers, combined with their low wages, puts their incomes at extremely low levels of subsistence. In many instances the daily wages amount to no more than a few cents per day. In Peru's sierra, for example, workers in outlying districts are paid a tiny fraction of the going wage rates, and wage rates decrease with the distance from major towns or villages. It has been established by the 1961 census that 86 per cent of the rural workers in Peru earned between $58 and $291 U.S. per year, although these figures are probably inflated, as they are estimated from the workers' reported average *weekly* earnings.[19] In Guatemala higher wages are not paid even when workers are "scarce," because the wage scale depends mainly on the social responsibility of the employer.[20] Even in modern Mexico, the wages paid landless workers, including migratory workers, are minimal and total wage incomes do not exceed thirty to forty dollars a month when they work full time.

In general, workers are no better off whether they are paid a daily or a piece rate. Employers prefer the latter when they wish to extort a maximum effort from the men. The workers incorrectly believe that they are getting more when they are paid by the piece, as evidenced by the following observation of the Brazilian sociologist Geraldo Semenzato:

> The so-called best period for piecework is the harvest and processing of cacao, but it happens that generally during this period there is a major influx of workers . . . which results in a decrease in the rate paid (say) for a box of cacao. The work paid on a production basis is in-

19 CIDA, Peru Report, op. cit., p. 273.
20 CIDA, Guatemala Report, op. cit., p. 177.

tense and highly supervised and requires from the worker an enormous effort. In fixing the payment, the producer takes into account the salary normally paid the worker per day of work, the production in terms of quality and quantity, requiring always a higher production . . . It is relatively common for the worker to be confronted with a fall in the rate of pay per unit to be produced when the landlord can count on a larger number of workers and hence with the same quantity of work [in less time]. . . .[21]

The worker's error derives from the fact that he may earn more per day, but work fewer days, or that he may have to put in a greater effort for the same pay. Statements of landlords regarding daily wages and piece rates confirm that they calculate the latter closely, always with the result that the "take-home" pay is about at subsistence levels.

Another disadvantage arises for the workers when landlords do not pay punctually, or when they fail to pay the agreed rate, or even fail to pay altogether. This occurs in large areas of the sierra of Ecuador, for example: "In the majority of the haciendas where huasipungueros predominate, the head of the family almost never receives his wage at the end of the day. The overseers or owners 'settle the accounts' from time to time—every two or three years. The cash wage is a fiction . . ." Or: "Incomes from daily wages (two sucres) are nominal, in the first place because [the workers] are paid after long delays, and secondly because instead of cash the workers are supplied with *panelas* (sugar and other items)." It is also noteworthy that in the sierra, wage "payments" have become a method for measuring the workers' debts, and in fact "cash wages" have taken on the additional function of tying the workers to the farm. It is also reported that "in none of the haciendas with huasipungueros do wages reflect the eight-hour day provided by the Labor Code. The huasipungueros on livestock farms especially work almost twenty-four hours a day. In agriculture the work-week is not in effect. Only the actual days of work are counted."[22] When the administrators cheat the workers

---

[21] CIDA, Brazil Report, op. cit., pp. 276 ff.
[22] CIDA, Ecuador Report, op. cit., pp. 144, 138–56.

out of their due, the owners normally close their eyes to these malpractices, since they are more in need of their supervisors than of the workers.

Perhaps the worst facet of landed elite-peasant relations is that estate owners sometimes mete out physical punishments either directly or through their representative, or by calling for police or military forces. This makes the estate owner accuser, judge, jury and enforcement agent, all in one. Violence has become an accepted phase of rural life in Latin America. As a result, fear and terror have become components of the lives of many campesinos.[23] Individual workers are punished for real or alleged misdeeds or for carelessness, partly to terrorize the men and "set examples," partly to deprive them of their belongings. The severest sanctions are saved for efforts to unionize farm workers. Acts of terrorism also serve to deprive peasants of their land, both in established farming communities and in the frontier areas.

In Ecuador, for example, punishment on one typical estate in the sierra was found to consist of extra workdays. It may be suspected that in some cases these punishments are merely pretexts for pure and simple robberies. The workers must work off, free of charge, any penalties imposed upon them; these penalties are enforced by the employees of the estate, who take from the workers such personal belongings as hats, ponchos, utensils and other items. On occasion the mayordomos and administrators attack the workers verbally or physically when an animal has strayed onto the hacienda's pastures and damaged a seedbed, and they even do damage to the animal so that its owner will take greater care in the future and comply with his duties. If a worker loses any of the landlord's animals over which he has charge, his punishment is to pay the market value of the lost animal. Since the peasant cannot pay in cash, the landlord arbitrarily confiscates his livestock, estimating their value at very low prices and withholding wages until the debt is repaid.[24] In many

23 In this context, see "Some Relationships Between Psychobiological Deprivation and Culture Change in the Andes," by Alan Holmberg. Cornell Latin American Year, 1966, Cornell University, Ithaca, New York.
24 CIDA, Ecuador Report, op. cit., pp. 226 ff and 239.

instances, estate owners refuse systematically to put up fences on their estates—not only in Ecuador, but throughout Latin America—and refuse to allow their peasants to build fences, in order to insure maximum flexibility in the land tenure pattern. This flexibility is always an advantage for the estate owners, since it makes it clear to the peasants that they have no rights in the land.

Obviously not all landlords exercise the "right" to sanction a worker, nor are all harsh practices found at the same time on the same estates. However, they are encountered often enough to indicate that there is a consistent pattern of repression or incipient and actual brutality. Within the existing social structure there is no countervailing power which impedes landlords from resorting to violence.

CHAPTER 14

The Economics of Repression: A Brief Digression

The Brazilian sociologist Carlos Alberto de Medina affirmed that the estate owners make their largest profits from their laborers. Perhaps Medina's conclusion is exaggerated, but there is little doubt that the lack of peasant bargaining power is financially profitable for the landed elite. We shall give a few simple examples to demonstrate the veracity of his argument. Their significance is not so much that they show the short-run gains to the landed elite, as that they explain the long-range losses to the campesinos as they accumulate overtime.

A characteristic case is the obligation of peasants to turn over a share of the product to the landlord in return for the privilege of using his mill to grind corn or yucca into a meal. For example, on an estate of 4,200 hectares in the state of Maranhão (Brazil), where poverty and feudalism are everywhere, 202 tenants, all living at subsistence levels, are charged one fourth of the meal for the use of a mill, in addition to having to furnish their own time and labor. Two economists—who, incidentally, are of the antiquated opinion that feudalistic tradition in Brazil is "probably a net social advantage" and that the country owes a substantial debt to the landed elite—stated that in this case this charge is "insignificant," after comparing it to the total gross returns of the tenants (1.2 per cent before paying rentals), and concluded that there was no exploitation of the peasants.[1] However,

[1] W. H. Nicholls and R. Miller Paiva, "The Structure and Productivity of Brazilian Agriculture," *Journal of Farm Economics*, May 1965; and "The Itapecuru Valley of Maranhão; Caxias, *99 Fazendas*," *1963* (Nashville, Tenn.: Vanderbilt University, Graduate Center for Latin American Studies,

there are other ways of looking at the same problem and arriving at the opposite conclusion. A simple mill can be set up with the relatively small investment of less than $200 U.S. In our particular case, if the mill was worth $300 U.S. and each tenant paid $1 U.S. in kind annually for its use, not counting his time and labor, the mill would be paid off, conservatively speaking, in one and a half years if all the tenants on the estate used it—a reasonable assumption, as ground yucca is a staple food there. Once amortized, the net annual profit in the small investment would equal roughly the annual family income of one tenant and his family. One must also take into account the conditions surrounding this small business venture. If the payment of the one-fourth charge makes a difference between an adequate amount of food for the tenant's family and a meager or even insufficient diet, then the charge would turn out to be exorbitant. If the milling charge is part of the owner's systematic policy of keeping his workers at a subsistence level—including his prohibiting the tenants from purchasing their own mill on a co-operative basis—it would be a pure case of "exploitation" if the tenants run out of food and later have to purchase additional meal at market prices, perhaps the very same meal which they had turned over to the landlord, giving him an additional profit.

But there are other cases where landlords obtain much more significant returns from their workers, sometimes without any investment or effort. We have already mentioned the Ecuadorian estate that receives an estimated five thousand days of labor totally free of charge, and the free fertilizing of another estate in the sierra of Ecuador. Such "incomes" to the landed elite reach astronomical proportions if they are computed on a regional basis, as for the Indian Andes of Central and South America, where the described practices are common. A more complex example involves the systematic violation of the minimum wage laws, which is often justified by the hacendados on the grounds that they furnish their resident workers with a house or garden plot or both. At

---

1966), Chapter II. The two authors were taken to task for their incomplete views of Brazilian agriculture by the sociologist Carlos Alberto de Medina, in *America Latina*, July–September 1968, pp. 146–53.

times a deduction for the "rental" of a house is specifically authorized by law, as is the case in Brazil. But in most cases, the wage paid is below the minimum wage rate whether or not a house is furnished, so that the hacendados' justification is misleading. While the law may authorize a deduction of a rental for a house, it does not authorize a deduction for the garden plot. But such rentals *are* deducted, in fact, because the sum of the actual wage paid plus the rental for the house furnished still remains below the minimum wage rate. In other words, the employers deduct more than the authorized rental for the house. This again shows that the existing wage legislation is not adapted to the conditions of rural labor.

The Brazilian law that may serve as an example allows the rural employers to make financial gains in several ways. Firstly, rental for a house is deducted for every worker living on the premises, regardless of how he lives. For example, a father and son living and working on the estate have the rental deducted twice, although they may live in the same house. Secondly, the law does not distinguish between rooms and houses. This means that workers living in barracks, which are common on plantations, each must pay the full rental of a house. In the third place, the rental deduction from the daily wage—the customary form of wage payment in agriculture —implies that the total rent paid by the worker increases as his wage income increases. The more days he works, the greater his total house rent. And finally, the rental deductions authorized by law are exorbitant in view of the quantity and quality of living quarters furnished. Prior to 1963 employers of rural labor could deduct about 30 per cent from the wage, but new legislation reduced this to 20 per cent if the house furnished offers minimum conditions of health and hygiene—a totally unenforceable law under the conditions that prevail in Brazil—and even the 20 per cent is exorbitant. Given the employers' insignificant investment in workers' houses—usually they are made from material available on the estates and built with free labor furnished by the workers themselves—the multiple rental deductions, which may exceed several times the number of houses available on the estate, represent a pure profit to the owner. It was estimated that on one cacao plantation, the mere "rental income" of a large cacao producer with thirty resident workers in one year was over ten times higher than the yearly cash wage earnings of one worker, and it rises rapidly if the workers worked more days and earned more.[2]

The extra rent deducted for a garden plot—the difference between the minimum wage rate and the sum of the actual wage paid plus house rental—can become another pure profit for the estate owner. For example, in the same cacao region of Brazil, it was estimated that a resident worker would pay off the real estate value of a garden plot in about four or five years, and on a per-hectare basis, the owner's income from plot rental exceeded his net income from the remainder of his estate by a substantial margin.[3]

Could the landed elite pay higher wages to their workers —e.g., the legal minimum wage rates? It is a difficult question to answer. The very management of estates is often a deterrent to better returns for rural workers in kind or cash over the long run, because of declining yields. No doubt some marginal estate owners would have to sell out if they had to pay better wages. But generally estate owners' incomes are high, and the hacendados reinvest an insignificant portion of the gross agricultural returns on their estates and pay few, if any, taxes. The remainder is used to sustain a high level of living. Hence, if gross estate returns were to remain constant, larger wage bills would merely reduce the landed elite's level of living and their consumption expenditures. These, of course, can be greatly reduced without any threat of poverty to the owners. Their reduction might even be of considerable benefit to the national economy. In many cases, of course, estate owners could theoretically continue to obtain their previous returns from the estate, and still pay higher wages after increasing their yields, simply through better farm management. But this is obviously speculation. Paying higher wages is against the rules of the game of a landed elite whose economic, social and political foundation is a cheap, obedient and partly unemployed labor force.

[2] CIDA, Brazil Report, op. cit., pp. 410 ff.
[3] Ibid., p. 412.

CHAPTER 15

The Disorganization of the Campesinos

With a few exceptions, a contract of employment between an estate owner and a campesino is the result of an individual "bargaining" process. Better terms of employment, including minimum wage laws, could be obtained if the bargaining power of the rural workers could be increased through the organization of effective labor unions or peasant leagues and rural co-operatives, and if the terms could be effectively enforced through a well-functioning network of labor courts. Since such organizations or agencies would threaten the status of estate owners, attempts at establishing collective bargaining processes are systematically suppressed by the landed elite by means which range from bribing peasants or their leaders to eliminating them. Only a tiny fraction of the rural work force is organized. Landlords vigorously oppose unionization, even when the workers' demands are modest. The lack of peasant organization stands in sharp contrast to the closely knit collective action of the large producers, who are organized into commodity associations or general landowners' groups. These groups have great influence on national or local agricultural policies, including the "management" of rural workers. They are backed by powerful financial resources and, if necessary, by the local police or the army. Their activities range from blacklisting workers who join or are active in unions, and "vigilante" action, i.e., armed self-defense against the workers, to opposition to government policies or agencies set up to assist the workers.

Even in countries where labor unions or co-operatives have made the most progress, the proportion of workers or smallholders who belong to them is usually very small.[1] Most countries (except El Salvador, where peasant organizations are forbidden) have legislation which authorizes the peasants to form associations, including syndicates or smallholders' leagues. But often the legislation is very restrictive and does not, in practice, allow for easy formation of such associations. In many cases, the legislation does not conform to the principles established by international agreements to which the countries have subscribed. Specific legal obstacles include lengthy delays to officially recognize duly constituted labor unions. According to the latest information, in 1967, eleven countries out of nineteen (including Cuba, but excluding Puerto Rico and Haiti) had ratified Convention No. 11, concerning the Rights of Associations and Combination of Agricultural Workers of 1921; twelve had ratified Convention No. 87, concerning Freedom of Association and Protection of the Right to Organize of 1948; and twelve countries had ratified Convention No. 98, concerning the Application of the Principles of the Right to Organize and to Bargain Collectively of 1949. Only a few countries have ratified all three conventions. But even in countries where such conventions were ratified, national legislation was not always adjusted to conform to their principles, as the International Labor Organization has shown. For example, in Costa Rica the workers' federation, Rerum Novarum, complained in 1964 that the authorities had broken up meetings of union leaders in the plantations of the Compania Bananera, which controls large enterprises in the Pacific banana belt, on the grounds that the leaders were "extremists who advocated hatred, confusion and discontent in order to upset the social peace which prevailed in the plantations." Usually "social peace," in the minds of the landed elite, means the undisturbed exercise of arbitrary and autocratic labor man-

[1] In recent years, only Chile has seen a significant development in peasant organizations. It has been claimed that after 1964, within four years, well over half of the country's farmers had been organized into unions, credit societies, pre-co-operatives, co-operatives and land reform *"asentamientos."* Rural wages of farm workers increased substantially on the average. For a detailed account of Chile's peasant movement, see Almino Affonso, *Movimiento Campesino Chileno,* Vols. I and II.

agement practices. A similar case involved the Standard Fruit Company of Honduras. It is apparent that "leftist views" are used as a pretext to slow down or hinder union activities. In some countries, such as Venezuela, unions are recognized officially only after delays of up to one year, although the law provides for a period of thirty days.[2]

In most of Latin America, the organization of rural labor unions was still in its infant stage in the early 1960's and many of the existing associations were forcibly dissolved in the mid-1960's. For example, it is reported that only a very low percentage of the workers in Ecuador are organized, and statistics on rural syndicates, particularly in the sierra, where they were more numerous, are fragmentary. Most union activities are of a clandestine nature and the organization of local unions is not spontaneous because of landlords' repressive tactics, but is aided by influences from outside the rural sector. Given the isolation of rural people, collective action without such outside assistance would be nearly inconceivable. Even with it, the viability of rural unions is not high. Often organization of local associations arises in response to the landlords' abuse of the workers. In some cases it is based on existing communal or social organizations that become active when these abuses become intolerable. One form of resistance is the strike. It seems to occur relatively frequently and is generally accompanied by violence. One Ecuadorian observed that "the strike in the rural areas assumes the character of a real insurrection. When this occurs the workers throw out the landlord and his immediate collaborators. The intervention of the police only serves to give them more courage and under those conditions, transitional measures and arrangements have little effect. . . . The organized indigenous workers present their requests at the time of planting or harvesting because only at those times can a strike be effective." At times the workers' demands are addressed to parliament or the president of the republic or even the Church. But these are not always transmitted to

[2] Xavier A. Flores, *Le Role des Organisations Agricoles dans le Development Economique et Social des Zones Rurales*, ILO (to be published). See also ILO, Plantation Workers (Geneva, 1966), for more details.

the authorities and in any event, the authorities cannot always take care of the conflicts, in view of their limited personnel. The requests reveal that workers claim only those rights to which they are entitled under the law; words like the following: "we have formed a union," "we are assembling in accordance with the terms of the labor code," "we are acting within the very terms of the labor law," "we wish to organize within the terms of the law for our own defense," "the employers have to adhere to this law," show a preoccupation to adjust to the law which is worth pointing out, particularly if one takes into account the fact that these requests originate from organizations that are virtually forbidden by the employers and the local authorities. This is also significant, since the majority of the workers' requests arise out of the employers' refusal to grant elementary human and legal rights. The reactions of the employers toward union activities seem to have one common denominator: refusal initially to admit the existence of labor unions, denying a right recognized by law, and discouragement of the workers' participation by threats, persecution and even attempted murder of union leaders or other persons who appear to the employers and local authorities to be dangerous. Workers interviewed in the field stated that "the estate owners mislead the workers by giving them to drink and eat so that they don't join the organization and if they persist, says the administrator, they'll have to leave the hacienda. He uses some very bad words against the workers." Or: "That day, the [representative of the syndicate] visited the farm and the boss came out to kill him." Another worker added: "Now that we are organizing again the boss says again that we must leave the place or says also that houses of those who make trouble will be burnt and they are giving money away so that they will kill [the local leader]."[3] With this tradition of violence, it is small wonder that unionization in Ecuador is carried out clandestinely and does not reach large proportions.

In Guatemala too the right to organize and to strike is recognized by law, but the legislation is not effective in agri-

[3] CIDA, Ecuador Report, op. cit., pp. 89–97.

culture. There are serious difficulties that impede the organization of rural labor unions. Government policy with respect to unions has been one of "utmost caution." The strong workers' organization of 1952–54—when a land reform was being carried out—whose specific purpose was to do away with the great dependence of the workers on the haciendas, was suppressed because the government feared the influence of the communists. Though the constitution in no way prohibits the unionization of rural workers, there are now practically no agricultural unions. Potential leaders do not participate in the reorganization of the movement for fear of reprisals. The large landholders do not forget the events of past years and interpret any attempt at organization as being in the interests of international communism.[4] As a result of their unfortunate experiences, the peasants and particularly the workers have become very skeptical about the effectiveness of politics and unions to achieve their ambitions. They remain at the margin of the nation's activities. And their suspicions create an obstacle which will be difficult to overcome before fundamental changes can be brought about.[5]

Thus, peasant organization finds one of its greatest handicaps in the fierce opposition of the landed elite. But no less important is the extremely low income—and particularly cash income—of the campesinos. It is noteworthy that peasant associations often develop first among workers with rights to land, as they are in a better financial condition to join unions. This was the case for example with the ligas camp[oê]nêses in Brazil. The precarious financial situation of farm workers—whether plot holders or landless—is a nearly insurmountable obstacle to the formation of peasant organizations. Even if the monthly contribution to a peasant union were to amount to only one day's wage of one of the members of the worker's family, this would mean a significant item in the family's budget. Under the circumstances, *the monthly membership fee for the union could mean the difference between eating or not eating for one or several days. In many cases, this*

---

[4] CIDA, Guatemala Report, op. cit., p. 90.

[5] Ibid., pp. 177 ff. For Colombia and Brazil, see CIDA, Colombia Report, op. cit., pp. 228 ff; and Brazil Report, op. cit., pp. 309 ff.

cash sacrifice simply cannot be afforded. For this reason, rural labor unions have more non-dues-paying members than financial supporters among the peasantry.

The structure of labor courts or similar agencies dealing with labor conflicts is entirely inadequate and allows the landed elite to violate laws with almost total impunity. Attempts to strengthen these agencies are also systematically discouraged. Even where they exist, only few rural labor conflicts reach them. When they do, the implementation of labor laws tends to be lax. In industrialized countries, courts are severe in forcing employers to pay wages rightfully earned by workers. But Latin American courts have not yet reached the independence necessary to enforce the law. They frequently condone compromise offers of employers which are considerably below the amount for which workers sue or which may be owed them. Employers make such compromise offers only after it has become clear that they are in the wrong. Such compromises are legally acceptable and shorten judicial procedures and, under the conditions which prevail, must be considered small victories for the workers. But they obviously do little to discourage employers from evading their obligations. Delays in these proceedings are notorious and the judges commonly biased in favor of the employers.[6] In the region of the Indian Andes, the personnel of agencies dealing with labor conflicts is openly prejudiced against Indians.

The co-operative movement in rural Latin America is equally weak. In many countries, co-operatives are still regarded as subversive. The most recent statistics seem to reflect a slight improvement in the status of co-operatives in absolute terms. But good statistics are difficult to obtain. In Peru, for example, agricultural co-operatives are not listed separately and no accurate data seem to be available. There were apparently 104 co-operatives "related to agriculture," with about 7,500 members, 64 of which were officially recognized in 1965. But not all of these were agricultural co-operatives in the sense that they were formed by peasants.

[6] For an interesting case see CIDA, Brazil Report, op. cit., p. 285. See also ibid., pp. 318 ff.

It is clear that the co-operative movement in Peru lacks economic and political significance. According to official statistics, 40 per cent of 102 of these co-operatives had less than 40 members; 30 per cent had between 41 and 60; 13 per cent between 61 and 80; 2 per cent had over 400 members but none had more than 500 members. Their financial basis in all cases was practically insignificant. This in a country with a rural labor force of 1.4 million in 1960!

On a regional basis, according to a recent report of the ILO, the number of co-operatives in twenty countries (excluding Cuba) rose from about 2,100 in 1948 to about 5,000 in 1963, and the number of co-operators increased about five times, from about 235,000 to 1.1 million in the same period. However, the number of members decreased by about 200,-000 between 1960/61 and 1963. Most of the earlier increase was due to developments in Argentina. As a result, average membership rose from about 111 to 214. In some countries, however, the average membership is considerably smaller, reflecting the low bargaining power of most of these associations. In fact, in ten of the twenty countries, the average membership in co-operatives did not exceed 100. Only in Puerto Rico did it exceed 500.[7]

In none of the countries has there been a major "breakthrough" in co-operative growth since 1963; at the end of the decade the co-operative movement was probably about at the same level as in its beginning. It is estimated that only about 1.15 per cent of the rural population had membership in co-operatives in these twenty countries, reflecting an almost total lack of organization of the peasantry with respect to economic activities, such as the acquisition of inputs or the marketing of outputs.[8]

We conclude this Part by emphasizing that in Latin America's latifundio agriculture the relationships among people, and between people and land, are ruled by power, not by law. Power and lawlessness are synonymous. As Pearse

[7] Xavier A. Flores, op. cit.

[8] In Cuba the co-operative movement marked a strong increase. According to Sergio Aranda, *La Revolucion Agraria en Cuba* (Mexico: Siglo XXI, 1968), the co-operative movement has been joined by a large number of smallholders and other peasants.

said: "An open society in which citizens may claim universal rights is incompatible with the personal rule of the patrón on an estate in which the writ of the public law officers, in effect, does not run. The helot class must be effectively and publicly discriminated against so that its members continue to feel isolated from the society even when outside the bounds of the estate."[9] Lawlessness begins with the chaotic status of property titles or real estate registers, which introduces an element of confusion with respect to "who owns what and how much," and allows a powerful landlord simply to claim land which is not his. It ends with the elimination of peasants and peasant leaders who are active in organizing the otherwise defenseless campesinos. The rule of power in turn is a reflection of the extraordinary imbalance in the distribution of wealth and incomes. Most of the power is used for the preservation of the status quo, which must be maintained with respect to both the distribution of physical resources and the impotence of the *campesinato*. Agricultural development and latifundismo, then, seem to be incompatible. Part IV will discuss this subject.

[9] Pearse, op. cit., pp. 27 ff.

PART III

THE LAND REFORMS OF THE 1960'S

The Statutes of 19 February 1861 provided not only for the emancipation of these millions [of bonded peasants on private estates], but for their endowment with land, and for their social-economic organization. These laws of 1861 were so verbose, so full of variables, so loaded down with qualifications and exceptions, and in general so astonishingly involved and complicated, that it is difficult to understand how any serf could ever by any possibility have known what rights might be hidden in this legislative haystack.

G. TANQUARY ROBINSON, *Rural Russia under the Old Regime,* Chapter V, "The Emancipation," p. 65.

Author's Note

Part III contains repeated references to the processes of Peru's land reform under the 1964 legislation. Shortly after this manuscript was completed, the old statute was replaced by two land reform decrees, issued by a new military government in 1969.[1] These decrees seem to introduce an entirely new note into the land reform panorama of Latin America[2] although a considered judgment on their importance and impact on Peru's agrarian problems—after they have been in force for over a year—is still premature. This new legislation presents in some respects a departure from previous concepts and procedures. It is the basis for a more ample and rapid land reform than the previous one. It has eliminated some (but not all) of the defects of the complicated law of 1964. It can be modified again by new decrees, and it is to be expected that this will indeed happen in the future.

Our analysis of Peru's 1964 legislation, however, continues to be of considerable value. It is typical for most of Latin America's land reform legislation; it has historical significance because it explains how the processes of reform are being stalled by legal, administrative and political institutions; and finally it serves as an illustration that agrarian legislation must

[1] Decrees 17716 and 18296 of May 1969, reissued as Decree 265-70-AG of August 18, 1970. Other decrees complement the land reform legislation: 17752 of July on water; 17395, 17713 and 240-69 of June and November 1969 on cooperatives; 37-70-A of February 1970 on Indian communities. The new legislation on water is particularly important, as it nationalizes this resource and abolishes all acquired rights to it.

[2] See Edmundo Flores, "La Reforma Agraria del Peru," *El Trimestre Economico*, July–September 1970, pp. 515 ff. For a less political but more detailed analysis, see T. Carroll, "Land Reform in Peru," USAID, *Spring Review Country Paper* (SR/LR/C-6), June 1970, Washington, D.C.

be examined in light of the realities of the agrarian problems of a country, rather than exclusively in legal terms.

Peru's new decrees—still relatively complicated, with 215 articles—attempted to shorten the time period required to expropriate estates and to redistribute the land to the peasants, although expropriations continue to be handled on an individual basis and are time-consuming. In many cases, the reserves of the landowners (*tierras inafectables*) can be reduced to zero, and by and large, the capital assets of an estate, including livestock, are expropriated along with the land. The appraisal value of the land is low and in some cases expropriations are near confiscatory. But the expropriation price of cattle and other assets must be paid in cash, which puts severe limitations on the volume of land reform in a country where the national budget is strained.

The decrees also provide for severe sanctions for landowners who evade the law or disobey the authorities. They prohibit the ownership of land by private corporations. A significant change consists in giving the highest priority in the redistribution of land to co-operatives, Indian communities and other groups of peasants who are to operate the land jointly, rather than to small individual owners. The law also provides for participation by the peasants or workers in the net profits of agricultural enterprises. Furthermore, the law sets the basis for regional development schemes rather than development of individual haciendas, as most Latin American land reform laws envisage.[3] In fact, the land reform institute has initiated a policy of planning and executing land reform on an area basis.

The radical departures from previous concepts incorporated in the legislation, however, have not as yet been paralleled by similar action in the field, although ambitious targets have been set by the government (at first 500,000 families were to be beneficiaries in five years, but this is now scaled down to less than 300,000).[4] But there are some exceptions. One has

[3] Article 92 of Decree 265-70-AG stipulates that in land reform zones the land reform institute must prepare zonal development plans which are to accompany the new agrarian structure.

[4] The total number of potential beneficiaries is about 1.2 million families.

been the "intervention" (for subsequent expropriation) by the state in the powerful sugar monopolies. This intervention may have broken the back of a landed elite which for generations has dominated the agricultural plantations of coastal Peru, if not the economic policies of the entire country. In addition, expropriations of haciendas in both the coastal irrigated valleys and the sierra now proceed at a more rapid pace, although perhaps not rapidly enough to prevent a counter-reform movement from gaining strength. Redistribution to the peasants has been slow, although some of the expropriated estates are already being managed by the state with some token co-operation of peasant representatives, in anticipation of their final adjudication to the peasant groups favored by the law. The declared policy of the government has of course greatly increased peasant expectations. But the state has still been very cautious in its support of, or appeal to, peasant organizations. The participation of the peasants in the land reform process is therefore still in an embryonic condition, and there is as yet no effective grass-roots movement to get the campesinato to identify itself with the program.

If area land reform schemes could be successfully carried out with the active collaboration and support of the peasants on a national scale, accompanied by fundamental changes in the structure of supporting services (credit, marketing, etc.), Peru's land reform could become a new symbol for Latin America's peasantry. This means particularly a new orientation of the economy toward the support of the new co-operatives. But there is as yet no clear trend in this direction.

CHAPTER 16

Land Reform and Progress

It has long been evident to observers of Latin America that land reforms are both an essential prerequisite for improving the welfare of the campesinos and a cornerstone of general economic, political and social progress. It is also obvious that the so-called operation of the forces of the market not only fails to secure for the peasants greater access to the land and other agricultural resources or to the markets of goods produced on their farms, but in fact tends to bring about increasingly greater inequalities in the distribution of wealth and incomes. This must have become clear from the analysis of trends in Latin American agriculture during the 1950's and 1960's.

The theory that progress must be both preceded and accompanied by social reforms has long been defended by social scientists and politicians who, not being intellectual slaves to a given social system, have understood that progress consists in distributing the benefits of society to the largest possible number of beneficiaries and eliminating the institutional barriers set up to prevent their diffusion. This theory has known varying degrees of popularity, depending on political conditions. But even when it is least popular, it is always given a certain amount of lip service.

Shortly after the Second World War the United Nations put the matter succinctly. It stated that

> to a very large extent, the problem of the underdeveloped countries of the world is the problem of poverty of their farm populations; that unduly low standards of living in rural areas are not confined to the underdeveloped countries; that they can be found also in countries which

have reached a high level of economic development. But in the underdeveloped countries the problem is of a different dimension, because the economy of these countries is mainly agricultural. Among the most important factors which affect rural living standards is the agrarian structure. This term is here used to mean the institutional framework of agricultural production. The agrarian structure may reduce the standard of living of the peasant by imposing on him exorbitant rents or high interest rates; it may deny him the incentive or opportunity to advance and it may check investment because it offers him no security; it may lead to the prevalence of farms which are too small to be efficient units of production or too large to cultivate intensively.[1]

Almost two decades later, the Inter-American Development Bank commented on the "sluggish rate of overall agricultural growth" on the Latin American continent, one of the poorest in the world, and noted that there is growing evidence of the need for structural reforms in the rural sector. While the ideological controversy over reform objectives and strategy continues, three major arguments in favor of changes in the traditional agrarian structure are gaining increasing acceptance. They are the fuller employment of natural and human resources, greater integration of rural populations in the market economy through improved income distribution and the anticipated effect of higher rural incomes and increased social mobility on political stability."[2] Coming from an institution whose main function is that of a banker, this is an important admission. Even the Inter-American Committee of the Alliance for Progress (CIAP), whose sympathies for land reform are somewhat lethargic, confessed that "the accomplishments with regard to land distribution programmes are clearly inadequate in comparison with the magnitude of the rural problems."[3] No doubt this organization felt obliged to make reference to such a delicate concept as land distribu-

[1] Excerpts from "Land Reform, Defects in Agrarian Structure as Obstacles to Economic Development," E/2003/Rev.1.ST/ECA/11 (New York 1951), pp. 4-5.

[2] IDB, "Socio-Economic Progress in Latin America," Social Progress Trust Fund, Seventh Annual Report, 1967, p. 29.

[3] CIAP, "Report to the Interamerican Economic and Social Council" (CIES), Twelfth Meeting, Vina del Mar, June 1967.

tion because of the increasingly explosive agrarian situation in the hemisphere, which cannot be ignored.

A theory of development in which progress becomes a function of necessary basic changes in the man-made institutions shaping a traditional agriculture cannot be based, on statistical or mathematical evidence. It can only be based on logic, supported by historical evidence and experience. Man-made institutions that resulted in progress—e.g., greater economic justice and security, expanded participation of the masses in the political and economic processes—were brought about by the abolition of antiquated institutions which hindered progress. Whether antiquated or progressive, institutions have their supporters who have a "vested" interest in them and will fight to the bitter end to preserve them. The more "basic" the institution, the more bitter the fight. For that reason a change in favor of progress is normally accompanied by great violence, even by revolutions. In societies where democratic processes prevail, new benefits are often brought about through peaceful institutional changes. Even then, political pressure or the need for political support is a strong factor in bringing about change. As an example, social security was expanded in the mid-1950's to farmers in the United States, although they had not specifically pressured for it, to broaden political support for the party then in power. It meant an almost revolutionary change for the better in United States agriculture and undoubtedly had sharp economic repercussions on the pattern of consumption, expenditures and investments of farm people. But such democratic processes do not prevail in Latin America, least of all in the agricultural sector. Of course not everyone agrees with the meaning of progress. Most people—particularly the poor—would agree unanimously that unemployment and old-age insurances are a definite sign of social advance. But heirs to large fortunes whose economic security for life is guaranteed them from birth, or permanent army personnel who can look forward to retirement and a good pension at the age of fifty-two, would consider it a sign of pampering the masses. Progress is a value-laden concept for which there is no objective definition.

It is necessary to examine the status and performance of

he various sectors of society from several angles in order to
iscuss progress. But this is exactly what many people can-
ot undertake. For example, only in rare cases can the rich
r the powerful put themselves in the position of the poor or
veak and identify with their problems or preoccupations.
Only a few people with moderate to large incomes could
ossibly imagine what a farm worker with an annual family
ncome of $200 U.S. or less, working under semi-feudal
erms of employment, would consider as progress. The atti-
ude of the landed aristocracy in Latin American nations—
although they must be aware of the extent and nature of the
ural masses' poverty is one of indifference, ignorance or lack
f interest, or at times pride; they see in it evidence of super-
aatural forces at work to punish the poor (who are bad) and
eward the rich (who are good). For the rich and powerful,
he disadvantages and lack of privileges of the poor or weak
re not proof of lack of progress. Thus the theory of the
unctional relationship between social reforms and progress,
vhich may seem obvious to the masses does not have much
ntellectual or political appeal for the landed elite. They are
nore likely to consider progress to be changes which rein-
orce and perpetuate their elite status.

There is not complete unanimity with respect to the mean-
ng, nature and scope of land reform. In fact, the more the
ssue is debated, the more confused people are likely to become. It has been said that land reform defies a precise defini-
ion, because "reform" is whatever reformists have in mind.[4]
To one "reformer," land reform may mean the introduction
f hybrid corn;[5] to another it may mean large public investments in manufacturing plants in his own region (as one
member of the landed elite of southern Brazil stated in all
seriousness). Another reformer may point to the two essential
aspects of a "true land reform," which are, first, the expropriation of all latifundios, and, second, the free redistribution
of the land to the campesinos. Perhaps the best "definition"

---

[4] Solon Barraclough, "Lo que Implica una Reforma Agraria," ICIRA (FAO),
Documento No. 2 (Santiago, Chile), pp. 5–8.

[5] Edmundo Flores, "La Economia de la Reforma Agraria y el Desarrollo
Agricola," ICIRA (FAO), Documento No. 32 (Santiago, Chile), p. 32.

of land reform—best because it is most directly related to the agrarian problems of traditional agricultures—consists of the three objectives implicit in the concept: *greater social equality or justice, the redistribution of political power*, and *improvements in the economic performance of agriculture* (including higher levels of income for the peasants).

The economic, social and political changes to be brought about by land reforms cannot be marginal; they must be massive in order to be successful.[6] With respect to the achievement of greater social equality, a massive reform in Latin America implies principally a redistribution of land, the basic agricultural resource, through the elimination of both privately held estates and the tight control over land exercised by a small landed elite. A new land tenure system would be set up to eliminate absentee landlordism. This new system might include family-type enterprises, co-operatives, collectives or state-operated farm units, or a combination of these. In most countries throughout the world which have gone through land reform, several systems coexist side by side. Credit and other farm inputs would be made available to producers not on the basis of wealth, social prestige or political affiliation, but on the basis of need and the actual or potential contribution the receivers can make to aggregate output. Agricultural workers who do not gain access to land—because they prefer to work for wages, or because there is not enough land to be distributed, or because the new tenure system includes state-operated units with hired labor—obtain full employment at satisfactory wage levels, better housing, education and social security benefits. In the process, of course, farm work will become a much more prestigious occupation.

Redistribution of political power means, among other things, the end of the estate owners' exclusive control over decisions regarding agriculture and the working or living conditions of farm people; the right of campesinos to form co-operatives or labor unions, to elect local or national government representatives of their choice, and to have a more

[6] See, for example, J. K. Galbraith, "Conditions for Economic Change in Underdeveloped Countries," *Journal of Farm Economics*, November 1951, pp. 695 ff.

decisive voice in community activities and development. In view of the conditions which now prevail in Latin America, such progress could only be brought about through drastic and far-reaching changes in the institutional framework and the political power structure.

Once such changes have been achieved, they form the basis and provide a climate for a sharp increase in output and greatly improved economic performance. The major reason is that they create entirely new incentives for the rural masses. The rewards can be greater because of the elimination of idle human and physical resources that now characterize Latin American agriculture. The production and distribution processes can also be reorganized to conform with the needs of a growing and modernizing society. Historical experience seems to confirm that this is the impact of a true land reform.

CHAPTER 17

Land Reforms Before 1960

Between 1910 and 1960, three Latin American nations lived through drastic land reforms. Of these, the Mexican reform was the most violent. It started with the revolution of 1910, which ended a period of severe peasant repressions during the second half of the nineteenth century and the first decade of the twentieth. At that time, almost all of the land in Mexico was controlled by a few thousand hacendados, and a large portion was in foreign hands. It is estimated that up to one million people died during the revolution, which Frank Tannenbaum described as a war of extermination (of the peasants).[1] In nine years, one third of the population of the state of Morelos, where Zapata began his agrarian revolution, was destroyed. Land distribution to peasants began before 1920, but more farmland was turned over to the peasants under the ejidal land tenure system of the 1930's under President Cárdenas—that is, more than fifteen years after the end of the revolution—than at any other time. The process of land distribution still continues, but it is perhaps no accident that the period of highest intensity was during the Great Depression of the 1930's.

The Bolivian reform began with the revolution of 1952. It ended most of the feudal labor relations in that nation. By and large it was much less violent than the Mexican Revolution. For one important land reform area, the canton Ancoraimes near Lake Titicaca, it is reported that after 1953 there were no cases of large-scale violence, although in some instances peasants used force against the landlords' efforts to

[1] *Peace by Revolution: Mexico after 1910* (New York: Columbia University Press, 1933; paperback, 1966), p. 178.

bypass the land reform legislation. According to one estimate, 3,000 people were killed during the initial turmoil. The Bolivian Government also armed the peasants so that they would better defend their gains under the reform.

The Cuban reform began shortly after the overthrow of the Batista regime in 1959, with the first land reform law of May 1959. The change of regime was preceded by several years of guerrilla warfare. But after the fall of Batista, no major violence was reported in the execution of the reform. In October 1963, private property in excess of sixty-seven hectares was abolished by a second land reform law.

Of the three reforms which brought radical changes to the agrarian structure of the countries, the Cuban was the most drastic. For the first time in Latin American history, it created a socialist agricultural sector, side by side with a private sector. The latter now controls about 30 per cent of the farm-land. The socialist sector is based on state-owned farm enterprises. The immediate impact of the unexpected Cuban land reform was electrifying. It brought about great changes in national and international agrarian policies in the Americas. It seemed to mark the beginning of a vast reform movement on the entire continent. The drastic nature of the Cuban reform was quickly understood by Latin America's peasants; it abolished the large private estates, many of which were owned by foreigners and which are always associated in the peasants' minds with their oppression, and it was aimed at securing direct and immediate benefits for small peasants and rural workers.[2] But its drastic nature was also fully realized by the landowning class. Calls for abolishing latifundios and the traditional agriculture had been made for decades throughout the hemisphere. In Brazil, for example, at least forty-five major bills on land reform were introduced in the legislature between 1947 and 1962, as well as a series of decrees, amendments or messages. During the same period, 110 important speeches were made in Parliament on the subject, of which eighty-five were given in 1959! But few people took them seriously.

[2] Eric Jacoby, "Cuba: The Real Winner is the Agricultural Worker," in *Ceres* (FAO), July–August 1969, pp. 29 ff.

Nor can it be said that the landowning class was entirely unaware of what a land reform meant. The Colombian legislators, for example, were fully conscious of the three objectives of land reform mentioned earlier, because Article 1 of the land reform law of 1961 stated specifically that its objective is to reform the social agrarian structure through measures designed to eliminate and prevent the unequal concentration of land ownership or its excessive subdivision; to increase production; to bring about better conditions of work for farm workers; and to lift the level of living of the campesinos. The article did not speak of electrification, irrigation or road construction, pilot settlement projects, education, pure-bred livestock, or greater efficiency of the pricing system as being land reform. So it can be assumed that when members of the landed elite speak of these measures as being equivalent to land reform, they do so to sidetrack the real issues of domestic land tenure problems. They know that a real land reform means breaking down the monopoly of land-ownership and politics by the landed elite.

Land Reform Laws and Date of Enactment in Selected Countries

Country	Year Enacted
Brazil	1964[a]
Chile	1962[b]
Colombia	1961
Costa Rica	1962
Dominican Republic	1962
Ecuador	1964
Guatemala	1962
Nicaragua	1963
Panama	1962
Peru	1964[c]
Venezuela	1960

[a] Preceded by partial legislation on a land reform institute (SUPRA) in 1963.

[b] Replaced by a new law in 1967.

[c] Preceded by partial legislation in 1962 and 1963, and replaced by new legislation in 1969.

Practically all countries passed new national land reform legislation soon after the Cuban land reform. They organized land reform institutes and carried out some land reform projects. This occurred even in nations, like Peru, with a highly traditional agriculture where land reform had hitherto been taboo. Peru's law was passed in 1964,[3] but it was preceded by partial legislation (decrees) which applied only to an area in which there had been peasant uprisings. In the Dominican Republic a law was passed in 1962, and in Chile, land reform was legislated into existence first in 1962 and then again in 1967. Today only El Salvador has no land reform legislation.

Restlessness of the peasants as well as fear on the part of the landed elite were important factors in hastening legislation. In some countries, the law was passed after considerable unrest and violence. The most outstanding peasant movement took place in Peru and involved an estimated 300,000 campesinos, men and women. Elsewhere, as in Colombia, legislation was devised to pacify the rural sector by the promise of large-scale reforms, in anticipation of more unrest.

[3] A new law was promulgated in Peru in 1969. See Author's Note preceding Part III.

CHAPTER 18

The Alliance for Progress and Other Events

An equally important factor in land reform was the enlighten-
ment of public officials in both Latin America and the United
States. For the first time it was admitted at the highest levels
that economic development was being hampered by the backwardness of agriculture. Backwardness in agriculture was
recognized not only as a cause of low aggregate output and
low productivity per hectare or per worker, stagnating per
capita production and levels of technology, but also as a function of extreme inequities in the distribution of agricultural
resources and incomes. In Colombia, for example, even conservative politicians closely tied to the landed oligarchy began
speaking of needed adjustments in the agrarian structure, paying lip service to the new ideological fashion, although they
did not necessarily mean that these adjustments would be in
favor of the masses of campesinos.

A great impulse stemmed also from an apparent change
in the policy of the United States toward Latin American
economic development. This had an important bearing on national policies, because of the obvious influence which the
United States exercised over Latin American economic, political and social programs. Shortly before the Cuban revolution economic development was viewed in the United States
principally in connection with desirable increases in productivity.[1] But by September 1960, in the Act of Bogotá, the
problem of land tenure (i.e., agrarian structure) and agri-

[1] See, for example, "Report to the President," by Dr. Milton S. Eisenhower,
27 December 1958, United States–Latin American Relations. U. S. State Department, publication 6764, Inter-American Series 55. January 1959, Washington, D.C.

cultural development was tackled more directly. The act recommended a special program for social development directed toward the carrying out of measures for the improvement of rural living conditions and land use. But the act was hesitant, and the measures recommended consisted principally in "studies" of the situation and the acceleration of programs which are marginal to changes in the agrarian structure, such as land reclamation, land settlement or tax measures.

The Act of Bogotá contained the seeds of ideas expressed with great vigor and precision in the Charter of Punta del Este of 1961, the legal foundation of the Alliance for Progress. Concern with the impact on progress of social, political and economic inequities was evidenced in the Charter's call for an "effective transformation of unjust structures and systems of land tenure and use," with a view to "replacing latifundio and dwarf holdings by an equitable system of land tenure so that . . . the land will become for the man who works it the basis of his economic stability, the foundation of his increasing welfare and the guarantee of his freedom and dignity."[2]

The Alliance for Progress did not fulfill its promise to become the cornerstone of an effective transformation of the unjust agrarian structures of Latin America. It has been attacked as being ineffective, as a tool of American imperialism, as hypocritical. But as an historical document, the Charter plays a unique role and has great significance; no one can object to the desirability of peaceful and systematic changes in the structure of traditional agriculture, although one might object that this is not easy or even possible to achieve. The Charter set the basis for American policies followed during several years with respect to agricultural development, and it serves as a bench mark from which any subsequent deviations from its principles can be judged.

The Charter recognized explicitly that the distribution of resources and incomes is inequitable in Latin American agriculture; that per capita incomes and rates of growth are low; that unemployment is high and labor relations deficient; and that the solution to these problems lies in "profound eco-

[2] Title I, Objective 6.

nomic, social and cultural changes." Land reform was considered an important instrument to bring about such changes in agriculture. Hence land reform seems to have been considered the basis of sustained agricultural growth at which the Alliance was aiming. The Charter, then, is a sophisticated international agreement. It clearly recognizes that development is a function not only of more capital investments, more trade, higher productivity and other purely economic variables, but also of political and cultural variables, such as social justice and the freedom of men working through the institution of representative democracy.

The Alliance was intended to be a mutual arrangement, "a great co-operative effort" of help and self-help. The United States pledged its financial assistance in return for the Latin American countries' mobilization of their own resources to accelerate agricultural growth. In order to marshal their resources, the countries agreed to formulate development plans and programs and were "encouraged" to undertake programs of comprehensive agrarian reforms. The Charter did not clearly state that major financial assistance was to be forthcoming only if reforms were undertaken according to development plans; this must be inferred, however, from the text of the Declaration to the Peoples of America, in which it is said that the countries agree "to make the reforms necessary to assure that all share fully in the fruits of the Alliance for Progress," and that "as a further contribution, each of the countries will formulate a comprehensive and well-conceived national program for the development of its own economy."

Three important issues arose in connection with the Alliance. The Charter did not specifically state that plans and programs of development must include targets and mechanisms for reform.[3] In fact, it seemed to treat reforms and development plans as two relatively independent issues. In subsequent years, most Latin American countries have indeed treated them as such, although the Committee of Nine,

---

[3] See, however, "Reunion extraordinaria del Consejo Interamericano Economico y Social al Nivel Ministerial," Punta del Este, Actas y Documentos, OEA/Ser.H.XI.1, pp. 714 ff. (Planning Experts' group.)

an Alliance panel of high-level experts whose principal function was the formulation of development programs, and later CIAP, repeatedly pointed to the need for establishing land reform targets and even suggested such targets in at least one case (Colombia) for inclusion in the development plans.

Furthermore, the Charter and other subsequent documents did not specify when a land reform was to be considered a land reform. Only experience could tell when the leaders of the Alliance would regard changes in the structure of a nation's traditional agriculture as a land reform. Hence there was an inherent danger that the mere enactment of land reform legislation and a few colonization or land distribution projects involving only a few beneficiaries would be considered adequate as evidence of the nation's marshaling its resources for land reform in order to qualify for financial aid. The danger was not only that aid would be given without due regard to the principles of the Charter, but also that an ineffectual program of land distribution to peasants would maintain, with the blessing of the Alliance, the basic structure of latifundismo, and with it, the traditional obstacles to agricultural growth which the Charter so well recognized. Subsequent developments showed that this indeed took place. In order to assist the leaders of the Alliance in formulating guidelines for land reform, a special committee (CIDA) was organized in August 1961. Its members were representatives of five international organizations[4] engaged in agricultural research and technical or financial assistance in Latin America, and its work program was established during the same year at a meeting of high-level experts. The studies and missions of this group now form an impressive documentation on land tenure conditions in relation to agricultural development; they have been used in some cases to formulate land reform targets for most of Latin America.

Although the scope of the required land reforms was not specified in the Charter, this document must be interpreted as a clear-cut mandate to bring about peaceful, rational reforms which aim at *changes in the structure of traditional agricultures within the established legal framework, including*

[4] FAO, ECLA, IDB, OAS and IIAS.

newly enacted land reform legislation, and consequently within the existing political and social power structure. It attempted to channel reforms into controlled programs which, unlike Cuba's reform, would not imply a fundamental change in the political, social and economic foundations of the Latin American nations. It is this inconsistency which was the downfall of the Alliance. In essence it left it up to existing governments to break up latifundios for the benefit of the peasants, although in most cases the governments owed their very existence and survival to the latifundio-owning class.[5]

In summary, then, the Alliance was a warning that if current trends in agriculture were to continue, social and political conflicts would multiply. But it did not take into account the political, economic and social power of the landed elite and its allies, and their resourcefulness in finding ways to maintain the status quo. This power enabled them to start a large-scale counter-reform.

Soon after the signing of the Charter of Punta del Este, a totally different political movement of great significance made land reforms in Latin America almost impossible, at least for the time being. Peasant unrest, large-scale invasions of land and political pressures for changes in the agrarian structure were common in the early 1960's. Peru and Brazil were the scenes of the largest peasant movements; but in Colombia, Ecuador, Chile and Venezuela, too, the discontent of the landless peasantry renewed both open and hidden conflicts. Although the Peruvian and Brazilian peasant movements assumed great proportions, their scope and development have not been brought to public attention in a systematic fashion. In Peru, open violence seems to have begun in 1960, on the coast, in the sierra and in the selvatic region. It became most severe in 1962 in a semi-selvatic area of the department of Cuzco and soon covered most of the altiplano. Events thereafter are shrouded in secrecy. Great military operations seem to have been mounted in 1962 and 1963 which resulted in the death and imprisonment of many peasants and peasant

[5] Edmundo Flores, "Land Reform and the Alliance for Progress," Center of International Studies, Woodrow Wilson School of Public and International Affairs, Princeton University, 20 May 1963.

leaders. The vestiges of the operation could still be detected as late as 1966 through the presence of military contingents in the areas most affected by the violence, and the obvious passiveness and reticence of the peasantry. Since military operations were directed against the peasants and their leaders, they implied strong assistance to the landed elite and must be so interpreted.

In Brazil, military and police action in 1964 against peasants, peasant leaders and organizations ended the pressures emanating from the rural sector in favor of land reform. But still less is known about this operation than about the Peruvian one. It is a fact that the major campesino organizations, such as the ligas camponêses, which had been active in pressuring for land reform, were broken up and their leaders killed, tortured, imprisoned or exiled. In the years following the military coup, only small organizations were permitted to exist, but they do not have the backing of the peasantry and therefore have little political influence. Again, the beneficiaries of the repression of the peasant movement in Brazil were the latifundistas. In Colombia, large-scale but unpublicized operations by the forces of law and order are reported to have been directed against the so-called *"repúblicas independientes"* in the mid-1960's. These "repúblicas" were peaceful nuclei of peasants operating land collectively in relatively isolated regions of the country. The operations conducted against them are reported to have caused many deaths. Many regard them as provocations organized by the forces of law and order for no apparent reason, except, perhaps, to allow the landed elite to take over this land.

By the second half of the 1960's, peasant organizations in Latin America had not significantly gained in either numbers or influence. By and large, their position is now much weaker than it was in the beginning of the decade, while the political position of the landed elite has grown much stronger. The near destruction of the campesino movements in the years following the Punta del Este conference of 1961 brought about a radical change in the political base which a large-scale land reform movement could have counted on as a springboard. Whereas the landed elite seemed to be on the defensive for a few years following the Cuban revolution, the tables were now turned and the elite's political power was enhanced. The counter-reform made real land reforms politically improbable by 1965.

It is no accident that, in historical perspective, the counter-reform occurred at a time when many Latin American governments were ruled directly or indirectly by the military. By December 1968, of nineteen Latin American nations, ten had purely military regimes, four were under heavy influence by the military, and five were countries with non-political establishments, if one follows the classification of Lieuwen.[6] Between March 1962 and June 1966, nine duly elected constitutional civilian presidents had been deposed by military coups. Lieuwen attributed this "new wave of militarism" in part to the Alliance for Progress, "for it was the view of many Latin American military leaders that the United States government's public advocacy and support for crash programs of material development and social change, conducted through the medium of authentically democratic regimes, was tantamount to encouraging political instability and social disintegration."[7] This view is of course not valid, since political instability and social disintegration are the consequences of an antiquated agrarian structure and the oppression of the peasantry, not of the Alliance for Progress. The near destruction of the peasant organizations in many countries is undeniable; what is less certain, however, is whether the military upsurge can be blamed entirely for the success of the counter-reform. The argument is valid only to the extent that the hand of the latifundistas has been strengthened by military action. But in other countries, with civilian governments, land reform has also made little progress, and it is evident that the landed elite has at its disposal many methods to forestall the redistribution through expropriation of land to the peasants, even without resorting to excessive force.

[6] E. Lieuwen, "The Latin American Military," Subcommittee on American Republic Affairs, Committee on Foreign Relations, U. S. Senate, 90th Cong., 1st Sess., 9 October 1967, p. 4.

[7] Ibid., p. 6.

CHAPTER 19

Land Reform Legislation in the 1960's

The Alliance for Progress sought to bring about changes in the structure of agriculture, within the established legal framework and power structure. Because of the importance that law and power assume with respect to land reform, it is necessary to analyze, in light of the realities of rural Latin America, the legal basis of the reform programs, as well as the scope, ease and speed with which reforms can be carried out.

Land reform laws must first aim at abolishing the existing undesirable land tenure structure—i.e., they must do away with latifundios and their by-product the minifundios—and establish the legal foundations for a new tenure system. The first implies principally the expropriation of large estates, including those owned by public entities. It also implies the determination of the land which should be exempt from expropriation, and the consolidation of smallholdings. It includes provisions for abolishing undesirable tenure arrangements between landowners and peasants who work under some lease (possession and use) contract, or between employers and other rural workers who must fulfill feudal or semi-feudal obligations. It must also provide for the amount and kind of compensation which the expropriated estate owners are to receive. Finally, the laws may provide means to enforce these various provisions.

The creation of the new tenure system requires provisions for the types of new farm enterprises to be organized and what their size shall be; who will receive the land; the tenure relations between the land and the peasants who farm it; how the rights in the land will be stabilized (property lists and provisions on boundaries); the relations among the peasants (e.g., with respect to inheritance); and the financial and other obligations of the beneficiaries to the state, or of the state to the peasants. Where irrigation is important, the laws must also provide for regulations about access to water and its use.

Because land reform is time-consuming, the laws also usually provide for priorities in the expropriation and redistribution of land, and they can regulate access to potential farmland not yet in use, in order to fix future land tenure conditions in unexplored regions. Finally, provisions must be made for an agency in charge of the program and its functions.

Other problems related to a land reform are rural labor relations, housing, co-operatives, taxation, credit, production and marketing. But these ought to be governed in most cases by separate laws and programs, as they are not part of land reform *per se*.

An intrinsic part of the established legal framework and power structure is the existence and protection of private property of farmland, regardless of size or number of properties owned by one person.[1] Although land reform laws in Latin America have not modified this basic element of Latin economics, they have attempted to introduce an important change in the legal panorama of private ownership of rural real estate, i.e., greater protection of small rural properties than of large properties. Hence the laws aim to preserve

[1] Opponents of land reform often argue that reforms are directed against private property and are therefore unlawful. This is incorrect. If reforms aim at establishing family farms which are privately owned, or even co-operatively owned, they actually aim at an expansion of private property, but for the benefit of the peasants, not the landed elite. Land reforms are against private property only if they nationalize all the land, but this has occurred in only a few countries, as normally the land tenure system is mixed, after the reform has been carried out. Land reforms can be against large properties and still protect their owners by providing for compensation for expropriated real estate. The extent of this protection depends on the type of compensation, and this in turn depends on the power structure. If landlords retain power, as they have in Latin America, compensation is high and usually payable in cash. This serves a double function: to protect the landed elite's investments and to reduce the possibilities of large-scale expropriations when the financial resources of the land reform institute are limited.

private ownership of land, but still allow the expropriation of large privately owned estates (and at times of "uneconomical units"). It has been thought necessary to justify such expropriations on formal grounds. The legislators have turned to the concept of the "social function of land" in order to rationalize the type of expropriation of estates which is theoretically allowed by law. In the process, this concept has become a tool to justify the expropriation of only a few estates and to exempt the majority of them. In other words, the "social function of land" has become an anti-reformist tool.

In order to understand why this complex concept was introduced into the legislation, it must be noted that the constitutions of Latin American countries generally have allowed expropriations of privately owned urban or rural property "in the public interest," with compensation to its owners in cash. These cases are always exceptional cases—for example, government plans for the construction of public edifices, highways or large dams. When the constitutions were written, they did not refer to expropriations of estates in a broad land reform process. The latter can also be justified within the existing legal framework only if the "public interest" is involved. For this reason, the concept of the social function of the land appeared to be useful. It assumes that expropriation of farmland as such can be in the public interest. This, of course, implies an expansion of the meaning of public interest.

In the process of introducing this new concept, the legislators have not always been logical or consistent. Agricultural land *per se* does not have a social function. It is its use which is of interest to society, and its use is determined by its owners or users and by society as a whole. Some of the laws speak of the social function of property or land.[2] Others speak more correctly of the "use of land in the public interest," with the concept of the social function of land more or less in the background. It would be still more accurate to refer directly to the owners of land and their use or non-use of their property in the public interest. But none of the laws have taken

[2] Ecuador's law states that private property of farmland fulfills its social function if it complies with prerequisites such as efficient use of land, etc.

this logical step, presumably out of concern that this would implicate the landed elite too directly.[3]

Land reform laws have specified that land "fulfills its social function" in some cases and not in others. Usually they provide that when land has been put to productive use, and when its quality is being maintained, it fulfills its social function; but not so when it remains unused or when it is not used efficiently or adequately. What the law states, then, is that expropriation is in the public interest if land in estates is not used in the public interest. Identifying the social function of land with the use of land means that attention is now focused on efficiency and intensity of land use, or, better, on output and productivity on individual enterprises, rather than on the social inequities inherent in an unequal distribution of land (i.e., the basis of land reform), which have little to do with the "social function" of the land. A further consequence is that expropriations now need not be undertaken on a large scale to wipe out these inequities, but only on an estate-to-estate basis, each case being judged on its own merits.

Consequently, the process of land reform is slowed down considerably, and, above all, *expropriations of estates can continue to be regarded as essentially exceptional occurrences.*[4] Some laws have confused the equity issue in land reform still more by adding that land does not fulfill its social function for such reasons as "the existence of anti-social or feudal methods of land exploitation" or "land concentration," or "the existence of minifundios." The Brazilian

[3] When private property is sanctioned by society, owners of property may use it in their own interest and for their own benefit as long as this does not clash with the public interest. Law and custom determine when private interest clashes with public interest. The exact determination of this point depends on the stage of development of the economy. Historically, societies have tended to impose greater obligations on owners of property to keep the public interest more in mind, which implies that owners of private property are increasingly restricted in the use of the property for their own benefit and interest.

[4] It is also interesting to note that the concept of the social function of land has not been related, in Latin America's land reform legislation, to the idea of "the land to the tillers." In some countries where land reforms have taken place, the land was considered to fulfill its social function if and when it was being operated personally by its owner or tenant. Obviously if used in this sense, it would allow for a much broader redistribution of estates, since it goes directly to the heart of the land reform problem, namely, the unequal distribution of the land, and absentee ownership and management.

Estatuto da Terra of 1964 declares, for example, that "land-ownership (*a propriedade da terra*) fulfills its social function if it [sic] contributes to the welfare of the owners and the workers who work there and their families . . . and if it [sic] observes the laws which regulate the just labor relations between those who own it and those who cultivate it" (literal translation). To say that the *land* or ownership of it does not fulfill its social function (or is not used in the public interest) because labor relations on the estates are anti-social or there is land concentration is totally invalid when the concept of the social function of land is basically tied to its use. The use of the land cannot be equated with either the use of people hired to work for the employer-owner of the land and the terms of their employment or the number of properties owned. If it were, it would put the blame on the land, when in reality it should be put on the owners, or, more accurately, on the society that permits such a state of affairs. These legal provisions, then, are obscure and difficult to apply. Perhaps the legislators intended to prove that they were aware that the issue of social injustices could not be entirely dropped from the texts of the laws. But in this case, it has been mere lip service and the outcome was a juxtaposition of words that do not accomplish anything.

Actually there is no need at all to use the concept of the social function of land. It would be sufficient to say that an owner acts against the public interest if he monopolizes land or exploits his peasants. In the absence of a clear provision to this effect, the monopolization or concentration of land-ownership is not even officially recognized as being anti-social, much less, illegal, and therefore does not become a reason for expropriation. The land reform laws passed during the 1960's in Latin America do not make it illegal to own a great deal of land (as the Cuban law did), although by implication they admit vaguely that it is anti-social. If a land reform states—as does Colombia's law of 1961, Article 1—that it will "reform the agrarian structure by means directed toward the elimination of the unequal concentration of land," it is not necessarily stating that land concentration or lati-fundios are unlawful. In fact, this formulation has no legal force whatever, and in an agriculture dominated by latifundistas, it has little moral impact. Roughly the same comment could be made about exploitation of peasants.[5]

We conclude that the concept of the social function of the land, although apparently introduced to pave the way for large-scale expropriations, serves in reality to divert attention from the injustices inherent in a sharply unequal distribution of land resources and to draw attention to the less controversial uses of land.

We should examine further the process by which the legislators have used the concept in order to make large-scale expropriations of land difficult or impossible. Leaving aside semantic and logical confusions, the use of the concept of the social function of land has as its first objective the diversion of land reform to the outlying districts because there the land does not usually "fulfill its social function," since it is not used adequately or at all. Secondly, and more important, it justifies the exemption from land reform of all land in large estates which *does* fulfill a social function because it is being used or "adequately managed."

The first point must be examined in light of the provisions of the laws which establish priorities for expropriations and settlement. The Colombian law is typical. Its highest priority for land distribution to campesinos is on the publicly owned land. (This is not land reform at all but colonization—but this did not deter the legislator.) If "it becomes necessary," farm people can be settled on privately owned land which can be expropriated—but only in this sequence: first, on unused land; then, on land which is inadequately used; then, on land cultivated by small tenants and sharecroppers; and finally, on land which the owners voluntarily cede to the land reform institute. Only as a last priority can land which is "well managed" be expropriated. But the legal (quite apart from the political) obstacles to such expropriations are for-

---

[5] Most countries have laws which declare illegal the existence of exploitative relationships (and usually this is evident from their constitutions). They also have minimum wage legislation. The land reform laws which mention exploitation therefore recognize the existence of such illegal practices notwithstanding these laws. What is needed is not more legislation, but more enforcement.

midable.[6] This is how the concept of the social function of land has been used through actual legal provisions to make land reform in traditional, good farming areas almost impossible; to make reform a doubtful venture for the campesinos because they may be unable to succeed[7] on the poor land on which they are to be settled; or to make land reform a very costly business for the economy, since the outlying regions require large investments in infrastructure if the land reform beneficiaries are not to remain entirely marginalized. Furthermore, terms such as "efficiently used" or "adequately managed" are vague and normally undefined in the laws, and it is questionable whether definitions are useful in the context of a real land reform. If they were to be tested in court, it is unlikely that they would be interpreted in favor of the campesinos, given the existing rural power structure. The most visible result of the use of such terms is that they are apt to reduce reform to a mere token, if the standards of efficiency or adequacy of land use and management are set low.

No less serious is that the concept enables landowners quickly to transform any estates that do not fulfill their social function—e.g., those which are not being used—into estates which *do* fulfill it and thereby exempt them from reform. This is very important in view of the fact that, by oversight or intention, the laws never refer to the date at which the use, non-use or inadequate use is to be considered relevant. In some cases, estates can be exempt simply because under the conditions prevailing in Latin America, reform proceeds very slowly and the owners are given time to make the necessary adjustments, such as putting cattle on the land or giving out some portion to sharecroppers. In some countries, like Ecuador or Chile, the legislators have carried their assistance to the landed elite to an even greater extreme and provided that estate owners who make an effort at improving their farm operations are to be exempt from reform. This

[6] J. R. Thome, "Limitaciones de la Legislacion Colombiana para Expropriar o Comprar Fincas con Destino a Parcelacion," Land Tenure Center, LTC, No. 14, University of Wisconsin, Madison, Wisc., November 1965.

[7] Or, to use the terminology of the legislators, the land of the land reform beneficiaries would not fulfill its social function.

eliminates from land reform the issue of social justice for the campesinos. Thus the laws make the bulk of the large estates untouchable for the land reform institutes.

The "social function of land" is a deterrent to social justice for the campesinos not only because it shifts the reasons for expropriations onto the more neutral grounds of land use, production and efficiency, but also because it introduces thereby *a new concept of social justice for the landed elite,* i.e., that it is unjust to expropriate land which is more fully utilized. The landed elite can now claim that it is unjust to deprive them of land which has been acquired by them or their forefathers, and which has been improved by their efforts and superior management capabilities. Such a claim has great propaganda value. Since usually only the campesinos know how this land was acquired in the first place, and few people realize whose labor has actually been incorporated in the estates, and that the superior management capabilities of the landed elite is a myth, the argument seems convincing and land reform appears to be unjust. Of course, this is incompatible with the fundamental goal of the elimination of injustices inherent in the unequal distribution of land. Another underlying reason for the focus on land use is the hope that the landed elite itself will "reform" and exploit its land so that it will fulfill its social function and make a real land reform unnecessary. Even if this were to be the case, it would prove to be of little comfort to the campesinos, not only because the expectation is hardly justified, but also because the inequalities would continue to exist and so would the exploitation of rural labor.

Even though existing land tenure institutions vary from country to country, and within each country from region to region, and although differences must somehow be accounted for in land reform legislation, it is clear that such legislation can remain relatively short and simple and still deal effectively with the basic reform issues at stake. The laws need only set out in broad outlines the legal basis of the program. They cannot provide rules for every detail or take into account all the variations which may be encountered in the field. The land reform institute should be given latitude to solve the many practical problems which arise in the execution of the program. Examples for short and incisive reform laws or bills exist. For example, in 1962, the Christian Democratic Party of Chile submitted a bill to Parliament which contained sixty-two articles and provided for two new types of land tenure systems: private (small) property and communal property. But the bill did not become law. The Cuban land reform of 1959 (later amended by the law of 1963) contained sixty-seven articles and a few brief provisions regarding their implementation.

In the legislation of Latin America during the 1960's, other than that of Cuba, brevity and simplicity are not a common trait. Why are Latin America's land reform statutes so awkward? In the first place, the laws often contain provisions on matters which are extraneous to land reform proper and which would have been best treated in separate laws. Secondly, the legislation was exposed to months, or even years, of parliamentary debate. Compromises had to be made to accommodate different political views and economic interests.[8] Another, more important factor was that the legislators, many of whom are members of the landed elite or closely associated with it, did not intend to entrust the implementation of the land reform program to a land reform institute without regulating all possible issues and circumscribing exactly the limits of its activities. This has resulted in legal texts of extreme complexity and very difficult application. Many provisions are obscure, contradictory or of little use, and give evidence of hasty drafting and unclear thinking. One also cannot entirely exclude the possibility that some of the provisions were purposely drafted by lawyers with the intent to "muddy the waters." If the text of a statute is unclear or contradictory, the landlords have many opportunities to challenge the law or its constitutionality, and postpone or even prevent its implementation.

Legislation became more voluminous with time, as it be-

[8] See R. Mac-Lean y Estenos, "La Reforma Agraria en el Peru," XV Congreso Nacional de Sociologia (Estudios Sociologicos sobre la Reforma Agraria), Tomo 2, Instituto de Investigaciones Sociales, UNAM, Mexico, 1964, pp. 437 ff.

came more apparent throughout Latin America that the time for real land reforms had passed. The new Chilean law, promulgated in 1967 after several years of preparation and public debate, consists of 356 articles. Its text is "very lengthy and complex" and includes provisions not related to reform.[9] Brazil's Estatuto da Terra contains 128 articles, of which only a small number deal with land tenure changes.[10]

In many cases, the "control" which legislators tried to impose on land reform has been carried very far. In several countries, e.g., Colombia, the land reform institutes quickly became aware of the legal obstacles to expropriation and redistribution of estates to the peasants, and attempted to have the law modified. When the climate for land reform is not favorable, any amendments may create further obstacles to the process of reform. In some cases the institutes had to rely on antiquated legislation still on the lawbooks to carry out a portion of their program, which made the new legislation appear superfluous.

The poor legal technique used in the preparation of land reform legislation is obviously of particular significance, because of the policy of peacefully carrying out reforms "within the established legal framework."

The concept of the social function of land has paved the way for a slow piecemeal change in small sections of agriculture, and the reform laws do not provide, therefore, for a complete overhaul of the agrarian structure. This is an inherent feature of the laws which we shall now examine further. In fact, some of the changes which the laws provide are of doubtful benefit for the peasants. This conclusion can be traced to three facts: provisions regarding the expropriation and redistribution of land and priorities for expropriation; the organization and functioning of the land reform agencies; and the financial basis established in the laws for the execution of the programs. It is of course not possible to

[9] "Exposicion Metodica y Coordinada de la Ley de Reforma Agraria de Chile," Estudio Realizado por el Departamento de Derecho y Legislacion Agrarios del ICIRA, Editorial Juridica de Chile, 1968, p. 5 and pp. 325 ff.

[10] Twenty-eight of its 128 articles deal with land reform; the rest, with cadastre, taxation, colonization, etc.

examine here each country's legislation in detail. We can only examine a few typical cases and keep in mind that there is considerable similarity between the laws of various countries. There is little doubt that the later statutes have relied extensively on the land reform legislation issued during the first years of the decade.

We shall first examine the land reform priorities and the limits of expropriations. The laws have tended to restrict land reform to a small portion of the land potentially available for redistribution to peasants, and to relegate reform to the outlying and poorer agricultural areas. This has been achieved principally by four types of provisions: the priorities established in the legislation with regard to where land reform is to begin; the conditions or requirements necessary for the expropriation; the exemption from expropriations that takes land out completely from the reform program; and the rights accorded owners of expropriable land. These limitations are not always explicitly stated, but they become obvious when the laws are subjected to close analysis.

The Cuban law of 1959 stated in its first article that latifundios are illegal and that privately owned farms cannot exceed thirty *caballerías*, i.e., about 400 hectares. The limit was later reduced to sixty-seven hectares. Thus Cuba eliminated with almost one stroke the control of a few private landowners over the land resources. The same law also provided that the land reform agency could expropriate, first, state owned land, then privately held land cultivated by sharecroppers and similar workers, and all privately owned land not exempt from expropriation.[11] Of the other Latin American laws, not even Chile's new law of 1967 approaches such sweeping reforms. Colombia's law is characteristic of Latin American legislation. It provides, as we stated earlier, that peasants obtain access to land first on the public domain. Only "if it appears necessary" will they be settled on privately owned land. If land which is privately owned is to be redis-

---

[11] The Chilean bill of 1962 presented to Parliament by the Christian Democratic Party stated that privately held farmland could not be in excess of eighty hectares of good land and had to be cultivated by the owner. But this bill did not become law.

tributed to the peasants and has to be acquired or expropriated, the priorities under the laws are as follows: unused land; land which is inadequately used; land cultivated by small tenants or sharecroppers; and land which the owners voluntarily cede the land reform institute.

Generally, expropriation of privately owned land is the exception and colonization of public lands the rule. Ecuador's decree of 1964 also provides first for expropriation of land unused for three consecutive years, then for that of inadequately used land. However, even these areas can be taken out of the land reform program if the owners present "investment plans," presumably for the improvement of the estates. But there is no provision which determines what is to occur if these plans are not carried out, and the decree contains no deadlines with respect to the intensity of land use under the investment plans. The Peruvian law of 1964 has similar rules. In Chile, land owned by a private owner in excess of eighty hectares of irrigated land (or its equivalent) is "subject to expropriation" under Article 3 of the law of 1967. Farms which are not exploited or are inadequately managed can be expropriated in their totality, except for farms not exceeding eighty hectares, which are granted a grace period of three years after the promulgation of the law.

It is significant that the Colombian law does not speak of *farms* on which land is unused or inadequately managed, but of unused *land* or *land* inadequately used. As a result, only that portion of an estate which is unused or poorly used is expropriable. This usually implies that the poorest land is available for land reform, since the owner can be presumed to cultivate his best soil, or that only such land is available which has not been cleared of trees and stones. The law defines unused land as land which is "visibly" not exploited in an organized manner. It can be assumed that if the owner of such land who is threatened with expropriation were to organize quickly a small livestock enterprise, thus "visibly" exploiting his land in an organized manner, he would immediately be exempt from expropriation. Such practices are facilitated by the law's failure to relate the degree of land utilization to any time period, such as the date at which the law is promulgated, or a given period preceding that date. Considering that the Colombian statute is so detailed with respect to all phases of expropriation, the failure to include this significant detail of a time period represents a large loophole for the estate owners. The Peruvian law of 1964 does actually refer to farms, not land, but the language of the law is not consistent. Other countries have texts similar to that of Colombia.

Such vague provisions have three inherent dangers. The most serious is that they do not do away with latifundios or minifundios, the traditional agrarian structure which land reform must seek to modify. This can be costly for the peasants, who, instead of receiving land in the best and most developed agricultural area, obtain unproductive land or land principally in undeveloped areas without infrastructures, and must invest their own efforts before they can produce incomes which might never be adequate. It would be costly for the nation directly to bear part of the costs of developing these farm areas. As we have seen, there is no scarcity of good, relatively well-developed farmland in Latin America. Hence this approach threatens the success of the land reform beneficiaries and makes it appear as if "land reform" is harmful to the peasants.

The simple declaration of priorities for unutilized or underutilized privately owned land does not automatically insure expropriation of such land, because of the complex and slow expropriation procedure. Thus Chile's statute, which speaks of expropriable land for farms in excess of eighty hectares, clearly indicates that ownership of this excess land is not illegal *per se*. It is available for expropriation only after the authorities have made an administrative decision to that effect.

With the exception of provisions referring to the expropriation of estates which are farmed by sharecroppers, colonos, small tenants and the like, the laws fail to set up objective criteria for expropriation. Instead, they rely on conditions (such as "inadequately used land") which have to be interpreted by means of value judgments. Presumably these conditions will be interpreted by the land reform institutes or the courts, and their interpretation or definition then depends on the standards adopted.[12] If the standards for "adequately used land" are low, a great deal of land would be exempt from expropriation. In this manner, the land reform laws leave the amount of land which is actually available for land reform undefined, and introduce a strong element of uncertainty into the process of land reform.

No less significant is that a number of laws exempt entire blocks of land from expropriation and land reform. Such an exemption does not necessarily have to be spelled out in detail, because it becomes simply the result of the provisions on priorities which automatically exempt good farmland from the reform. But in some cases, the legislators have taken this additional precaution in order to be sure that some estates or groups of estates are saved from reform. Exemptions can be unconditional or conditional. They are unconditional when the laws lay down the criteria governing the exemption in an unequivocal manner. The Ecuadorian decree of 1964, for example, exempts estates up to 2,500 hectares, plus an additional 1,000 hectares of pastures for estates located on the coast. In the sierra it exempts up to 1,800 hectares. Livestock enterprises, however, may be allowed to exceed these limits. The law also exempts farm enterprises which are well managed and which furnish raw material for their own processing plants and other "well-managed enterprises." These are obviously far-reaching exemptions, even to an extent where it becomes highly questionable whether latifundios can be expropriated at all for the purpose of land reform. The Peruvian law of 1964 has a very complex system of exemptions and refers confusingly to both farms (*propriedades rurales* or *predios rústicos*) which are poorly managed or abandoned, and land (*tierras*) which is unused. Apparently all or part of estates which belong to stock corporations or persons in joint ownership (*condominio*) are exempted, on the assumption that there are as many farms as stockholders (or persons participating in the condominio), each of whom can retain

---

[12] The Chilean law of 1967 attempted to circumvent this difficulty by establishing a definition of a "poorly managed farm," including a more objective criterion, such as percentage of land in crops. But this is an exceptional case.

the maximum reserve allowable under the law. Small wonder that before and after the promulgation of the law many
estates were rapidly transformed into such exempted entities!

Exemptions are conditional when they depend on factors
which, although specified by the legislation, are unpredictable.
For example, the Colombian law provides that the land reform institute will expropriate privately owned land only if
it is usable for cropping or livestock "on a small scale,"[13]
exempting other land. Similarly, the expropriation of well-
managed farmland is subject to a variety of preconditions
to be determined by the institute. The Ecuadorian law even
allows an expropriation to be annulled under certain conditions, e.g., if the compensation price has not been paid as provided by law. In those cases, the property reverts to the
owner. In other words, the legislators seem to have anticipated
that expropriations would not be final! According to Peru's
law of 1964, large blocks of land can be exempted in the case
of farms belonging to certain processing industries, once the
President has authorized their exemptions. The exemption
can be applied also to land which produces industrial crops
even if it does *not* belong to processing industries. In Chile,
the President can authorize exemptions up to twenty years
in the case of farms whose owners present investment plans
for the improvement of their farm enterprise, but the owners
must comply with the approved plan. In Brazil the provisions
referring to exemptions are complex and difficult to interpret. The statute appears to exempt many medium-sized
and large multi-family farms, in land reform priority zones,
which fall under the definition of "rural enterprises," i.e.,
estates which are reasonably well managed. Estates which
are not yet "rural enterprises" are also exempt in non-priority
areas, if they are on the way to becoming such enterprises.
According to authoritative opinions, it is uncertain whether
with the existing legislation *any* expropriation can effectively
be carried out.[14] An examination of the land reform legis-

[13] *"No adquirira sino tierras que sean adecuadas para labores agricolas e de
genaderia en pequena escala,"* Article 57, para. 2.

[14] See FAO, "Informe al Gobierno de Brasil sobre Aspectos de la Reforma
Agraria en Brasil" (Informe de la Mision de la FAO, April–May 1968), Rome:
R.U:MISC/69/17, 31 March 1969, p. 32.

lation of the 1960's leaves the distinct impression that there is a tendency for the exceptions (i.e., exemptions) to rule, and for the fundamental measure of land reform, the expropriations, to be allowed only occasionally.

Of course, the costs of the exemptions are borne by the peasants who have no land. However, in a sense all expropriations are conditional—and therefore land is exempt until further notice—since they are subject to a number of procedural steps which in turn are subject to unpredictable administrative decisions (although by law all farmland is "susceptible" to inclusion in the land reform program—a very vague formula indeed). In practically all cases, expropriations of privately owned estates must be preceded by a number of administrative activities and decisions.

The Peruvian law of 1964 can serve as a typical example of a complicated expropriation procedure. Land reform through expropriation of privately owned land takes place only in an area which the President has decreed to be a land reform zone. (The same is true in Brazil.) Such a decree must be based on a previous study undertaken by ONRA, the major organ of the land reform institute. The study must show that the zone deserves to be selected ahead of other areas. For this, ONRA must take into account a number of factors, such as population pressure or the existence of abandoned farms in the area to be proposed as a land reform zone. Logically, such a priority could only be established if the institute were obliged to make a study of the entire country. But the law does not require this. The law neither specifies the time limits within which the study must be completed, nor requires the President to issue the decree within a specified time limit. For this reason, the entire procedure depends not on the text of the law but on the political pressures prevailing at the time. If the institute were to make a serious study of all the factors required by the law, it would have to spend months or years to satisfy fully the legal requirements, because of the lack of adequate information. In reality most land reform zones are selected not because of the factors enumerated in the law but for political reasons, such as peasant pressures and violence. To include the legal provisions on the declaration of land reform zones, therefore, makes no real sense, except on the assumption that the legislators did not want to allow the land reform institute to make decisions on priorities, and that they wanted to avoid a speedy reform.

But once an area has been declared a land reform zone, the law establishes an approximate time schedule for the procedure to be followed up to the moment of expropriation. It has been calculated that under the law of 1964, the time necessary to bring about an expropriation is *from 392 days, or thirteen months, to 490 days, or sixteen months, excluding both the time necessary to declare the zone a land reform zone and the time needed to distribute the land to the peasants.* However, this period could be extended by an unspecified number of months or years if landowners take advantage of various legal means to question administrative decisions in court.[15] Furthermore, the thirteen to sixteen months do not include the time necessary for the President to issue a decree legalizing the expropriation with the approval of the Minister of Agriculture. And the law does not specify within what period the President is to issue the decree. Finally, it is to be observed that the plan for expropriating estates does not necessarily refer to the entire land reform zone, but may be related only to a smaller subzone.

Expropriation, therefore, is always on an individual basis. The laws on land reform in Latin America do not provide for a broad expropriation of estates in a given region, much less in the country as a whole. *They provide not for a broad-scale land reform, but for an atomized program of small land reform projects.*

Latin America's laws provide for special treatment for estate owners, by allowing them to retain a selected portion of their estates in reserve. According to Colombia's law, for example, each owner can retain at least 100 hectares, whether the land is well managed or not. In fact, the owner of poor farmland can request an additional 100 hectares—an example

---

[15] In some countries, the institute can take possession of an estate which it decides to expropriate, even though the owner objects. This can theoretically speed up the procedure.

Approximate Administrative Procedure Necessary
Before Expropriation of Privately Owned Estates,
Prior to President's Decree, Peru[a]

Sequence of Procedure	Time Period Allowable by Law (days)
Cadastral plan	70
Legal and technical justification	30–60
Provisional plan of affectation[b]	15
Notification of owners	7–15
First appeal of owners	60
Revision of provisional plan	45
Appraisal of land	60
Second plan of affectation (prelim.)[b]	10
Adjustments of second plan	60
Second plan of affectation[b]	10
Final plan of affectation[b]	10
Resolution of Consejo Nacional Agrario of ONRA	15–90
TOTAL	392–490

[a] Based principally on Articles 62–77 of the law of 1964.
[b] Area of each estate which could be subject to expropriation.

NOTE: This does not include the time needed for owners' court appeals, or the time required for establishing a land reform zone, or the actual distribution of the estate to peasants.

of equity in reverse. The owner can retain his reserve in a single piece although the law usually also provides that the land that is expropriated should be of about the same quality as that of the owner. However, if the owner retains the buildings and other non-real-estate assets with his reserve, to which he is entitled by law, he retains in effect a going concern (although reduced in size) which gives him a considerable advantage over the land reform beneficiaries. The Nicaraguan law of 1964 declares that the owner can retain 500 hectares of first-rate land (or its equivalent), plus a forest reserve. The Peruvian law of 1964 provides that the owner can retain 100 hectares of irrigated land (or, 1,500 hectares of pasture), but under certain conditions he may request that the expropriable area be reduced by 20 per cent. Depending on the size of the farm, this can add a considerable amount of land to that already retained by the owner. He will be compensated in cash for permanent crops and installations as well as livestock. Such provisions impose a heavy financial burden on the land reform institute. The Chilean law of 1967 is equally generous with respect to the estate owners' reserve. It distinguishes between the normal reserve, which grants between 80 and 100 hectares of irrigated land (or its equivalent), depending on the number of sons working on the enterprise if the land is well managed by the owner himself,[16] and an "extraordinary" reserve of up to 320 hectares of irrigated land in the case of farm enterprises which are exceptionally well managed and provide social benefits, such as the participation of workers in the gross production of the farm.

Obviously, such provisions are not beneficial to the peasants, who will receive the bare land not retained by the owners, and will have to start their farming operations from scratch. In Mexico's land reform, similar provisions have led to a situation where the former hacendados or their heirs retained the best portions of their farms and often with it the control of water in irrigated districts. Over the longer period this has led to a new situation of severe inequality which could have been prevented if the power of the hacendados over the peasantry had been evaluated more realistically. A much better solution would be to leave decisions on the land to be retained by the hacendados (if they are to keep any land) to the land reform institutes. They could then divide up the land much more fairly among the peasantry.

With all these clauses on priorities, exemptions and reserves, it is *extremely difficult to estimate in any given country the amount of land which by law can actually be included in a land reform program*. Still the question is of crucial importance. It is obvious that under the best of circumstances, a relatively large proportion of privately owned land in multi-family farms will *not* be available for land reform. For Peru, CIDA estimated tentatively that about one third to one

---

[16] The term "managed by the owner himself" is another clause to exempt some estate owners from the reform.

fifth of the land in multi-family farms would be available for expropriation. But this computation is an approximation, or rather a speculation. It does not account, for example, for the effects of the law regarding the unknown number of exempt stock corporations, or the provisions regarding the rights of owners to claim more exempted land.

In summary, there can be little doubt that the laws tend to leave the traditional agrarian latifundio-minifundio structure largely untouched.

We turn our attention now to a few administrative aspects. The greater the autonomy and resources of an agency, the greater its potential scope of action. The land reform laws of the 1960's have not provided for strong, autonomous land reform agencies with adequate financial resources. This has tended to put strong brakes on the progress of the various land reform programs.

Generally speaking, the implementation of the laws is in the hands of the land reform agencies themselves. However, some of the most important decisions are not made by them. Since the landed elite in Latin American society retains its effective power, this arrangement proved to be fatal in several cases.

All activities of the institutes are subject to approval, or are decided upon, first, by a board of directors in which several sectors of the economy are represented. As a result, these sectors exercise a close surveillance over all land reform, colonization, irrigation and other projects which the institutes undertake. A typical case is the Peruvian, which, although it has an institutional arrangement *sui generis,* manifests the kind of administrative and political problems faced by most land reform institutes in Latin America. The Peruvian law of 1964 provides for an unwieldy complex administrative organization in which many public and private bodies intervene. In practice, however, this has not worked out, because some government agencies were hostile to land reform and refused to co-operate with the institute. The organization of the institute itself is therefore tailored to a slow-motion land reform. As far as the public sector is concerned, at least five distinct bodies or organs forming the institute are in direct charge of the program,[17] not counting the interventions of the judicial system that the law requires or authorizes. At least seven major government agencies have auxiliary functions connected with the program and four public agencies occasionally enter into the land reform process—not to speak of semi-public and private agencies or groups represented in the various organs of the institute, either with the power to formulate decisions or in the role of advisors.

Peru's land reform institute, under the law of 1964, provides for a policy-making organ which also has executive functions. This Consejo Nacional Agrario (CNA) makes decisions on major and minor matters. It appoints all higher officials, in the central and regional offices, of ONRA (Oficina Nacional de Reforma Agraria), the organ which is actually in charge of land reform. Only one out of nine voting members and four non-voting members of the CNA represent the millions of Peruvian campesinos with the right to take part in the decision-making processes of the institute. But the one delegate of the campesinos who represents a government-patronized peasant organization (FENCAP) only speaks for a portion of the campesinos of Peru, inasmuch as several large campesino organizations which existed prior to the enactment of the law disappeared after the successful suppression of the peasant movement of the early 1960's. The inclusion of two delegates of the two most powerful estate owners' associations, the Sociedades de Agricultores and the Asociaciones de Ganaderos, who represent the small upper echelon of Peruvian agriculture and are notoriously hostile to land reform, shifts the decision-making power of the CNA heavily in favor of the estate owners' economic, social and political interests. In fact, the *institute has an efficient, built-in sabotage system, from the point of view of the campesinos.*

[17] Under the law of 1964 the organs of the institute were: the CNA (Consejo Nacional Agrario); the Consejo Tecnico de Reforma y Promocion Agraria, mostly a consultative body; IRPA (Instituto de Reforma y Promocion Agraria); ONRA (Oficinal Nacional de Reforma Agraria); and SIPA (Servicio de Investigacion y Promocion Agraria), three organs of an executive nature, of which ONRA is most directly concerned with the expropriation and redistribution of land; the Consejos Zonales de Reforma Agraria, also of a consultative nature; and CORFIRA (Corporacion Financiera de Reforma Agraria), which handles all financial matters.

This lack of balance is not improved by the fact that the peasants are not represented in the other organs of the institute.

The activities of the executive director of ONRA are limited to carrying out the decisions of the CNA, which appoints him. It is also significant that the director and his staff in the capital and in the regional offices are isolated, by law and in practice, against any influence of the campesinos or their organizations, except, as indicated earlier, through their thin representation in the CNA. Peru's law contains no provision for including peasants or peasant leaders in the formulation, preparation or implementation of land reform projects, whatever their nature, nor does it provide for any mechanism whereby the peasants can take the initiative for setting up such projects. Projects are therefore carried out without the active intervention or co-operation of the peasantry. This means that they must be acceptable to the landed elite.

The same situation prevails in other countries. In Colombia and Ecuador, for example, even the armed forces have a voting member on the board. Thus the combined civilian and military forces lined up against the peasantry are formidable. It is therefore impossible, by law, that land reform processes can ever "get out of hand," from the point of view of the landed elite. It is therefore not surprising that in several instances officials who were enthusiastically prepared to assist the peasants and who had by far the best contacts with the peasants, were gradually eliminated from the institute, and that the executive directors' tenure was usually of short duration, except when they were obviously catering to the wishes of the landed elite. More serious still is the exclusion of the peasants from all reform processes. With the sole exception of Venezuela, where peasants can request a land reform project on particular enterprises, the campesinos have no right to take the initiative; any initiative on their part would be considered illegal and would bring down on them the forces of law and order. In this light, the laws have made the peasants more the victims than the beneficiaries of land reform.

In Peru, under the law of 1964, the governing board of directors cannot make certain important decisions, because they are left to the President himself. The most important of these are the expropriation of land and the declaration of a land reform zone, without which no land reform program can begin. A similar procedure is required in Brazil with respect to priority areas. In the final analysis, therefore, the progress of land reform is in the hands of the President. Under various political pressures, including pressure from the landed elite, the President can withhold his signature from expropriation decrees for an indefinite period of time, as the law contains no provision obligating him to sign them within a specified time. In fact, in several countries there have been long delays, and some expropriation decrees are still awaiting the final presidential decision. The Colombian law recently (1968) attempted to speed up this phase of the expropriation procedure by replacing the presidential decree with an approval of the Minister of Agriculture. But this may make matters worse.

In summary, the restrictive provisions of the land reform legislation, limiting the scope of the reform, are compounded by an unwieldy administrative mechanism and obviously biased institutional arrangements in favor of the landed elite.

CHAPTER 20

The Financing of Land Reform

Let us now turn to the third factor inherent in the legislation of the 1960's which forces the land reform institutes of Latin America into a piecemeal reform, i.e., their *financing*.

If land reforms are carried out on a massive scale, as, for example, in Cuba, they claim a large proportion of a country's physical, financial and human resources. A real land reform can be compared to a war effort: it draws on almost all sectors of the economy for support. When land reforms are accompanied by a large-scale shift of political power in agriculture away from the landed elite, the most important economic problems become the issues of capital investments for immediate and long-run agricultural growth, increased productivity of land and higher returns to previously underpaid agricultural labor, and creation of incentives for producers and rural workers.

On the other hand, historical experience shows that when land reforms are carried out in agricultures controlled by the landed elite, as was the case in Latin America during the 1960's, attention is focused on the compensation of expropriated landlords. It has been stated that "the importance of compensation payments in the financing of land reform is obvious, for this aspect often forms the focus of landowner opposition to reform and may well hold the key to the successful initiation and implementation of an entire land reform program."[1] This statement oversimplifies the issue. It could be taken to mean that if compensation is satisfactory to the estate owners, landlord opposition will disappear and make

[1] *Progress in Land Reform*, Fourth Report, United Nations, E/4020/Rev.1.ST/SOA/61 (New York: 1966), p. 98.

way for a successful land reform. It might be taken to imply that estate ownership is merely an investment and has only economic benefits. There are some estate owners who, for adequate compensation, would be willing and in some cases even anxious to dispose of their rural real estate. But this is not true of the landed elite as a group. Estate ownership provides landlords not only with adequate economic returns, but also with a basis for political power and social status. No amount of compensation can make up for the loss of status and power, particularly in countries where alternative investment and job opportunities yielding equivalent political power and status are limited. Landlord opposition to land reform has concentrated on compensation because it raises one equity issue—landowners should not be expropriated without a just reward—against another—the search for equal distribution of land and access to it. A strong case could be sustained for expropriating landlords with only very reduced compensation. Hence one ought to formulate the issue as follows: where landlord compensation is an important matter, the probability that land reform is not seriously considered is very high. The compensation issue is a "smoke screen" behind which landlords as a group hide their opposition to any and all agrarian reforms, knowing that no government could afford to pay the compensation which would fully make up for the loss of estate ownership. Opposition to land reform is not only based on economics.

The financing of land reform is a complex issue which has been dealt with in several publications.[2] Here we shall limit ourselves principally to comments on the effects of the financial provisions of the land reform laws on the progress of land reform and their relation to land reform needs. Atten-

[2] See, for example, T. F. Carroll, "Issues of Financing Agrarian Reform: The Latin American Experience," World Land Reform Conference, Rome, June–July 1966, FAO/WLR/66/5-WM/46788. J. Strasma, "Financiamiento de la Reforma Agraria en El Peru," *El Trimestre Economico*, July–September 1965, pp. 484 ff. See also United Nations, *Progress in Land Reform*, Fourth Report, Chapter II; Third Report, Chapter V, E/3603/Rev.1.ST/SOA/49 (New York, 1962). See also "Seminario sobre el Financiamiento de la Reforma Agraria," Panama, 25–30 May 1964, IICA-CIRA, Bogotá, 1964.

tion will also be drawn to one or two specific cases as illustrations of the limiting effect of the laws.

Land reform laws always contain provisions on at least some aspects of the revenues, assets, expenditures or investments of land reform institutes and their related activities. These provisions can be classified as follows: (1) the financial endowment of the institute, including the financing of the compensation of landlords; (2) the agencies, if any, authorized to handle the financial aspects of land reform; (3) the expropriation and compensation of estates or of smallholdings for land consolidation programs; (4) the financial obligations of the beneficiaries of land reform; and (5) the nature and costs of services shouldered by the government. Few attempts have as yet been made to analyze these provisions in detail. Still, it would seem that they have a strong bearing on the scope and nature of the programs which the legislators had in mind: the financial provisions provide a dollars-and-cents framework for the reform.

If we focus first on the resources made available to the land reform institutes, an examination of the pertinent clauses demonstrates the narrow concept which legislators seem to have had of the scope and nature of land reform. This cannot be substantiated merely on the basis of the quantities of funds allocated by law. It must be demonstrated in light of the general and specific rules regarding the various phases of reform (e.g., priorities regulating the expropriation of land or the price at which land is to be expropriated) and the various functions of the institute, as well as in light of the specific land reform needs of the country.

As a general rule, it is evident that the allocation of resources to the programs has been made without a clear concept of actual land reform needs and without benefit of land reform planning. Take as examples the Brazilian and Colombian legislation. The documents which accompanied the legislation prior to enactment made reference to the poor distribution of land, the former in brief, general terms, the latter by citing census statistics.[3] But they contain no indication of the

---

[3] Brazil: Estatuto da Terra, Ministerio de Agricultura, INDA, Departamento de Imprensa Nacional, 1965, p. 8, item 10. Colombia: Reforma Agraria, Senado de la Republica, Imprenta Nacional, Bogotá, 1961, pp. 81 ff.

number of campesinos to be benefited annually or over the aggregate period during which the land reform was to be carried out. In Colombia or Peru it might appear that the legislators thought of a ten- to twenty-year program, if one takes certain financial provisions of the law—the provisions concerning budget allocations, the issuance of bonds and their amortization, for example—as indices. But in the absence of such indications, it would seem that the legislators thought of land reform as an indefinite program. Neither during the preparation of the legislation nor later, when the laws were being implemented, were plans made concerning the aggregate or the annual achievements. The only exception seems to be a plan prepared by the National Planning Board of Ecuador, which established a target of 250,000 farm families to be settled over a period of twenty years on 4.5 million hectares.[4] But the Ecuadorian decree on land reform of 1964 exempts so much land from the reform program that these targets can hardly be achieved, if at all, and it must be assumed that the decree did not take the targets of the planning board very seriously.

Land reform institutes obtain their funds principally from two sources: annual budget allocations and agrarian bonds issued by the state. For example, the Colombian institute, INCORA, receives annually from the national budget "no less than" 100 million pesos—only recently raised to 300 million— and a total of 1.2 billion pesos—later raised to 2.6 billion—in agrarian bonds, prorated, as mentioned, over several years. In Brazil, the agency receives exactly 3 per cent of the national budget revenues. No agrarian bonds are issued, as land must be paid for in cash. In Peru, under the law of 1964, a "minimum of 3 per cent" of the national budget revenues for a period of twenty years is assigned not to the main land reform agency, ONRA, but to the Corporacion Financiera (CORFIRA), which handles all financial aspects of the land reform program, almost like a bank. It is, of course, far removed from land reform processes. However, these funds are not all for land reform alone, as CORFIRA has to split the funds among

---

[4] Junta Nacional de Planificacion y Coordinacion Economica, Reforma a la Estructura de Tenencia de la Tierra y Expansion de la Frontera Agricola, Plan General de Desarollo Economico y Social, Libro Sexto (Quito: 1963).

various organs of the institute. CORFIRA can also authorize[5] the issuance of agrarian bonds in the amount of six billion pesos (gold). In Venezuela, the annual allocation of funds is left to the discretion of the executive, but the issuance of bonds is regulated by law.

In addition, institutes receive financial means from other sources. At times they can assume a certain importance, such as land acquired by the institutes, amortization payments made by land reform beneficiaries, or national and international loans. The total of these resources enters into the patrimony of the institutes, sometimes called the National Agrarian Fund.

The bonds' primary function is the compensation of estate owners. In Colombia the law also authorizes their use as collateral for certain activities undertaken by INCORA. In Venezuela, the institute can pay investments other than land acquisition with bonds. Generally, however, the other activities of most of the land reform institutes have to be paid principally out of the annual allocations from the national budgets. The size of the allocations is of particular importance in those cases where the expropriation price or compensation is paid totally or partly in cash. A brief examination of some of the compensation provisions and the related subject, the valuation of estates, is therefore in order.

Expropriation of estates by means of government bonds instead of cash has been the subject of bitter debates. Landlords are violently opposed to bonds for obvious reasons. Bonds lose their value through inflation, so that landlords have no confidence in them; their interest rates are relatively low; and holders may receive their compensation only in installments, unless the bonds are negotiable. In several countries, expropriation with bonds required a constitutional amendment. The opposition of the landed elite has frequently resulted in extensive compromises. (In Mexico and Cuba, landlords received only bonds. In Mexico, expropriation

---

[5] The text of the law is inconsistent. Article 220 says that the supervisory body of CORFIRA, the Consejo Superior, can "authorize" the issuance of bonds; Article 229 authorizes the executive to issue the bonds at the request (*solicitud*) of CORFIRA.

amounted to outright confiscation, because the bonds soon became valueless.) Cash compensation for expropriated estates may be for the land itself, for capital improvements on the land, and for inventory. In combination, they can represent a real obstacle to carrying out expropriations when funds are short.

The compromises made in Colombia in favor of the landlords' demands can serve as an illustration. The expropriation of privately owned estates other than those which have been idle for ten years and which can be taken over by INCORA without any compensation whatever, has by law a low priority. The law provides for cash compensation to the estate owners in the case of inadequately and adequately managed land, as well as for land cultivated by tenants or sharecroppers. In the last case, under a new amendment of 1968, half of the expropriation price is paid in negotiable bonds of the type B (2 per cent interest, twenty-five years). As a general rule, therefore, B bonds are now used only in the case of expropriation of idle land and land cultivated by certain types of small tenants and sharecroppers. In all other cases compensation is in cash, most of it payable within a few years. Estate owners can also select to receive negotiable bonds of the type A (7 per cent interest, fifteen years) instead of periodic cash payments, and obtain the bulk of their capital immediately. If they retain the type A bonds, they gain slightly in interest rates, but lose out in terms of amortization. If the recipients of B bonds sell them in the open market, they also gain immediate access to all or part of their capital, depending on the strength of the market. Since the interest rates of both bonds are low in comparison to commercial papers, it is to be suspected that the market for agrarian bonds is not very wide. On the other hand, if only a few estate owners are expropriated and only a few bonds are negotiated, the holders of the bonds can expect to sell them without losses.

In Peru, under the law of 1964, all estate owners receive compensation partly in cash and partly in negotiable bonds, regardless of the type of land expropriated. Except for livestock enterprises, where the institute can, if it wishes, buy the cattle for cash, the institute has to pay for cattle, permanent crops (plantations) and installations in cash if the owner does not wish to remove them. The law is not quite clear on this point, but it must be assumed that in the latter case, the institute has no choice but to pay cash for them. In any event, permanent crops, livestock and other installations are valued separately, and in some cases their value could easily exceed the value of the land.

In Ecuador, idle and inadequately managed land or land which does not fulfill its social function is paid in bonds; but well-managed land expropriated in areas with great population pressure is paid 50 per cent in cash and 50 per cent with the better type bonds. According to the new complicated Chilean law of 1967, practically all expropriations are compensated partly in cash and partly in bonds, in accordance with the type of expropriation, the conditions of the farm and other factors. The cash payments range from 1 to 10 per cent, and in exceptional cases up to 33 per cent. Some improvements are also payable in cash.

From the point of view of the peasants and in the interest of a speedy land reform, these arrangements do not seem to be at all satisfactory; with expropriations of the best and most conveniently located estates, which should be turned over to the peasants first, the financial burden on the institutes is heavier than for those concerning the poorer and distant farmland.

The effective financial burden on the institutes or the treasuries depends on the value assigned to the expropriated land. Here too, the legislator, or in some cases the executive, has been relatively generous in meeting the demands of the landed elite. Compensation prices are not "punitive," they are not designed to punish estate owners for anti-social activities and social injustices inherent in the latifundio system. Compensation is in most cases more than adequate, considering that the real estate and other investments have usually long been amortized; expenditures for long-run improvements have been minimal; owners have paid few taxes on their land or on agricultural earnings; and the operation of the estates has been carried out with a minimum of operating expenditures and often with free labor. Under the circumstances, expropriation can sometimes even be a reasonably profitable business proposition.

The price of an estate can fluctuate between the price set by the owner himself—the maximum—and a much lower figure, such as the declared tax value of the estate. The declared tax value is always a small fraction of the "real" value of the estate, to allow an estate owner to avoid the payment of taxes. On the other hand, the "market" value estimated by the owner tends to be above the "real" productive value of the farm, because he tends to include factors such as his control over the land, people and farm inputs, his political influence and role, and the land's capacity to absorb inflation. His price, therefore, represents a mixture of economic and non-economic elements. It is to be expected that in an agriculture dominated by a few large estate owners, the price of estate land is maintained artificially at inflated levels. It cannot represent the supply and demand of estate land, as few estates are ever bought and sold. In reality, the appraisal, i.e., the compensation price, like the compensation method, reflects the relative bargaining position of the landed elite, and not some simple economic features of the land. It might be added parenthetically that in no case can the campesinos intervene in the process of valuation, although they have a vital interest in this process whenever the expropriation price has some relation to the price they have to pay for the land which is turned over to them. Most land reform laws have adopted appraisals acceptable to the estate owners. In Colombia, in 1962, a decree on the appraisal of land which was not acceptable to the landowners was quickly replaced by a decree more favorable to them.

Often the law itself establishes the norms for appraisal of land, but in some cases it leaves the details to a regulatory decree. In Colombia, the law provides that the institute must request the appraisal to be carried out by professionals of the Geographic Institute and then proceed on the basis of two alternatives: if the owner agrees with it and if he does not. If he agrees, expropriation is speeded up, but there is the danger that the expropriation price will be high. If the owner fails to agree, the subsequent procedure includes another appraisal by three experts, one of whom can be designated by the owner. The law was revised in 1968 to allow the owner as well as the institute to request a revision of the first valuation, the costs being paid by the requesting party. But the law did not specify how the land was to be appraised. It apparently relied on the traditional methods used by the Geographic Institute, which in effect normally arrives at the "commercial value" of the estates. In 1962 the government issued a decree that the valuation of the land could not exceed 30 per cent of the cadastral value registered during the year preceding the expropriation. But in the words of the land reform institute, this decree created "a climate hostile to land reform," and was replaced by a decree which stated that the commercial value of the land was to become the upper limit of the price.

The Peruvian law of 1964 provides the basis for a highly complicated method of appraisal. The law was supplemented by two sets of detailed regulatory provisions approved by the Consejo Nacional Agrario of the land reform institute. The expropriation price of the estate must be the average of (a) the declared tax value (for rural income taxes); (b) the potential productive capability of the land; and (c) the value as determined in accordance with the most recent rules of the corps of appraisers. In the case of idle or unused land, the law authorizes a deduction from (b) of the amount of investments necessary to make the land productive. The capitalization rate is normally 9 per cent, resulting in relatively high appraisals. It appears that the law wished to rely on a method which did not include the commercial or market value, but a fair mixture of criteria. The result may be equally favorable to the owners, because of the great pressure exerted on the Peruvian Technical Corps of Appraisers by inflated land values. If the owner objects to the appraisal, a final valuation is undertaken by three experts, one from the College of Engineers, the second from the corps of appraisers and the third from the landowners' association of the region. It is difficult to avoid the conclusion that the composition of this group of experts is an invitation to landowners to object to the original appraisal and await the probably more favorable outcome of the second.

The Venezuelan land reform bases its expropriation price on the commercial value of the farm. In Brazil, the law authorizes the land reform institute to take into account the declared tax value, the new cadastral value and the market value of the estate, but does not indicate the relative weight of each criterion. In Chile, the new law of 1967 establishes that the compensation price is based on the appraisal which is in effect for purposes of real estate taxes (*"equivalente al avaluo vigente para los efectos de la contribución territorial"*), plus any improvements not included in this appraisal. Of the countries mentioned, this appears to be the appraisal price most unfavorable to the owners. In most laws of the 1960's, the expropriation price tends toward the commercial or market value of the estate, i.e., the price essentially fixed by the owners themselves.

Three general hypotheses may seem valid in light of the existing legislation as it has been described. These hypotheses are not mutually exclusive, but complementary. First, it is to be expected that if limited cash resources—i.e., resources other than bonds—are to be spent on expropriations of privately owned estates with relatively high-quality land in prosperous farming communities and with relatively high appraisal values, not many estates can be expropriated annually for redistribution to peasants. Resources would be quickly exhausted and few farm families would benefit. Secondly, if expropriations of private estates take place principally on abandoned, unused or poorly managed farmland, for which the laws prescribe the highest priority, the land may be obtained at relatively little cash cost to the institute, but the institute may be forced into spending its funds on infrastructural investments to get the land into shape for productive use prior to settlement. This in turn may keep the annual rate of settlement at low levels, since such investments normally take considerable time to carry out, particularly if the resources of the institutes have to be prorated over a period of years. Finally, if the expropriation of privately owned estates is rendered difficult or impossible on legal grounds or for political reasons, or both, the resources of an institute may be left unspent, which in turn may be used as a justification for cutting the land reform institutes' budgets in subsequent years, or they may be spent on non-land reform projects. In other words, if the land reform institute attempts to carry out projects through the expropriation and redistribution of privately owned land when the general political climate is unfavorable to land reform, its budget may be threatened or actually cut, until such time as the institute will use its funds on non-land reform activities.

It is not generally easy to separate the actual land reform activities of an institute from non-land reform activities. This is the result of the often inaccurate concept of land reform, but also of the fact that the laws prescribe many different functions for the institutes, some of which may have only an ephemeral connection with land reform itself: titles and cadastres, taxes, irrigation, road construction, credit, colonization and others. Land reform projects *per se* are only those which modify the property and power structure in the established farming communities through expropriations and redistribution of estate land. How far costs of settlement of peasants are to be counted as land reform costs, rather than general agricultural development costs, is not always clear. For example, if, as in Chile, the government provides that for three years beneficiaries will not obtain title for the land they receive, will land reform costs terminate once the settlers have been placed on the land, or only after government control and supervision has ended? Or in some cases, farm people cannot be settled without previous public investments. But even if an institute spends a large proportion of its funds on such investments in outlying districts, they are not necessarily land reform expenditures, especially if there are many privately owned estates with good or potentially good land in developed farming communities which are left untouched by the land reform program. In other words, irrigation, road construction or similar projects undertaken by a land reform institute in order to prepare land for settlement in subsequent years generally cannot be counted as land reform expenditures.

Colombia's INCORA annual reports contain balance sheets of the agency's assets and liabilities, and condensed tables of the investments and operating expenditures. The balance sheets do not reveal the actual transactions made annually by the institute, but they show the overall resources at its disposal at the end of each year. If consecutive balance sheets are examined and evaluated in light of the agency's program and the annual resources which it receives, they give a rough indication of the agency's nature and scope of activity. (The agency can have relatively few resources at the end of a period and still carry out a large-scale land reform if its yearly transactions are large.) The assets of the institute are shown in the table below. Total assets less agrarian bonds increased from about $27 million U.S. in 1962, the year of INCORA's establishment, to $72.5 million in 1967, or about three times. The latter figure includes about $20 million in "loans," most of it probably from INCORA's credit operations. Its agrarian bonds rose from $40 million in 1963 to about $52 million in 1967, although the annual reports contain no information on how the bonds were actually used. The major annual contribution of the government to INCORA during 1962–67 was to be a minimum of $7 million from the national budget and about $14 million in agrarian bonds, excluding any national or international loans which the agency could receive. However, during the first year of its operation, the institute received only a small proportion of the funds to which it was entitled from the national budget—20 million pesos or about $1.8 million U.S.—"owing to fiscal difficulties." This was not a significant amount of money to begin a nationwide land reform program in a country of the size and with the agricultural population of Colombia. No further delinquencies of this nature have been reported for subsequent years when INCORA's policies were already firmly established. At the end of 1967, INCORA had an investment in farmland (colonization and other settlement projects, and work in progress) of about $16.5 million. But a new item appeared during that year: $19 million in irrigation projects (presumably including the value of the land). Land assets alone rose from $4 million in 1963 to $17.1 million in 1966 and then declined slightly to the $16.5 million figure. These assets as well as irrigation projects are no doubt farmland acquired by INCORA to be turned over at a later time to peasant families, or they would not appear in the balance sheets, or at least not in this form, depending on how the land is turned over to the campesinos. Most of the land in irrigation and similar projects requiring lengthy preparation, according to INCORA, will not be ready until the early 1970's. The total INCORA holdings of land in 1967 were surprisingly small in absolute terms, although they represented 27 per cent of all INCORA assets (less bonds), or about 50 per cent if irrigation projects are included. This could imply that INCORA is rapidly distributing the land it acquires to the campesinos. But since this has not been INCORA's policy, it merely means that INCORA, with its acquisition of land, has temporarily become a major real estate owner.

Assets of Colombia's Land Reform Institute, INCORA
1962–67
(in U.S. dollars)

Year	Bonds	Land and Projects	Irrigation	Other Assets	Total Assets	Total Assets
1962	–	–	–	21.1	27.1	27.1
1963	40.1	4.0ᵃ	–	11.7	15.7	55.9
1964	45.0	9.3ᵇ	–	15.2	24.5	69.5
1965	40.6	8.8ᶜ	–	15.0	23.8	64.5
1966	55.1	17.1ᵇ	–	22.2	39.3	94.4
1967	51.9	16.5ᵇ	19.0	37.0	72.5	124.4

ᵃ Colonization and land distribution projects.
ᵇ Colonization and land distribution projects, farms and work in progress.
ᶜ Colonization and land distribution projects and farms.

In the aggregate, the data do not appear to reflect an operation commensurate with a national program designed to reform the nation's agrarian structure in an agriculture which in 1967 generated a gross income of about $1.4 billion, and in an economy of a total gross product of about $5 billion. Rather, they reflect a marginal undertaking obviously incapable of making a dent in the nation's agrarian structure.

The same is true of an accounting of INCORA's investment and other expenditures, which further elucidates the type of activities the agency appears to have carried out. During the first four years of operation, INCORA spent a total of about $48 million, or an average of only about $12 million annually, on its various activities. A little over one fifth, or $2.3 million annually, can be estimated for land reform itself and 17 per cent, or $2.2 million annually, for administration of all INCORA programs. In other words, administration consumed about the same as land reform. Nearly one half, or $5.5 million annually, was spent on activities not related to land reform. In 1966, INCORA spent a total of $23.6 million, almost twice as much as in the preceding years, but most of the increase seems to be due to infrastructural work projects and a relatively large-scale credit program financed in part by foreign loans. By the end of 1966, INCORA had spent $18 million on engineering works and $10.8 million on land acquisition. An increased proportion went to the former during the year 1966. Thus INCORA's budget is more like a general agricultural budget, although it is operated under the name of land reform.

If one were to divide the costs of land acquisition and settlement services (about $9.9 million up to 1965) by the number of farm families settled during the same period (1,127) INCORA spent close to $9,000 per family, excluding costs of administration. In fact, to justify the settlement of 1,127 families through the land reform program, INCORA spent a total of about $42,000 per family during the years 1962–65! The Colombian case appears to be typical for other Latin American countries.

It is apparent, then, that the resources allocated to the land reform institutes are not for land reform expenditures *per se* under prevailing conditions. The resources must also be regarded as far from adequate for the needs of the campesinos. Furthermore, the limited funds which the institutes are to obtain in accordance with the law are not even always allocated to them. The problem, then, is not only that of expanding financial resources, but that of governments fulfilling their obligations under the law. It is doubtful that failures to allocate sufficient funds to the reform programs is attributable only to economic factors. It is more plausible that they are politically inspired. Actual or threatened budget cuts can be envisaged as having two specific goals: to make it difficult for the institute to terminate projects or impossible to begin new ones and plan ahead; and to channel activities into areas where they could do the least harm to estate owners. Since the landed elite is well represented in the legislative and executive bodies, as well as in financial circles which influence the shaping of national budgets, these goals are not difficult to achieve. In some cases, an institute can even be persuaded to undertake projects which are actually beneficial to estate owners, such as penetration roads in frontier areas which enhance real estate values. This turns a land reform institute into an agency beneficial to the landed elite.

Failure to allocate funds seems to have coincided with the initial fear of the landed elite about what land reform institutes would be doing and how they were going to function. Once it is ascertained that their policy is not to expropriate land but to invest in irrigation and colonization schemes, and once it is established that the laws do not really operate in favor of the campesinos, or benefit only a handful of them, two alternative courses of action are open. Resources can begin to flow more freely to the institutes to be used in nonreform projects, or funds can be withheld in order to starve the institute out of a useful existence. The malfunctioning of the institute (i.e., of the law) can then serve as an argument to withhold further funds on the grounds of "inefficiency" of institute directors and personnel. Given the nature and content of the laws, the probability that the institutes would engage in real reform, or that the institutes' directors would aggressively but peacefully bring about the "effective transformation of unjust structures and systems of land tenure and use" (in the language of the Charter of Punta del Este) is exceedingly low. But the landed elite does not take any chances. This conclusion tends to confirm the validity of the other two hypotheses mentioned earlier: a few expropriations of good, privately owned farms in prosperous communities would quickly exhaust the institutes' resources; and settlement of campesinos on poor land in outlying districts, which is legal priority, causes the spending of a large part of reform funds on infrastructural improvements, leaving few resources for actual settlement. However, the real relationship between the law, finances and the scope and nature of land reform cannot yet be established with precision, because so little land has thus far been expropriated, paid for and redistributed to the campesinos, although all the funds allocated were spent by the institutes. The discussion must remain on the theoretical level as long as the institutes engage mainly in non-land reform or pre-land reform activities.

Finally, there seems to be a tenuous relationship between the amount of money spent and the success of land reform so far in Latin America. Success is much more dependent on political factors, including campesino support and the speed with which reforms are carried out. In fact, with real campesino support, the costs of land reform to the institutes might well be reduced drastically. Unless a reform is carried out swiftly, as in Bolivia in the early 1950's, when almost all of the land was distributed within a few months and peasants were armed to protect their rights, the landed elite can benefit from delays and launch anti-reform strategies or block the reform through a variety of means which can range from violent repression of campesinos and their organizations to withholding funds from the land reform institutes. It is obvious that anti-reform strategies have contributed sharply to raising the costs of Latin America's "land reform" programs.

CHAPTER 21

Land Reform Laws and the Campesinos

The land reform legislation of the 1960's not only excludes the campesinos by law from all phases of the national land reform programs, but also seems to have incorporated certain views and attitudes about the role of the campesinos which reflect the thinking of the landed elite. Its members are often heard to reflect that farm people are not ready to assume major responsibilities of the management of land without their control. Hence *they are "not ready for land reform."* It is also said that only a very small proportion of the peasants are capable of exercising the functions of entrepreneurs. This opinion is the basis for the rationalization that land reform must proceed at a snail's pace. It coincides of course with many estate owners' concept of land reform, i.e., the creation of a small number of highly capitalized and specialized model family-type operations with purebred imported cattle and other refined inputs. The Chilean land reform law of 1962, which preceded the present law of 1967, actually provided that there would be two groups of land reform beneficiaries: the few who would become medium-sized operators and all those who, on the edge of the land reform or settlement projects, would occupy tiny garden plots (*huertos familiares*) and work for the remaining estates or the newly established units.

Although the argument that the peasants are not ready for land reform is of doubtful value—all the farm work in agriculture having actually been carried out for generations by the peasants, and the contribution of absentee estate owners to the agricultural production processes being highly overrated by the landed elite—it seems to have been included in some form or another in the legislation. The pace at which reform can proceed is the same as the pace at which the land reform institutes are supposed to select, train and settle peasant families able to fulfill the requirements for meeting the demands of an allegedly complex production and marketing system.

The Chilean law of 1967 states specifically, for example, that one objective of the redistribution of expropriated estates is to prepare and train the beneficiaries of the land reform projects so that at the end of the trial period of settlement, they will be able to assume all the responsibilities of ownership and entrepreneurship. Therefore, the law provides that the peasants who receive land will acquire ownership only at the end of three years, during which period they operate under government control and supervision. From the peasants' viewpoint, this introduces a strong element of uncertainty in the land reform process, although it is compatible with the belief that peasants must be taught how to farm. What this all adds up to is land reform on the installment plan.

In the desire to control both the peasants and the activities of the land reform institute, and to leave as little room for deviation as possible, the majority of the laws state that the settlement of peasants must be principally on privately owned units resembling "family farms." In most cases, other forms of land tenure are either not mentioned or are given a low priority. The Colombian statute of 1961 states, for example, that INCORA can use the land it acquires to constitute family farm units or co-operative enterprises, but in a special chapter devoted to family farms it also prescribes that INCORA must give preference to establishing family farm units. The Peruvian law of 1964 was more emphatic: settlement of peasants (*personas naturales*) must be on family farm units, with the exception of *feudatarios,* sharecroppers or small tenants, who may be assigned the smaller plots they cultivate and which they are allowed to receive in ownership under the law's Title XV. In outlying regions the settlers may be assigned "medium-size" enterprises. An exception is made for Indian communities as well as co-operatives previously authorized by the land reform institute. Brazil's law of 1964 provides that expropriated land can be redistributed as family farms or as units (*glebas*) to be exploited by groups of farmers organized in a co-operative; this formulation leaves the problem of the property of such co-operatively exploited enterprises unsolved. However, the second alternative seems remote, inasmuch as the legislation was specifically focused on the "democratic option," which favors private property (*"A opção democratica baseia-se no estimulo a propriedade privada,"* a statement of a rather cryptic nature), and the right of the farm owner to the fruits of his work.[1] Only the recent Chilean statute of 1967 provides for various forms of co-operatively owned or operated farm units as a second major land tenure system, although the text of the law gives clear priority to privately owned family farm units and leaves the decision to establish non-privately owned farm units in each particular case to the judgment of the land reform institute.

The disadvantage of Latin America's land reform legislation lies in the fact that land reform institutes are prevented from carrying out a more flexible settlement policy and it seems obvious that the legislators attempted to avoid the organization of large co-operatively or collectively owned or operated farm units able to deal effectively with the problem of sharply increased production and rural employment. Large units might have greater bargaining power in obtaining access to credit, machinery and other farm inputs, and would be a constant reminder to the government that they must be accorded the privileges which hitherto have gone almost exclusively to the landed elite. Experience has shown that with the survival and predominance of latifundismo "family farm units" established in land reform or colonization projects are, with respect to the farm inputs and output markets, in about the same marginal position as other smallholdings in Latin

---

[1] In the message accompanying the bill (Mensagem No. 33 de 1964, C.N. paragraph 15), a distinction is made between the democratic option and the socialist option. To identify the democratic option with the private property system is not quite accurate, particularly in Brazil, where it has led to one of the most unequal patterns of land distribution in the world. Only in a remote sense can it be claimed that for the estate owners the benefits of private property stem from the fruits of their own work. It is more correct to say they stem from the work of others.

America. Hence the inflexibility inherent in the law is a disadvantage for the peasants, and it is to be suspected that it is not accidental. New family farms could be successful if the distribution of land were to be accompanied by reforms of the input and output markets. But the land reform legislation of the 1960's was not accompanied by such reforms. It is true that most laws oblige the beneficiaries of land reform projects to belong to a co-operative. Usually this would be a marketing or service co-operative. But since settlement projects are practically always small—normally with a maximum of a few hundred settlers, as they are settled on individual estates, and not "wholesale" in large expropriated areas—such co-operatives are bound to be small and ineffective. The provisions in the land reform laws for the formation of co-operatives must be regarded more as lip service to the co-operative movement than as a serious attempt at reforming the market structure. These small co-operatives are not serious competition to the private channels of distribution of inputs or outputs, and the governments have been unable to support effectively these new co-operatives when private dealers set out to make them ineffective, as indeed they have done.

Although the land reform legislation of the 1960's aims at the elimination and prevention of the inequitable concentration of land ownership, there is evidence that it tends to preserve a cheap, abundant and obedient supply of labor for the large estates. This is inherent in the piecemeal or pilot project approach to land reform, which is not capable of changing the fundamental nature of the existing land tenure structures. But in addition, there are provisions in some laws which clearly attempt to maintain peasants in a condition of social and economic dependency on the estates.

One of these is the much heralded Title XV of the Peruvian law of 1964—a last-minute amendment to the land reform legislation designed as an apparent gesture to give farmland at one stroke to a large number of campesinos.[2] It provides

---

[2] This type of legislation—where "tenants" are supposed to become owners—has been passed by many countries throughout the world, generally with disastrous results for the peasants.

that feudal or semi-feudal farm workers, such as sharecroppers, small tenants or resident workers with garden plots (all lumped together under the name *feudatarios*) have the right to demand in property the farm plot which had been ceded them by the owners in return for free work or work at sharply reduced wages, for the owner. The contradictory text of the law indicates how hasty the legislators were. Title XV is entitled "Preferential Rights of Feudatarios," but the first provision of the title states that the feudatarios "shall become" (*se convertirán*) owners, implying that feudatarios have more than a preferential right and that with the law's enactment they would immediately become owners. The same provision also says that they will become owners only after the institute has paid the estate owners for these plots. If the right to become an owner of a plot were a "preferential right" of the feudatario, the decision to become its owner would be his. In reality, the decision is made by the institute, and finally by the treasury or the parliament, which provide the funds to expropriate the plots. Thus the "preferential right" of the feudatarios turns out to be a preferential right of the government. Actually, since the institute never disposed of adequate funds, the provision that estate owners must first be paid before the land is owned by the feudatarios has put the most severe damper on this program. Although some 120,000 feudatarios registered with the institute to claim their "preferential right," not a single one was to become the actual owner of his plot by mid-1966, except for a handful who obtained title to their plots after a voluntary transfer from the owners. ONRA distributed some 32,000 certificates in which the status of the peasants and the future right of property in their plot is established. But these certificates did not give their holders any rights which they did not already have under the law. So Title XV has not yet operated to the advantage of the campesinos. Since the institute did not have sufficient funds to pay the owners for the plots of so many peasants, the delay allowed many estate owners to dismiss their feudatarios on a large scale, as they were unwilling to give up even the small amounts of land involved. Resident peasants were occasionally dismissed by violent means which prevented many campesinos from exercising their right under the law, and thousands were afraid of claiming their rights for fear of being thrown out. The dismissal of the feudatarios was clearly a violation of the law, for which estate owners were not prosecuted, and the institute was unable to help them. In the long run, however, the application of the law would have helped the campesinos only in a limited way, since the plots are often very small, although it would have given them immediate security. Therefore, both the implementation and the non-implementation of the law are actually or potentially harmful to the campesinos. They are of benefit only to the estate owners, who continue to rely on a supply of cheap labor.[3] The Peruvian experience is of great significance for Latin America. In fact, its experience has been duplicated in many other countries throughout the world.

Another by-product of the piecemeal, pilot project land reform in Latin America is that the legislation provides inadequate protection for peasants who are left without any land on an expropriated estate which has been subdivided among its tenants or sharecroppers into "family-sized units." Some laws, like Colombia's, provide that neighboring estates may be acquired. But given the nature of the acquisition and expropriation processes, the redistribution of additional land to the excess peasant families threatens to be slow or costly, and the peasants may have moved away by the time additional land becomes available, *if* it becomes available. Thus a land reform institute may be pressured to crowd as many peasant families as possible into an expropriated estate, in order to avoid social conflicts, at the risk of making the "family-sized units" substandard in size. This is the route toward the establishment of new minifundios, and perhaps the opponents

[3] In 1968 Colombia amended its law of 1961 and in a much heralded move attempted to make most small tenants, sharecroppers and similar resident workers owners of their plots. However the Colombian legislation is less favorable to the peasants than the Peruvian, since the "preferential rights" of the peasants are subject to a previous expropriation of the estate on which their plots are located. Since INCORA's expropriations were rare, the peasants' preferential rights are therefore minimal. Nonetheless the effects of the law were similar to those of Title XV in Peru: it has been reported that the landed elite began evicting their small tenants even before the amendment was enacted.

of land reform are not far from the mark when they claim that land reform leads to the establishment of minifundios—although, of course, they pretend to ignore that the activities of the land reform institutes are not real land reforms.

Latin American land reform measures, then, may actually be harmful to the campesinos. This surprising conclusion can be reached only when one knows how the laws and latifundismo operate. Resident farm workers can be dismissed on a massive scale; the number of wage and migrant workers can be increased; land becomes increasingly inaccessible and the resulting unemployment or underemployment will help swell the number of slum inhabitants in the cities.

Finally, we must mention the unequal protection of owners' and peasants' rights. The land reform laws of most countries tend to be much more considerate of estate owners than they are of the peasants, the theoretical beneficiaries of the laws. The peasants' rights to land cannot be enforced against estate owners, who possess both legal tools and political influence to fight expropriation, indemnification and other decisions of the land reform institutes. In other words, the laws do not adequately correct an obvious imbalance in the power relations in agriculture. Most of the laws provide the estate owners with more legal weapons to hold up the reform processes than the peasants have to obtain land speedily. For example, the Peruvian law of 1964 provides that the landowners can object to the classification of their land (for purposes of expropriation) before the institute's highest board, with the possible result that the land could be exempted from reform. The peasants have an equal interest in expropriation, but they are not given an equal chance to insist that a particular estate should be expropriated. As a result, the expropriation procedure is a matter only between the land reform institute and estate owners, and not, as it should be, between the peasants and the institute. Theoretically, of course, the land reform institute represents the peasants' interests, but its structure and composition, and its very functioning within the existing political framework, make it unlikely that these interests are fully protected.

With the exception of Venezuela, the peasants' "rights to

land" under the laws are protected only when the institute carries out a land reform project. The initiative for expropriation projects usually lies with the land reform institute, although there were cases where peasant unrest influenced the institute's decision. But once peasant unrest had been suppressed, this factor no longer played an important role. If the peasants wish to exert pressure on the institute to expropriate land, they must use political and extralegal means. The implication is that the "rights" of the campesinos to land are more like "handouts." In fact, there is the distinct risk that the peasants who attempt to exert pressure on the institute will be regarded as acting in violation of the law. Only in Venezuela do the peasants have the right to request the taking over of an estate.

In accordance with these principles, the land reform laws do not contain sanctions for estate owners' activities directed against the laws, except in a few isolated instances. As a result, the landed elite's active or passive resistance to decisions of the land reform institute remains unpunished. The failure to provide for sanctions is a significant omission, as historical experience should have taught that legislation in favor of the campesinos has been systematically ignored and violated. Even if the laws were to contain sanctions against the landlords, they probably would not be enforced, given the existing political structure. But by failing to establish sanctions, the laws themselves unequivocally embody the general attitude that the estate owners must be protected against the peasants.

One of the few existing sanctions is in Peru's law of 1964. It obliges estate owners to allow inspection of their property and furnish information on their operations, subject to a fine, which may be as high as 50 per cent of the expropriation value. This provision protects the land reform institute in the execution of its activities, and only indirectly protects the peasants. But in fact, the landed elite has been successful in sabotaging the work of the institute through political and economic influence at the national as well as at the local level.

Estate owners who prevent campesinos from taking advantage of the benefits accorded them under the law cannot be prosecuted. For example, Peru's law declares that campesinos who violate the property rights of estate owners—e.g., through invasions—are excluded from the benefits of the law (and presumably cannot obtain any land). In fact, the campesinos who fall under this provision are treated much more harshly than non-campesinos who commit similar violations: they receive twice the penalty stipulated by the penal code and cannot be released on bond or obtain conditional liberty. The penalty is up to four years in jail. On the other hand, if estate owners simulate such violations or prevent campesinos from claiming benefits—e.g., by evicting them from the estates —no sanction is provided by law, and prosecution of the estate owners is almost unthinkable under existing conditions.

In this manner, the peasants become more the enemies than the beneficiaries of land reform. As strange as this may seem, the very land reform legislation stacks the cards against the peasants.

CHAPTER 22

The Land Reform Achievements of the 1960's: Development in Reverse?

We have felt it necessary to devote a considerable amount of space to an analysis of the land reform legislation of the 1960's, because the decade ushered in a policy of rational, peaceful change in the agrarian structures of Latin America, based on legal, orderly processes. It was therefore essential to determine, first of all, how the Latin American nations have attempted to carry out this policy. In the process, it was found that the land reform legislation is not a basis for real structural reforms in agriculture. We must now go one step further and evaluate the achievements of various land reform institutes which are empowered to carry out national land reform projects under the law.

Progress in land reform has been insignificant if one uses as criteria the peasants' demands and needs for more land, better jobs, full-time employment and higher levels of living. However, detailed information on progress in land reform is not readily available, and some of the available evidence is difficult to interpret. A major source of confusion lies in the multiplicity of functions of the land reform institutes. Under the name of "land reform," the institutes carry out a variety of activities, which are not always land reform activities. Therefore the annual reports of the institutes are not always a guide. For example, land reform institutes are usually required by law to carry out settlements of farm families in colonization projects in new areas on land not previously cultivated. At times it is difficult to distinguish colonization from land reform. If settlement of peasant families takes place on a single privately owned and subsequently expropriated estate, whose land had previously been little used, or remained idle and practically abandoned by the owner, such an isolated project is on the borderline between reform and colonization. In fact, it might even be argued that *an isolated expropriation and settlement project on an individual estate, no matter how large, which does not significantly modify the agrarian structure of a community can hardly be qualified as land reform.* In some cases, such projects even contribute to reinforcing the traditional agrarian structure in the area, when estate owners who are not affected directly by any expropriation, attempt to offset the "negative influence" of the projects on the campesinos by counter-reform measures directed against them.

In actuality, except in Cuba, no Latin American country has undertaken in the 1960's a program which has radically modified the agrarian structure of a large community or region, and the institutes' land reform programs have at best consisted of single settlement projects on either expropriated farms or public land. However, in order to arrive at some sort of evaluation of the progress of land reform and ignoring for the time being the differentiation between real land reforms and the atomized, pilot project land reforms which the laws of the 1960's permit, we might realistically define land reform projects as settlement projects which are carried out on expropriated private estates in well-established farming areas, and colonization as those projects which take place elsewhere.

Land reform institutes occasionally issue titles of property, build roads, make large capital investments in irrigation or drainage schemes or set up a listing of properties (cadastre). These activities always have beneficiaries. But not all of them are real land reform beneficiaries, and in fact none of them may be. The issuance of titles, for example, means in many cases a small improvement in the land tenure situation of the recipients, as the titles may increase their security of tenure in the long run and entitle them to receive credit with greater facility, if credit is made available to them. But all this does not significantly alter their economic and political status. It simply legalizes a previously precarious possession of land by the peasants. To protect possession of land is an obligation of the government, with or without land reform. If governments have been unable to improve the precarious situation of squatters who are exposed to the whims of the large estate owners or investors, this has been part and parcel of the latifundio system, which thrives on the insecurity of the campesinos. The titles are an improvement; but they are not land reform. It is never quite clear whether the peasants are the major beneficiaries of some of the other activities mentioned above, even if they do modify the existing structure of agriculture. For example, the penetration roads built in isolated regions to facilitate access to the nearest towns and markets may benefit the peasants in the short run; but they may be of even greater benefit to the owners of large estates and rural and urban investors, because in addition to the physical improvements, they reap large gains in terms of increased real estate values, and are in a position to fortify the latifundio system in the area. Thus, in the long run, the peasants are deprived of the benefits that might have accrued to them at first.

Few attempts have as yet been made to evaluate in quantitative terms for Latin America as a whole the achievements of the Latin American land reform institutes. But a recent starting point was the claim that "some 700,000 families in Latin America have been settled or resettled on their own land since the Alliance for Progress was conceived in 1961. Some 450,000 families have received title to land. A total of 3.6 million people have benefitted from settlement and resettlement programs."[1] The wording of this statement is not clear. It might indicate that the families who have received title to land (450,000) are counted as land reform beneficiaries and therefore have to be added to the 700,000 families who have been settled or resettled on their own land; and that they are not included in the 3.6 million people who have

[1] James R. Fowler, Office of Public Affairs, Bureau of Inter-American Affairs, U. S. State Department, July 1968, p. 8.

benefited from settlement and resettlement programs, since the issuance of titles is not a settlement or resettlement program. Perhaps the 3.6 million people are the same as the 700,000 families which have been settled or resettled, at the rate of about five people per family, which is a realistic figure. But obviously not all the 700,000 families can have been settled or resettled on expropriated private estates, and some must have been settled in colonization schemes. Assuming that about one half of the 700,000 families were beneficiaries of reform rather than colonization—a rather optimistic assumption—during a seven-year period (1961–68), the annual rate of land reform beneficiaries would have been 50,000 families. Since we established earlier that during the 1960's the annual increase in new families—of whom 75 to 90 per cent were estimated to be poor and therefore potential land reform beneficiaries—is estimated at about 271,000 for nineteen Latin American countries, or about 220,000 families, excluding Mexico and Bolivia, it becomes evident that, even if the statistics in the quoted statement were accepted, the annual increase in potential land reform beneficiaries would be much larger than the number of families benefiting from land reform settlement, and in fact no dent would be made in the poverty status of the immense number of farm families before adding new generations of rural poor. As a result, the total number of potential beneficiaries continues to increase sharply. There is reason to believe, however, that the number of land reform beneficiaries settled or resettled on their own land is in fact significantly smaller. This leads to an examination of the scope and nature of a few national land reform programs.

In Brazil, between 1964 and 1968, only 329 farm families were settled by IBRA, Brazil's land reform institute in Rio de Janeiro, although IBRA had long-range plans to settle about 12,770 families in fourteen settlement projects. Several of these actually resembled colonization rather than land reform projects. (IBRA also had eight additional projects for the consolidation of minifundios.) Actual settlements had taken place on only three of the fourteen projects. If it is assumed that each settler received 30 hectares on the average, the total area involved would be less than 10,000 hectares—an insignificant fraction of the 44 million in the hands of "latifundistas," as defined by IBRA's large cadastral survey, on which the institute has been engaged for years, or of the 130 to 156 million hectares in large multi-family farms, according to CIDA. Hence there is no land reform in Brazil and there are practically no land reform beneficiaries. Since Brazil occupies about two thirds of the Latin American continent and has the largest rural population, its failure to achieve any progress counts heavily in the overall evaluation of Latin America's land reform progress in the 1960's.

We shall examine next the land reform program of Colombia, for which there is more published information available than on most other Latin American countries, and which has often been presented as a model for the continent. Here too we shall find that progress has been insignificant, although propaganda has attempted to convey a different impression. In the first annual progress report of 1962, the land reform institute, INCORA, referred to a recommendation of the Committee of Nine of the Alliance for Progress, which after careful study concluded that in its first years of operation (through 1965), Colombia should have settled a total of no less than 35,000 farm families, and in the second five-year period, 100,000 families.[2] Furthermore, CIDA estimated that 961,000 families were potential land reform beneficiaries. Hence, under a twenty-year land reform program, about 60,000 families would have to receive benefits in terms of land or otherwise. This figure includes the annual population growth increase of 14,000 farm families, most of whom are poor.

The most reliable method of examining INCORA's achievements is to analyze the annual reports of the institute from 1962 to 1967 inclusive, which were quite comprehensive during the first few years, although much more reticent in subsequent years. Although these reports do not lend themselves

[2] See INCORA, "Informe de Actividades en 1962," p. 6 f.

to a detailed analysis of the separate activities of the agency, they provide sufficient insights to make general, if approximate, conclusions on the progress achieved. INCORA is not only concerned with land reform schemes, but it has also taken over some of the functions of the Ministry of Agriculture and credit institutions, or is in competition with them. This is largely due to the provisions of the law, which assigns INCORA a large number of functions. In part it is also due to political pressure to reduce greatly real land reform measures. Hence INCORA has become to all appearances the most important agricultural agency in the country, an agency devoted to change. In addition to activities connected with the settlement of peasants on private and public lands and their housing, it also has the following functions: credit and technical assistance to both land reform beneficiaries and other farm people; crop and livestock development programs; market organization, including road construction and co-operatives; land improvement, including irrigation and drainage to expand the supply of good land; and training.[3] The efforts of the agency are therefore not concentrated mainly on the settlement of farm people.

The land reform policy of INCORA underwent two important changes during the short period of its activities. It had been widely admitted that Colombia's main land tenure problem is the monopoly of control over the land and other agriculture resources. CIDA reported that 1.2 per cent of the farms, the large multi-family units, controlled nearly 45 per cent of the land; and an additional 4.5 per cent of the farms, the medium-sized multi-family farms, controlled a little over 25 per cent of the farmland, so that 5.7 per cent of the farms controlled 70 per cent of all farmland. This does not take into consideration the fact that several producers may belong to one (immediate or extended) family, or that several estates may belong to one owner, both of which reduce the control over the same amount of land to a still small number of owners or landowning families. Former Senator Carlos Lleras

[3] INCORA, "Seis Anos de Reforma Social Agraria en Colombia, 1962–67," pp. 21–38.

Restrepo, generally considered author of the land reform legislation, stated in presenting the legislation before the Senate in 1961 that

> *No es aventurado afirmar, pues, que la concentración de la propiedad rural es mayor de lo que muestran las imperfectas estadísticas disponibles* [It is reasonable to say, then, that the concentration of rural property is greater than is shown by the imperfect statistics that are available].[4]

In the face of these realities, in 1963, the second year of its operation, INCORA adopted the thesis that Colombia has a land tenure problem *sui generis*. It asserted that "in Colombia there is no monopoly control over the land," and that large landowners do not decisively control the political machinery in the country.[5] According to this new concept, the major "social problem" in Colombian agriculture now was the minifundio and the underutilization of resources.[6] INCORA even claimed that latifundios occupy only a small proportion of poor quality land. It does not take a confirmed reformist to understand that this new policy intended to minimize the importance of expropriations of estates and their redistribution to peasants within the overall "land reform" program. The minifundio problem and the underutilization of the resources is an inherent feature of a latifundio agriculture which prevents access to land to the campesinos and reduces the employment of its resources in order to maintain an excess obedient labor supply working at low wages.

The second major policy change took place in 1967 and 1968, after the Institute had encountered serious obstacles to expropriating and redistributing land belonging to the *terratenientes*, notwithstanding the latter's failure to "decisively control the political machinery in the country," as the Institute had claimed. So it strove to secure amendments to the law of 1961, particularly an amendment which would allow

---

[4] Tierra, *10 Ensayos sobre la Reforma Agraria en Colombia* (Bogotá: Ed. Tercer Mundo, 1961), pp. 29–37, especially pp. 29 ff.

[5] INCORA, "Segundo Ano de Reforma Agraria, 1963," pp. 13 ff.

[6] Ibid., p. 17.

small tenants and sharecroppers to claim in property the land they cultivated on behalf of the owners. The second "new look" therefore implied another shift away from real land reform.

Let us take a closer look at what INCORA actually accomplished between 1961 and 1968. During this period, the institute acquired about 2.3–2.4 million hectares of land "for its land reform program" through various legal means. Of these, nearly two million hectares were obtained under an old law dating back to 1936 (Law 200), rather than under the 1961 land reform law. The older legislation allowed the nation to reclaim private land which had remained unutilized. Of these two million hectares 1.3 million were acquired in four provinces where large areas are underdeveloped and which are therefore more appropriate for colonization than land reform. In addition, INCORA acquired 265,000 hectares through gifts or donations; 109,000 hectares through purchases; and only 44,000 hectares through expropriations. The expropriated land actually acquired under a real land reform program comprised only 1.8 per cent of all the land handled by INCORA, and only a tiny fraction of the land in multi-family farms. In the most prosperous farming areas, where latifundismo is powerful, INCORA acquired only insignificant amounts of land by any legal means, and none for land reform. In Valle, one of Colombia's richest areas, which also has large extensions of good but underutilized land, less than 5,000 hectares were acquired, of which 710 were by expropriation. The same holds true for Antioquia, Nariño, Santander or Tolima. In some rich provinces, no land at all was acquired by the institute. Whatever land reform programs have been carried out, as reflected by these land acquisitions, have therefore tended to take place in the outlying regions of Colombia. But land acquisitions *per se* do not reveal the entire scope of the program. We must translate the land acquisitions in terms of beneficiaries.

If INCORA had carried out the recommendations of the Committee of Nine—35,000 families through 1965, plus 40,-000 additional families through 1967, a total of 75,000 families—it would have required about 2.1 million hectares to accommodate the 75,000 families at the rate of thirty hectares per family. But apparently the 2.3–2.4 million hectares of land acquired were not distributed to 75,000 families, and in fact there are no statistics on how much acquired land was actually redistributed to farm families, to how many, and under what terms.

On the other hand, INCORA distributed about 66,000 titles of property, presumably to an equal number of farm families, involving a total of 2.2 million hectares. It is not clear whether these 2.2 million hectares are partly included in the 2.3–2.4 million hectares acquired by the institute, because it has not been reported whether the issuance of titles is only for peasant families who are exclusively squatters. Among the 66,000 recipients of titles there may be real land reform beneficiaries who received plots of land acquired by INCORA in land reform projects. But how many? However, among the recipients of titles are undoubtedly many occupants of land in precarious land tenure conditions who possessed their plots for a number of years, and who had cleared and improved them by their own efforts. They cannot be counted as land reform beneficiaries, as we explained earlier.

The number of actual beneficiaries can only be estimated approximately from the description of the projects scattered throughout Colombia contained in the institute's annual reports. By early 1965, INCORA had been authorized to carry out thirty-four projects, of which twenty-one were land settlement and thirteen non-land reform projects. Among the latter were projects involving assistance to spontaneous colonization. These projects cannot be included in the land reform balance sheet of INCORA's activities. Of the twenty-one settlement projects, several of which are borderline cases between land reform and colonization, only six appeared to have registered actual settlers, namely 1,127 families on about 23,600 hectares. In other words, in three years of operation, only 1,127 families—less than 400 annually—were real land reform beneficiaries. There are no precise data on the number of families receiving land in the years following 1965, but it is known that few, if any, expropriation decrees were signed. Assuming that in the next three-year period the total number of beneficiaries had doubled, about 3,380 families would have been settled by the end of 1967, or about 560 annually.[7] Hence we might conclude tentatively that of the 66,000 recipients of property titles, about 62,620 can be estimated to correspond to occupants of land in the public domain.

The land reform projects of INCORA were therefore the extent of the Colombian "land reform." In early 1965, twenty land settlement projects of the institute, excluding one project (Magdalena Number 4), were to use between 328,000 and 351,000 hectares for an estimated 18,200 to 19,400 beneficiaries. But this estimate may be on the high side. For example, it was reported that one project could not be carried out because of the opposition of the *terratenientes* of the area, although, in the historic words of INCORA, they do not "decisively control the political machinery in the country." The average planned project is small—about one thousand families. Since the majority of the projects, according to INCORA's own projections, require lengthy investments in flood control, drainage or irrigation, it is probable that the twenty projects will not be ready before 1970 or 1972. If this is the case, INCORA's land settlement or colonization schemes would imply an average annual rate of settlement of about 1,900 families between 1961 and 1971, or about 14 per cent of the annual increase in the number of rural families (14,000), the bulk of whom are poor. And this does not take into account the poor families existing in 1960. In other words, the total number of underprivileged families needing land or some other reform benefit increases at best by an estimated 12,000 families, net of rural-urban migration.

In summary, then, Colombia's land reform program resulted in a land distribution benefiting approximately 3,500 families in the period from 1962 to 1967, while the net increase in poor rural families (net of migration to the cities after deducting the land reform beneficiaries) amounted to nearly 69,000 families during the same period. If between

---

[7] An independent evaluation of Colombia's land reform undertaken by one of the international agencies in early 1968 arrived at an estimate of 3,785 families recipient of land under INCORA's land settlement program.

1962 and 1972, 20,000 families will have received land through true land reform (which is not yet certain), the number of new underprivileged farm families needing assistance will have exceeded the land reform beneficiaries by 100,000. Thus Colombia's land reform program has been entirely marginal.

A Balance Sheet of Colombia's
Settlement Plans and Actual Settlements
Through Land Reform

Planned Projects 1962–71[a]	
Hectares involved	351,000 (328,100)
Beneficiaries	19,414 (18,213)
Actual Settlements	
Hectares involved 1962–65	23,689
Beneficiaries 1962–65	1,127
(Beneficiaries) (1962–67)	(3,500 est.)

[a] Excluding project Magdalena No. 4. The figures in parentheses reflect adjustments in the projects made subsequently by INCORA. Where the annual reports of INCORA failed to state the number either of hectares or beneficiaries, they were estimated on the basis of 19.4 hectares of land per settler—an average ratio for all projects on which information was complete. *Source:* Annual reports of INCORA.

What dent has this program made in Colombia's aggregate agrarian structure so far? In the province of Córdoba two projects totaling about 74,000 hectares represent about 4.5 per cent of the total farmland, and only a slightly larger percentage of the land in multi-family farms. For Colombia as a whole, the planned schemes represent about 1.4 per cent of all farmland, 2.1 per cent of the farmland controlled by multi-family farms, and about 2 per cent of the underprivileged farm families existing in 1960. We might conclude that the landholdings of the landed elite were practically not affected.[8]

There is no evidence to suppose that Colombia's land reform activities will increase sharply during the next few years,

[8] See also "Colombia—A Case History of United States Aid," Survey of the Alliance for Progress, Subcommittee on American Republics Affairs, Committee on Foreign Relations, U. S. Senate, 91st Cong., 1st Sess., 1 February 1969, pp. 79 ff.

in terms of new settlement schemes. It must therefore be anticipated that the 1970's will see a slow implementation and termination of the schemes planned in the mid-1960's, and later, perhaps, land reform will come to a complete halt.

In Panama, the Land Reform Commission reported in 1966 ten small projects including an area of about 12,000 hectares; a little over 1,000 beneficiaries were to be settled on an average plot of ten hectares, but only a small portion of the settlers have as yet been given land. In Peru, some land reform, in the form of partly legalized invasions, took place prior to the passage of the land reform law, and the establishment of the land reform institute in 1964. The largest invasion and subsequent settlement took place in Algolán, where about 3,000 families from fourteen indigenous communities, and twelve groups of feudatarios regained possession of land. In another area of peasant uprisings, La Convención y Lares, expropriation of several large estates promised land to some 10,000 families, but by the end of 1966 these expropriations had not yet been made final.[9] Sixteen publicly owned haciendas in the Puno area (45,000 hectares, which is very little, given the ecological conditions of the area) and on the coast (720 hectares) were "expropriated" by mid-1966. No families had been settled on the Andean public haciendas by the end of 1966, nor had any privately owned farms been expropriated. Although under Title XV the institute registered about 120,000 resident peasants (feudatarios) and distributed about 32,000 temporary documents confirming their possessory rights, only four feudatarios actually received land by 1966, not through expropriation but through voluntary transfer made for the purpose of demonstration, in cooperation with the estate owner. Although the institute had jurisdiction over 213,000 square kilometers in three officially decreed land reform zones with a rural population of 1.3 million people, and had established in addition thirteen offices to implement Title XV and several irrigation projects in areas totaling 3.3 million rural inhabitants, there was practically

[9] Several of the land reform projects which were started prior to 1964 were taken over for further processing by ONRA in 1964.

no land reform progress. Prorated on an annual basis, the total settlement of farm families in Peru through the land reform institute and prior to its existence was probably no greater than a few hundred families between 1961 and 1967.[10]

[10] Actually information about the settlement of farm families in Peru is confusing. According to a CIDA evaluation of Peru's land reform since 1964, no private estates had been expropriated between 1964 and late 1966, although some publicly owned land was "expropriated" as mentioned. Hence, CIDA concluded that the activities of ONRA benefited only a few peasant families. However, ONRA reported in May 1968 that between May 1964 and May 1968, 353,000 hectares of expropriated land (estates?) were distributed to 11,163 families. (Another official figure for the period of May 1964–September 1968 is 314,000 hectares distributed to 9,224 families.) On the other hand, S. Barraclough ("Agrarian Reform in Latin America: Actual Situation and Problems," in *Land Reform, Land Settlement and Cooperatives,* Rural Institutions Division, FAO, 1969, No. 2, pp. 1 ff) states that "In Peru, about 14,000 'campesino' families (one percent of the number of potential beneficiaries) have received lands during the last four years either from colonization programs or the redistribution of large estates."

How can the CIDA findings be reconciled with the 11,163, 9,224 or 14,000 beneficiaries of "land reform"? The answer is no doubt that between the end of 1966 and May (or September) 1968, farm families were settled on land reform projects initiated prior to the end of 1966 and even prior to 1964. Hence these projects had a very long gestation period. However, a portion of the beneficiaries were settled on colonization schemes. If we accept the official figures at face value, the statement in the text would have to be modified to read that between 1961 and 1969, total settlement of farm families on real land reform projects per annum was about 1,500 beneficiaries (depending on the size of the colonization schemes). Obviously, however, even the higher figure represents only a tiny fraction of the annual increase in poor farm families.

CHAPTER 23

A Final Balance Sheet

These few examples should demonstrate that in countries that have had any "land reform" activity at all in recent years, it is difficult to evaluate accurately how many real land reform beneficiaries there were, and official statistics must be used with caution. It is particularly difficult to separate the beneficiaries of colonization schemes from the real land reform settlers. It might be argued that it does not matter how farm families get their land, as long as they get it. There is of course some truth in this, except that it overlooks the crucial point that colonization schemes or the issuance of property titles do nothing to modify the basic agrarian structure, with its tight control by a small landed elite over the agricultural resources and the peasantry.

On the basis of the available evidence, the number of settlers who received land through expropriations of privately owned estates, carried out by national land reform institutes established through legislation during the 1960's, was at best about 1,000 or 1,500 annually, and usually much less. In many countries there has been practically no land distribution whatever. Only in Venezuela were about 100,000 families given land, beginning before the Alliance for Progress. But in all countries, including Venezuela, "land reform" activities slowed down considerably as the decade drew to a close.

A generous estimate would seem to be that so far on the average, sixteen countries (not including Mexico and Bolivia) settled about 500 families as land reform beneficiaries per annum, and Venezuela, about 12,000—totaling, over a seven- or eight-year period, 140–160,000 families benefiting from the activities of the land reform institutes. This figure would be well below the *annual* rate of increase in the number of rural families in the seventeen countries, estimated at about 220,000 families, the overwhelming majority of whom are poor. Even if the average settlement rate in the sixteen countries were 1,000 instead of 500 (the latter figure being more realistic), no more than a total of 196–225,000 families would have been real land reform beneficiaries during the Alliance for Progress years. With the recent slowdown in the activities of most land reform agencies, the number of annual beneficiaries now threatens to decline rapidly.

The rate of settlement by the institutes has been so slow that at the present pace it would require generations to settle only 75 per cent of the poor families existing in 1960. In Honduras, for example, it would need a 155-year program; in Peru it would last indefinitely at the rate ONRA was functioning during almost three years (1964–66); in Brazil it would take 34,000 years; in Colombia, almost 1,300 years. But since these estimates do not even take into account the natural increase in the rural families, these programs can never catch up with the rural poor.

We should not overlook the fact that while land reform institutes were distributing land to the peasants, on whatever small scale this may have occurred, the landed elite was evicting peasants from their estates, and from the land to which they had access under some sort of lease arrangement, in order to prevent the peasants from claiming land to which the legislation gave them certain rights. Precise figures will never be known, but a good guess is that these evictions equaled the number of families receiving land from the institutes, and probably exceeded them by a good margin. Thus the action of the land reform institutes was canceled by the illegal action of the landed elite, and the peasantry was no better off at the end of the 1960's than when the decade started.

CHAPTER 24

Counter-Reform: The Other Side of the Coin

Some observers of the Latin American scene have claimed that the failures of the land reforms of the 1960's clearly demonstrate that a policy designed to modify radically the agrarian structure and bring about true progress is intrinsically doomed to failure.

These observers overlook two important points. First, traditional agricultural policies for increased production and marginal land tenure improvements have failed to increase production even at the relatively low rates prescribed by the Alliance for Progress, and have succeeded even less in diminishing or eliminating rural poverty. Secondly, and more important, in response to the peasants' and many political leaders' clamor for agrarian reform, the decade of the 1960's has witnessed the most intensive campaign to forestall or sabotage reforms that the continent has ever seen. We would like to call this campaign the "counter-reform."

Counter-reform refers to all the multi-faceted efforts which are undertaken by or on behalf of the landed elite to maintain the status quo in the traditional agrarian structure, and, in fact, in the entire existing fabric of Latin American society. Counter-reform is not merely a defense mechanism on the part of the landed elite. It can also involve an aggressive attempt to "modify" the agrarian structure or actively prostitute existing land reform programs to suit the aims of those who control the land and political power.

The success of counter-reform cannot easily be measured in quantitative terms, although it is obviously reflected in a general way in the achievements or failures of the land reform institutes. Counter-reform uses political or military pressures with the intention of making land reform impossible. It is a direct, if subtle and even elusive attack against the forces which wish to bring about true reforms. Land reforms are relatively well formalized programs whose agents, agencies, supporters and beneficiaries are known and easily identified. Counter-reform, on the other hand, is practically never formal. It is a policy, but not a program. It has its agents, but not agencies. It is diffused, usually anonymous and often unrecognized, except when it degenerates into large-scale military or police action directed against peasants or peasant leaders. But even in the last case, the instruments of propaganda which are quick to publicize or criticize the land reform institutes' activities can just as quickly conceal all counter-reform activities and stifle public opinion, as happened in Peru and Brazil. This is easy to achieve, since press, radio and television are usually under the political influence of, if not actually owned by, the landed elite or their associates. A land reform carried out in a society in which latifundismo remains the cornerstone, faces the obstacle of an existing political, administrative and military establishment fighting for survival. Here, then, reform and counter-reform forces are very unevenly matched.

Although counter-reform does not have a well-formalized program, its activities are definitely the result of concerted—if unpublicized—action. It is true that some counter-reform measures often arise out of an instinct of self-preservation on the part of individual estate owners. In contrast to the peasants, who are generally forbidden to organize, estate owners are highly organized on the local, national and international levels, and are closely integrated with the powerful financial, commercial, political, military and administrative sectors. Of course, all members of the landed elite do not see eye to eye on all issues with which they have to deal, and in some issues they may be bitter competitors. But they are united in their desire to preserve and defend latifundismo and keep the peasantry in their place of obscurity.

The estate owners alone have formed economic and political pressure groups more powerful than any other sector in Latin America, and they can count on an abundance of resources to give full expression and support to their favorite economic, social and political views. The commodity associations, for example, are formed principally for the defense of the crops their members grow—e.g., livestock, coffee or cotton. But they take an active interest in the defense of latifundismo in general and lobby for it. The same is true of the general landlords' associations, which are called Sociedades de Agricultores, where the term Agricultores stands for the wealthy, usually absentee, estate or plantation owners. These sociedades always have a hand in shaping agricultural policies. They interfere in the passage of land reform legislation and afterwards in its implementation. But the estate owners of Latin America also form an "International" which has ramifications in all the centers of power in the Americas. For example, the Asociaciones Agropecuarias Americanas Amigas (AAAA), with headquarters reputed to be in Chicago, has secret periodic meetings to establish common strategies against the peasantry and the land reformers. It is difficult to avoid the conclusion that international collective action by the landed elites of Latin America has had concrete results in terms of sabotaging land reforms. The AAAA is not an association of automobile owners!

It is, of course, hardly necessary for the estate owners to band together for concerted action, because the entire structure of the nation works to a large extent in their favor. Government agencies are headed by estate owners or members of their families at the national or local level. Such agencies are effective instruments of counter-reform for the landed elite. Governors of states or provinces who are also millionaire landlords with substantial financial interests in agriculture and allied industries, directors of public or semi-public lending agencies, judges on the national or local courts, heads of rural labor courts or Indian agencies, police chiefs or prefects of towns and villages can all be used to assist the landed elite in its efforts to "defend itself" against the justified demands of the peasants. Many of them are simply in the pay of the landed elite. Thus land reform institutes seem to be constantly fighting a losing battle.

The instigators of counter-reform use as many methods as they have seats of control. These range from eviction of peasants before they can claim rights to land under the national land reform legislation to prosecution (or threats of prosecution) of directors of land reform institutes on grounds of alleged mishandling of public funds or incompetency. Counter-reformers can also deprive institutes of their funds or prevent the heads of government from signing expropriation decrees, thus turning one government office against another.

Land reform institutes in Latin America begin with staffs of relatively young and enthusiastic technicians, eager to implement the national law and help the peasants, who become frustrated and are replaced by inveterate counter-reformers, spokesmen of the landed elite, who sabotage the institutes' function with endless and fruitless discussions and contrived work.

Counter-reform finds its assistance in unexpected and sometimes ironical quarters. In their eagerness to justify themselves morally in the public eye, counter-reformers have gingerly accepted the help of the intellectuals. In the naïve conviction that land reform can be solved scientifically by "taking the subject out of politics altogether," the intellectuals have attempted to give theoretical backing to the idea that land reform is a matter of increasing the economic efficiency of agriculture, and therefore a problem for technical experts rather than misty-eyed romantics and pursuers of social justice. The theory that reform can be made apolitical is as absurd as proposals to make the race problem an issue of clinical psychology by adjusting the persecuted race to the precepts of middle-class society. It is a hypocritical approach because it does involve politics of the status quo. Technical experts attempting to solve the problems of a feudal agrarian society objectively must first determine the optimum conditions under which land settlement can be successful. This requires systematic research and the use of the most modern and refined methods of analysis, preferably the use of electronic computers. Data on soil conditions, climate, water supplies and the conditions of the markets must be gathered, which takes years to accomplish, because most Latin American countries do not have such quantitative information readily available. The data must then be analyzed, which takes another couple of years, before the peasants can be helped. All is studied thoroughly, except that the intolerable social system and its impact on the lives and welfare of the peasants —the crucial issue in land reform—never enters the stubborn computers. The process must be repeated innumerable times, as land reform projects are carried out in regions with entirely different agricultural conditions. In this manner "technical reforms" reverse the process of land reform; instead of solving, through expropriations and redistribution, the political issue of the monopolization of landownership, they first establish to the satisfaction of the computers what is "best for the peasants."

This, however, is only one aspect of technical reform. Much effort is spent on proving to the public or financial and technical assistance agencies that colonization is a much more "economically sound" enterprise than expropriations of privately owned estates. Although colonization might be more expensive in terms of settlement costs per peasant family, so the reasoning goes, it would not do to interrupt the productive processes of going concerns, because this might result in lessening the agricultural output, and subsequently in harming peasants. It is of course possible that production on expropriated estates which are extremely well managed by modern farming techniques might temporarily fall. But as we have seen, such farms are few and far between, and they occupy only a tiny fraction of the farmland in all Latin American countries. Their decreasing output would be offset immediately by the industrious effort of millions of peasants on land which has hitherto been unproductive even in the oldest and best farming communities. But this logic has little impact on governments eager to invest their "scarce resources" in huge and costly irrigation and drainage projects for colonization in outlying districts. Nor is it effective with international agencies eager to help the governments to circumvent land reforms.

The counter-reform argument that land reform is bad for the peasants can be taken seriously only by an estate owner sitting in his air-conditioned office in Rio de Janeiro or Caracas. A peasant would regard it as a joke, in rather bad taste.

PART IV

REFORMERS, TECHNOCRATS
AND PROGRESS

Latifundismo—like slavery in the nineteenth century—is not going to fall of its own weight or disintegrate as a poor business proposition for the landed elite. Quite to the contrary. In a traditional system of agriculture, ownership of land—particularly large blocks of land—is financially very lucrative. As a general rule, the size of the landholding determines the size of its owner's income and wealth.

But latifundismo is going to fall at some unforeseeable time in the future because it is poor business for the Latin American nations as a whole. Generally, what is good for the latifundio owners is bad for Latin America.

Latin American nations now import more than a half billion dollars' worth of agricultural products from third countries.[1] Chile alone, with only a total population of 9.6 million in 1970 and a farm population of 2.8 million, imports annually over one hundred million dollars' worth of food, and its small land reform has so far done little to diminish the need for such expenditures. A few imports are luxury items: caviar, smoked salmon, fancy cheeses and champagnes; but many are staple foods consumed by the people of the hemisphere. These staple foods, fruits, vegetables and other products, could all be produced in more than adequate quantities in the Latin American nations. In a number of countries, ecological conditions are so varied that many varieties of produce could be grown, ranging from tropical fruits to moderate-climate crops for short growing seasons.

[1] ECLA/UN, *Agricultural Development in Latin America*, E/CN.12/829, 12 February 1969, p. 21.

But without food imports, there would be famines in parts of the hemisphere. The outlook is that food import requirements will grow in the 1970's.

Food imports would be justifiable if sufficient foreign exchange could be earned from exporting industrial goods, handicrafts or services. Except for Mexico's tourist trade, such exports are generally insignificant. Under these conditions, food imports are an absurdity. Latin nations are constantly short of foreign exchange, because the importation of agricultural products that can be produced domestically reduces their capacity to import capital goods to launch the agricultural and non-agricultural sectors on the road to progress. The absurdity is allowed to continue because to do away with it would require enormous changes in the economic practices of the nations. For example, agricultural performance must be improved radically through land tenure changes; unemployment must disappear; resources must be veered away from the monocultures; agricultural and non-agricultural entrepreneurs must reinvest their profits in their own countries instead of depositing them in the banks of the industrial nations; foreign technical and financial aid must cease to be the tail to wag the (economic) dog; governments must obtain the necessary powers to implement development plans.

It would be interesting to know just what is the potential of Latin American agriculture. This is one question which, although crucial, is difficult to answer. We can only give a bird's-eye view, using very simple assumptions, yielding a very approximate answer. One way is to compare the poor performance of the estate sector (i.e., the latifundios) with the much better performance of the family farm sector, ignoring for reasons of simplicity the other sectors of agriculture, and then estimate what the estates could achieve if their performance were roughly equal to that of the family farms. Of course this immediately imposes a number of limitations. We must keep in mind that the latifundios do not now produce the same agricultural products as the family farms; that they use hired laborers, and family labor only in a managerial capacity; that they have almost exclusive access to all the inputs other than land which contribute to raising output and productivity; and that they sell in markets where the terms of trade are more favorable to the sellers than those in which producers on family farms sell. One of our simple but still realistic assumptions is that resources in latifundios are underutilized or unused; at the minimum, latifundio land could be farmed as intensively as land in family farms in terms of the proportion of cultivated or crop land, and value of production per hectare in latifundios would be assumed to be the same as in family farms. Another assumption is that the land would be operated at the same levels of management and technology, and with the same labor inputs as those now prevailing on family farms.

The table summarizes, for six nations,[2] the status of family farms and latifundios, estimated increases in cultivated or crop land, employment and value of production on the latifundios. Due to the enormous underutilization of the resources in the latter, which the table reflects, it would apparently be possible to raise output to unexpected magnitudes. In our example, the value of production on latifundios could be raised from $1.4 billion to between $4.1 and $6.3 billion.[3] It is obvious that even a fraction of this increase could eliminate the now customary imports of staple foods. If the medium-size multi-family farms were included, a further sharp increase in output and employment could be obtained. And if levels of management and technology were also raised on all farms, total yearly output on the same amount of cultivated land, and on the millions of hectares of poorly managed pastureland on latifundios, could be raised to almost astronomical figures (although we must keep in mind that changes in the composition of output in the various sectors would affect the relative values of production). But in Latin America's latifundio agriculture, spectacular increases are improbable.

Latifundismo is also the greatest obstacle to general eco-

[2] Argentina, Brazil, Chile, Colombia, Ecuador, Guatemala.
[3] The table shows a minimum increase computed on the basis of straight averages for the six nations, a maximum increase on the basis of weighted averages. The difference is the consequence of differences in the structure of family farms in the various countries.

nomic growth, because it perpetuates the existence of rural masses living at, near or even below subsistence levels. These masses represent a very small market for domestic or imported industrial or consumer goods—a fact which is now understood by most economic planners and even some businessmen. But it is also necessary to understand that the economic advantages of sharply expanded rural markets appear

Output and Employment Potentials on Latifundios
in Six Countries
(in millions)

	Total Land in Farms (ha)	Cultivated Land (ha)	Crop-land (ha)	Active Labor Force	Annual Value of Production (U.S. dollars)
Present Status					
Family Farms	101.3	29.0	14.3	5.1	1,687.2
Latifundios	242.6	39.7	8.8	3.3	1,434.8
All Farms	470.9	113.4	40.8	18.8	5,319.0
Increase from Present Status on Latifundios to:					
Minimum	----	69.4	34.2	12.3	4,051.1
Maximum	----	107.4	57.7	37.8	6,311.8

NOTE: Unadjusted data from CIDA.

to businessmen and industrialists to be much smaller than the advantages of the status quo. If higher incomes for the peasantry require fundamental changes in the agrarian structure—which, as Barraclough pointed out, entail a large number of political "incognitos"—businessmen and industrialists prefer the status quo. In a sense, therefore, they are allies (if not members) of the landed elite. Furthermore, most Latin American and foreign owned businesses and industries operate in monopolistic or oligopolistic markets allowing extremely high profits. They are satisfied with a market growth rate which is roughly equivalent to the slow growth of the rural and urban middle classes. To expect strong pressures from the business community in favor of radical changes in the agrarian structure and a concomitant improvement in the economic well-being of the peasantry is therefore unrealistic under the conditions which now prevail.

The peasants' subsistence incomes keep savings at very low levels, reducing to a bare minimum the possibilities of investing in the improvement of output and productivity of land, capital and labor—i.e., outlays serve mainly to replace worn-out equipment. Contributions to government revenues for improved public facilities and services are insignificant. Again, it is of interest to note the consequences for the Latin American economies of the stagnating financial status of the peasantry. We can take as an example the Brazilian study of eleven townships which demonstrated that in 1959/60, average capital outlays per minifundio (including those for livestock) amounted to only $5.50 U.S. Two municípios reported no outlays at all on the minifundios. The impact of such minimal expenditures by so many farm families on improving agricultural production is assumed to be totally insignificant. They represent replacements rather than additions to fixed capital and livestock, and are barely sufficient to maintain output. Purchases from the non-agricultural sectors are therefore also minimal. Family farms reported for the same eleven municípios averaged annual capital outlays, including livestock, of about $59, also a low figure. It is probable that Brazil's minifundios and family farms are typical for the hemisphere.

Purchases by the poor rural labor force from the non-agricultural sectors—the implement dealers, the construction industries, the textile and food merchants and many others —could be increased significantly even with very moderate increases in their wages and incomes because of the large number of prospective spenders. Let us assume, for example, that in the seven major Latin American nations,[4] of the 6 million farm workers on smallholdings (exclusive of hired workers), each worker could, as the result of a deliberate policy of technical and financial assistance, spend an addi-

[4] Argentina, Brazil, Chile, Colombia, Ecuador, Guatemala and Peru.

tional $2.50 U.S. per month, or $30 per year; each of the 4.5 million workers on family farms (again exclusive of hired workers), an additional $100 per year; and each of the 8.7 million hired laborers an additional $50 per year as a result of a slight increase in wages. The total additional expenditures on tools, clothing, construction materials and food would amount annually to over one billion dollars. All the small-holders might not be able to continue to invest in their inadequately sized plots for many years; but producers on family farms would be able to increase their capital expenditures once initial investments had borne fruit, and similar advantages could be expected from the greater contentment of the hired laborers. The marginal productivity of new investments on the smaller farm units would probably be very high during the first few years. All this is not a recommendation for an agricultural policy to be pursued, but only an aggregate index of one short-run economic consequence of the landed elite's systematic policies to prevent the farm people's access to more resources, and to keep the labor force at subsistence income levels.

But latifundismo is not only poor business for the hemisphere; it is essentially a system of lawlessness which must inevitably lead to increasingly frequent and violent social and political conflicts. The hired laborers who do the farm work have no interest in improving the performance of the system, because they are not allowed to exercise any initiative of their own. The entire network of labor relations is, from the point of view of the hired rural workers, *a conglomerate of disincentives for better performance.* The resentment of the workers toward such a system must therefore be profound and indelible. For them, the solution is no longer the creation of new incentives for better performance, which they would undoubtedly regard as new methods of exploitation, but the creation of an entirely new structure of labor–management relations or of land tenure relations in general. If they own or cultivate small plots of land, any initiative to gain more land or capital now meets with often insurmountable obstacles. In a sense, it is also "punished," not only by dismissal (if they are small tenants or sharecroppers) or economic or corporal sanctions, but by their oppression by the entire system. The smallholder who wants better land than that which is assigned to him may find himself without any land at all. If he wants credit, he has to bribe the loan inspector, pay his transportation costs and meals, and spend innumerable hours, hat in hand, in the bank's offices, unless he borrows from his landlord or a merchant. If on occasion he does receive credit, he obtains the funds long after they are most useful to him, in small allotments, over a period of time determined unilaterally and often arbitrarily by banks geared to dealings with the landed elite. In addition, he must often pledge his little plot of land as guarantee of repayment. The prices he obtains for the produce he sells are a fraction of the prices for which the buyer resells it. Hired workers and smallholders cannot insist on their "rights," because they have them only in theory.

Latin American peasants have learned to be submissive and apathetic; Pearse, quoting José Pastore, speaks of the popular stereotype of the northern Brazilian peasant as characterized by an "internalized resignation, already a part of the cultural matrix, in face of the overwhelming power of the social sector that controls access to natural resources: The Northerner is a sufferer, but he is calm and patient."[5] Holmberg speaks of the "feigned behavior" of the Vicos Indian serfs, typical of subordinated groups, but also points out that their behavior changes abruptly when they are not in the presence of their patrons or other mestizos; in their presence, "serfs presented themselves as the most foolish and incapable of beings."[6] And the CIDA studies contain ample material from other countries to the same effect. A submissive and foolish-acting peasant is not material for agricultural development. He is material for rebellion.

The near impossibility of bringing about progress through peasant initiative shows how unrealistic, if not absurd, are proposals to "raise the educational level of the peasants" which are not accompanied by profound changes in the agrarian structure. Estate owners have neither room nor jobs for edu-

---

[5] Pearse, op. cit., p. 32.

[6] "Some Relationships between Psychobiological Deprivation and Culture Change in the Andes," op. cit.

cated peasants. The traditional paternalistic relationship between the landed elite and the peasants implies that the former are more interested in the latter's obedience than in their working efficiency.

There are obviously constant economic, social and political forces at work which tend to undermine this traditional paternalism and the entire agrarian structure.[7] For example, Pearse continues the above quotation by saying that those workers who live closer to the towns have come to aspire to a better life and see themselves not only as poor, but as "poorer than they should be, and as unjustly exploited." Submissiveness, in other words, is not necessarily ignorance. However, as we have pointed out earlier, the changes which occur are not always advantageous to the peasants, since they represent the same continuing latifundio system in slightly modified form. In fact, in the present-day agrarian structure, peasants resist changes in routine which are suggested or ordered by management or other authorities.[8] This resistance is motivated largely by the peasants' inherited distrust of management and all the institutions which are part and parcel of the latifundio system, including the public authorities. Distrust is based on the generation-long experience that changes bring about reverses, rather than improvements, for them and the community. *For the majority of the peasants, the greatest security lies in maintaining the status quo under the conditions that prevail.* Although this is also true for the landed elite, the situations are not comparable; whereas the peasants need radical changes to better themselves, and accept the status quo only as a method of survival, the landed elite must constantly reinforce the status quo to preserve its gains. For peasants, for example, there is greater security in using unimproved seeds which will yield a minimum of *certain* foods for the family than introducing new unexplored seeds with reputedly higher yields.[9] Changes in work routine are resisted because

---

[7] A good description of these various forces is contained in CIDA, op. cit., Regional Report.

[8] Pearse, op. cit., pp. 25 ff, also emphasizes this fact.

[9] It must be kept in mind that new improved seeds are often poorly adapted to peasants operating on small units with primitive equipment.

they result in demands for greater labor efforts without added remuneration. A change in the type of remuneration (e.g., from kind to cash) results in less take-home pay and less security. Lasswell stated that among the inhabitants of Vicos, the well-known land reform project in Peru, "generations of oppression had created profound skepticism regarding the motives of any outsider and particularly of the padrone."[10] Holmberg concluded that the experience in Vicos confirmed the hypothesis long ago expressed by Marx that the alienation of people from control over the means of production retards social and economic development.

Even campesino leaders are distrusted, because estate owners bribe them and because some leaders use their positions to launch themselves into political careers, only to betray those who initially supported them. The vicious circle of corrupt campesino leadership can be broken only after the traditional relationship between the landed elite and the peasants has come to an end.

Since distrust, submissiveness and clumsiness are the peasants' best self-defense, the landed elite is convinced that peasants are dumb, lazy, disobedient, incompetent and dishonest. But the peasants' attitude is simply the "road of least resistance" for survival in the face of chronic aggression. Hence the landed elite's opinions of the abilities and potentials of the peasantry are entirely in error. The misconceptions that the peasantry are lazy and incompetent, that they do not know how to handle money and are not fit material for entrepreneurship, or that they use any excess earnings for alcoholic drinks, are so much a part of the credo of the landed elite that it precludes them from any possible function in aiding the development of the peasantry. There are many examples which demonstrate that once the traditional agrarian social structure has been eliminated, along with the peasantry's hopelessness about a better future for themselves and their children, peasant performance increases miraculously. These examples come from all over the world, and in Latin America they come from Peru, Mexico, Bolivia, Honduras,

[10] Harold D. Lasswell, "Integrating Communities in More Inclusive Systems," *Human Organization*, Summer 1962, p. 117.

Chile and Cuba. They are not given much publicity for obvious reasons, as Latin America's propaganda machine is geared to extolling the virtues of landed elitism.

The economic and political power of estate owners even has a corrupting effect on some of the peasants themselves, because they see in the landowners' success a way of life to imitate. In this fashion, some of the values cherished by the landed elite are adopted by members of the peasantry. For some of these peasants, the road to wealth and prestige is not through one's own work efforts coupled with the ability to save and invest, but through the exploitation of the labor of others—and not necessarily beginning in agriculture. There is always the opportunity for a few fortunate individuals, who are willing to accept and imitate the behavior pattern of the "establishment," to travel this road to success; and the "establishment" favors their success in order to raise false hopes with the remainder of the peasantry.

The outlook now for the 1970's is that, in the aggregate, the status of Latin America's peasants will not change for the better. In fact, there is strong evidence that it will deteriorate. Access to land is more closed than ever. Unemployment appears to be rising. Real wages and incomes are declining. Security of tenure becomes shakier. Peasant organizations are not only discouraged, but repressed. Worst of all, however, is the widespread acceptance by national governments, private entrepreneurs and international agreements, of agricultural policies and programs which, in the name of "agricultural development," only aggravate an already intolerable situation.[11] To this vital issue we must now devote a few paragraphs.

We are now witnessing, and shall continue to witness for several years to come, a great battle, obviously fought with very different equipment, between the Reformers and the Technocrats; at this moment it appears that the Technocrats and the agricultural policies they recommend and implement have the upper hand. We need not at this stage devote

[11] For a parallel view on developments in the industrial sector, see David Felix, "Economic Development: Take-Offs into Unsustained Growth," *Social Research*, Summer 1969.

much attention to the objectives and programs of the Reformers, except to remind the reader that the programs of
structural reforms ("land reforms") carried out in the early
1960's under the electrifying impact of Cuba's revolution and
the much milder Alliance for Progress have come to a near
standstill. The programs are still "on the books," because not
even the most violent anti-reformer can afford to ignore entirely the issue of social reforms, and it still has many fervent
supporters.

The Technocrats are the Modernizers of agriculture, the
"Green Revolutionaries" the "Food Drivers." They are the
devisers of programs to supply more and better inputs in the
hope of improving the sad performance of Latin America's
agriculture without modifying its basic structure. They are
the defenders of the "technology *ueber alles* syndrome of
our age, the notion that all social problems have solutions,
usually technological ones."[12] Hence the Technocrats are
the anti-Reformers of the 1960's and 1970's.

As Barraclough has pointed out,[13] special efforts to increase agricultural production and efficiency are not new in
recent history. But a new generation of Modernizers seems to
have emerged in the mid-1960's to offset and bypass land reforms. It is perhaps not surprising to find among its propaga-
tors the crusading conservative W. W. Rostow. As United
States representative in the Inter-American Committee on the
Alliance for Progress (CIAP), Rostow attempted to reword the
issues in obscure but new terms. These issues, according to
the 1961 Charter of Punta del Este, were related to the dependence of improvements in agriculture upon "programs of
comprehensive agrarian reform leading to the effective transformation . . . of unjust structures and systems of land tenure
and use." Rostow considered agricultural development a problem of "modernizing rural life," and advocated the reduction
of "urban rural market barriers" through national integration
programs, stating that "a critical and hitherto neglected aspect
of the linking of urban and rural life must be the moderniza-

[12] Ibid., p. 268.
[13] Barraclough, "Why Land Reform?", *Ceres,* op. cit., p. 21.

tion of marketing arrangements and institutions."[14] "Integration" apparently implies here that the rural sector should contribute to, and benefit more fully from, economic development. In this sense, it is obviously synonymous with "economic development," and Rostow's sentence becomes meaningless. Rostow used the term integration differently from its normal use by economists, who refer by it to the consolidation of production and marketing functions vertically and horizontally. Rostow may also have thought of it in this sense, but if he did, he was apparently not well acquainted with the mechanisms of Latin American markets, which are already highly integrated (i.e., monopolized), both with respect to the input markets from which farm people buy and output markets to which they sell. If he did not use it in the normal sense, it is illusory to think that market integration and the modernization of marketing arrangements and institutions can be brought about without fundamental changes in the agrarian structure. Or perhaps the intention was to identify land reform with improvements in marketing —a notion which would parallel other mistaken concepts about land reform.

The lack of clear thinking behind this new term (but not so new concept) of the Modernizer did not prevent its reappearance in a much more important political document than Rostow's original policy statement, i.e., the Declaration of the Presidents of America (Punta del Este, 1967), an international agreement to determine new approaches to saving Latin America's stagnating agriculture. But this time, it was expressed with more precision. In contrast to the 1961 charter, the new declaration relegated reforms to the third place and elevated Modernization to the role played by reforms in the Charter. The declaration stated that "in order to promote a rise in the standard of living on farms and an improvement in the condition of the Latin American rural people and their full participation in economic and social life, it is necessary to give greater dynamism to agriculture in Latin America

[14] See Ernest Feder, "Land Reform under the Alliance for Progress," *Journal of Farm Economics*, August 1965, pp. 664 f.

through *comprehensive programs of modernization,* land settlement and agrarian reform."

After indirectly paying lip service to the problems of land distribution, the declaration then abandoned this controversial subject and continued, in an obvious reversal of the 1961 Alliance policies, to define what it meant by Modernization programs. In so doing, it began where Rostow had left off, and departed from his overemphasis on modern marketing schemes:

> Such programs will be oriented toward *increasing food production* . . . in sufficient *volume* and *quality* to provide adequately for their population and to meet world needs for food to an ever-increasing extent, as well as toward *improving agricultural productivity* and toward *diversification* of crops which will assure the possible competitive conditions for such production.

The text of this important document then enumerated the following measures ("Action Program") to achieve these goals:

(a) the formulation and execution of domestic and international policies and programs;

(b) improved credit systems and facilities for production, marketing, etc.;

(c) price incentives;

(d) greater use of inputs and expansion of industries for inputs and processing;

(e) adequate tax systems;

(f) improved education;

(g) community development programs and co-operatives.

Thus the Modernization of agriculture obtained a much broader meaning than that first attributed to it by Rostow. The document's most remarkable feature is that it contains all kinds of measures "oriented toward increasing food production," except adjustments in land tenure arrangements. We shall comment further on the meaning of modernization in the context of the realities of agricultural programs and policies, but we must first examine what repercussions the declaration, which represented principally official United

States views on Latin American agricultural development in 1967, had on the United States domestic scene, or whether the official views were not influenced, at this stage, by the conservative approach to agricultural development prevalent in United States circles of prestige and authority. In this connection, reference must be made above all to a document published by Iowa State University,[15] whose importance lies not so much in its content as in its sponsorship, which included the Agricultural Development Council, the Ford Foundation and the Rockefeller Foundation. *Latin American Agricultural Development* is a selection of "economic" analyses of the agricultures of eight countries, with particular emphasis on aggregate output over periods of years; trade balances; indices of production of major crops, areas in various cultivations, and their regional distribution. However, the analyses make little reference to the peculiar obstacles to Latin America's agricultural growth which we have suggested in the first two Parts, or to the specific institutional arrangements which are inherent in Latin American agriculture. No reference whatever is made to any of the disastrous trends now apparent in Latin America as they affect the status of the peasantry. It was apparently the view of the thirteen authors of this monograph that economists are not equipped to discuss any issues for which there is no quantitative, computerized information available, even though such issues may be crucial to the economic performance of the agricultural sector. It is therefore with amazement that the reader discovers nine policy recommendations[16] which are as suitable for United States agricultural development as they are for Latin America's. These recommendations are to

(a) raise productivity;

(b) develop adapted agricultural production technology and get it applied;

(c) establish consistent and stable government policies toward agriculture;

---

[15] L. B. Fletcher and W. C. Merrill, *Latin American Agricultural Development and Policies,* International Studies in Economics, Monograph No. 8, Iowa State University, September 1968.

[16] Ibid., p. 90.

(d) sharpen priorities as to how, where and by whom output is to be increased;

(e) improve trade patterns and policies;

(f) organize efficient supply industries;

(g) invest in farm people (education);

(h) utilize land resources (tax reforms);

(i) reduce marketing losses and improve marketing systems.

Furthermore, to our amazement, nothing is said in this valuable, high-level document about *how* development is going to be implemented in the recommended manner, in societies in which the premium is on the conservation of the status quo. There is nothing in these recommendations which acknowledges the realities of Latin American agriculture. One is still more astonished at the similarity of these recommendations with those of the Action Program of the Declaration of the Presidents of America of 1967, although the former are worded in more sophisticated language, as behooves economists of the academic world. In fact, six of the points of the Action Program are clearly reproduced in the nine recommendations. The Action Program recognizes some needed improvements in community and co-operative development, but the Iowa document swerves at the end toward Rostow's nebulous emphasis on better marketing arrangements.

What are the likely social and political views behind these economic analyses and recommendations, which prompt the sidestepping of the most important issues of Latin American agriculture and which are neither efficiency, improved inputs and modern supermarkets, but the blatant inequalities in wealth and income and the oppression of the peasantry? In this respect, the Iowa document is revealing in two ways. One is the comment that the agricultural development which would occur if Latin American countries followed the nine recommendations, may "lead to a more equal income distribution in the long run."[17] The second is the recommendation to

---

[17] Ibid., p. 87.

"sharpen priorities as to how, where and *by whom* output is to be increased."

I should like to take up the second point first. It is strange that economists who have studied the economics of agricultural production in such detail have not detected that in Latin America the priority as to "by whom" output is to be increased does not require any further sharpening, since the landed elite and the institutions allied with it have for generations already decided this priority in favor of the landed elite itself. Since owners of estates have almost exclusive access to land, capital and labor, and to the *new* land, capital and labor which are to bring about further "development," it is realistic to assume that the priority given them with respect to the inputs decides automatically the priority of "who" is producing the output; a similar reasoning applies to the "how" and the "where" of agricultural production. Of course, the "by whom" refers only to the producers, the farm entrepreneurs who are thought to turn the wheels of the economies and agricultures; no reference is made to the output and productivity of the millions of workers who are employed under different types of contracts, and in whose hands are the real productive processes of the agricultural sector. If this particular recommendation were to be formulated in terms of the realities of Latin American latifundismo, it would have to give first priority to increasing output on the neglected smaller farm units, and to increasing the performance of the hired farm workers, on the assumption that the marginal productivity of new investments on smaller units would be immeasurably larger than those on the fossilized estates, and that better terms of employment and labor-management relations would prove an important bonus for the hired laborers and their employers. A more daring addition to this recommendation would also declare that most of the land in latifundios and half of the available credit funds, fertilizers, machinery and equipment were to be put at the disposal of the peasantry, which now outnumbers the landed elite by a very large ratio. A further addendum might recommend special institutions for strengthening the bargaining power of the peasants. Of course, all this would have required a previous analysis and discussion of agrarian problems and land tenure conditions—precisely the issues which the economists of the Iowa report wanted to avoid.

Not satisfied with overlooking an already sharply focused priority—an oversight which itself makes the recommendations suspect of being squarely behind the landed elite—the document adds that "strategic inputs and programs must be . . . made available . . . *to those producers who can take advantage of them*. Research, extension and credit programs will have to be geared to *the highest priority . . . producers*."[18] This is no longer a mere oversight, but an endorsement of traditional agriculture, since the only producers who can now "take advantage" of strategic inputs and programs are the members of the landed elite. They are the real "highest priority producers." One is obliged to conclude that this document places the burden of increased output (i.e., development), as in the past, on the landed elite. If this conclusion is correct, it can be further assumed that the Iowa report is an anti-reform pamphlet, although, like so many other economic studies, it poses as an innocent and "apolitical" economic analysis of Latin American agriculture.[19]

Is agricultural development based on more and better inputs, greater efficiency, adapted production technology, improved trade patterns and policies, and more education and taxes likely to result in a more equal income distribution? Again it seems that such an assumed cause–effect relationship is based on a misconception of how a traditional agriculture operates. As Ballasteros pointed out, "it can be demonstrated

---

[18] Ibid., p. 90.

[19] The Iowa document is only one example of subtle anti-reform literature clothed in a mantle of economic respectability. Another interesting example is OECD, "The Food Problem of Developing Countries" (prepared by its secretary general, Thorkil Kristensen), Paris, December 1967. It states (or understates) that land tenure problems which are "often politically very difficult because they are directly linked with the sometimes [sic] conflicting interests of various groups of people," and particularly the nature of the farmers' rights and responsibilities, "can be dealt with through legislation, if need be, supplemented by government credits to help farmers buy their farms." It adds that it seems on the whole easier to introduce the new techniques, including the high-yielding varieties of certain grains, "with good results on farms that are reasonably big" (pp. 77 ff). It does not explain the word "easier." Easier than what? The words "land reform" are not mentioned.

with mathematical precision and predicted with the highest degree of accuracy that the modernization of agriculture with the existing distribution of resources and political power, must inevitably lead to more poverty, more unemployment, and more repression of the rural masses."[20] The developments of the last two decades demonstrate almost beyond doubt that the so-called forces of the market, guided by the landed elite with the aid or non-interference of government, result in greater, not lessened, income and wealth disparities. Since the "forces of the market" operate for the benefit of the landed elite much more than for the peasantry, economic policies and recommendations which ignore these forces follow the logic that "what is good for the landed elite is also good for the poor peasantry." One important financier in the United States expressed this reasoning in only slightly different form when he said that "economic growth results in profound social reforms"[21]—an illogical statement typical of successful financiers who pose as intellectuals and great social leaders. We conclude, therefore, that the defenders of the Modernization of Latin American agriculture are also the propagandizers of the new version of the nineteenth-century trickle-down theory applied to agriculture, according to which the rural working classes will benefit from the improved welfare of the rural well-to-do.

Given the political situation of the beginning of the 1970's, it is to be expected that the Modernizers, the Green Revolutionaries and the Food Drivers, whose support stems from international agreements and national policies and programs, the implement makers and dealers, the fertilizer companies and the lending agencies, all opposed to social reforms for good reasons, will have a determining voice in shaping decisions on Latin America's agricultural or "agrarian" programs of the next few years. These programs may be classified in two groups: (1) programs to strengthen the latifundio

[20] Juan Ballesteros P., "Productividad Marginal, Eficiencia y Inocencia Politica," in *Investigación Economica* (UNAM, Mexico), Vol. 27, No. 107/8, pp. 401 ff. This article is a witty commentary on the Iowa document.

[21] David Rockefeller, "Falsas Etiquetas que Traban el Progreso de la Alianza [para el Progreso]," Inter-American Press Association, Lima, 27 October 1966, pp. 19 ff.

sector by pumping more "modern" inputs into agriculture and thereby improving the poor performance of this sector, combined with so-called economic incentive measures to call forth a greater effort of the landed elite; and (2) marginal or fake programs of "land tenure improvements," in an attempt to keep the peasantry happy.

Among the major categories of "output-improving" inputs let us discuss new technologies, fertilizers and improved seeds, credit and education, and their effect on the peasantry.

There seems to be little doubt that the next few years will witness a redoubling of efforts to import, manufacture or assemble, and sell high-priced agricultural machinery and equipment, particularly motorized machinery such as tractors and harvesters, in continuation of a marked process which has taken place over the last two decades. It must be emphasized, of course, that we are not in the least opposed to the mechanization of agriculture. We only doubt its usefulness under the conditions which now prevail in a traditional agriculture like Latin America's. Many experts believe—and the Food and Agriculture Organization of the United Nations has repeatedly stated—that spectacular improvements in agricultural production can be obtained in the agricultures of developing nations through the introduction of simple, inexpensive tools to replace the antiquated instruments used by peasants in the cultivation of their crops. But this recommendation meets head on with enormously powerful forces in the economies of the underdeveloped nations and industrialized countries, like the United States, all focused on the expanded use of modern equipment regardless of the conditions under which it is to be employed. The truth is that the developing nations of Latin America and other parts of the world have become the dumping ground for tractors and other equipment, on the theory that farm management will benefit from it.

The pressures for increased sales of machinery stem largely, but not exclusively, from the manufacturers and dealers of this equipment. The large factories of heavy farm equipment have geared their output to international as well as domestic markets, and they have dealerships in practically all the major towns and cities of Latin America. Some countries are licensed to operate assembly plants. Obviously the local dealers are interested in increasing sales of the equipment to justify their existence, and in this respect they join the factory owners in pressuring farm producers into purchasing it. The importation of tractors and other equipment is further facilitated and subsidized by national governments—usually under pressure from the developed countries and local businessmen—through reduced tariffs and international aid agreements, some of which even offer equipment free of charge. For example, a recent USAID loan contracted by Colombia was to be "used to finance imports needed by Colombia's commercial farms" and was aimed at "encouraging private investment in large-scale commercial agriculture."[22] Obviously these imports and investments represent to a large extent expenditures on heavy, motorized farm equipment.

It is crucial to note that most of the imported or domestically assembled equipment—powerful tractors, big harvesters, etc.—is geared to the needs of large-scale farming, rather than peasant agriculture. The terms of sale of modern equipment and the very cost of this equipment exclude their purchase by peasant producers. Normally the equipment can be bought only with cash or large cash down payments, with the balance to be paid off within a few months or, at best, a year. Only the landed elite has access to the resources needed for these transactions, either by dipping into their reserves, which may come from non-agricultural incomes, or more often by obtaining loans from institutional lenders. These lenders in turn are geared entirely to dealings with the landed elite. It is common knowledge that the bulk of agricultural credit is made available to large producers with social and political prestige. There are no significant programs in existence to enable peasant co-operatives or small partnerships to acquire this type of equipment. Although the peasants are generally better credit risks than the members of the landed elite, institutional lenders lend money to co-operatives only on the condition that each member is fully responsible for the entire sum of the loan, which is an effective way of telling the peasants

---

[22] "Colombia—A Case History of United States Aid," Survey of the Alliance for Progress.

that they are not among the banks' favorite clientele. If peasant producers risk losing their land in the process, they will normally not enter into such transactions. Thus the institutional framework is entirely hostile to the peasants' acquisition of modern tools. There are a few programs to facilitate the peasants' use of tractors, including some publicly owned tractor stations. But such schemes are always in the nature of pilot projects, and are insignificant in the overall framework of peasant agriculture. If they are successful, their success is quickly covered so as not to evoke in the peasantry false hopes that the programs could be expanded on a broad scale. As a result, smallholders in Latin America do not have the use of tractors, except in rare instances.

On the other hand, there are domestic social and political factors at work which are subtly exploited by the farm equipment manufacturers and dealers. For many large landowners, it is now prestigious to own one or several tractors, just as it has been prestigious to have in one's employment a large number of "hands" or "hoes." At the same time, many employers openly admit that they regard the acquisition of such equipment as a "solution to their labor problem" since it necessarily diminishes, sometimes radically, the use of labor.

We conclude therefore that the pumping of more technology into a latifundio agriculture is entirely landed elite-oriented.

Since we have previously characterized latifundismo as a system of enormous physical and human waste, it should also be noted that the "infrastructure" of more mechanization in such an agriculture does not allow the fullest exploitation of modern machines. Obviously mechanization of agriculture requires more than mere distribution of tractors and other machines. Although there has been some improvement in recent years, the importation of spare parts for all this equipment is sadly lacking, and a good portion of the equipment lies idle and rusting away. In an agriculture where the tractor is a prestige item, its purchase is much more important than its maintenance and full use.

The impact of mechanization ("modernization") on the peasants, particularly in the short run, is nearly catastrophic under the prevailing conditions. It has certainly contributed to the deteriorating status of the peasants during the 1960's. Mechanization is bound to increase the blatant inequalities in the distribution of wealth, and therefore of income. But more serious still is its impact on employment. In agricultures where labor is overabundant, mechanization is bound to increase unemployment and landlessness; it also increases seasonal and migratory labor, the least desirable form of employment from the point of view of the peasants, when commercial farms cultivate crops which need labor mostly at harvest-time. Greater unemployment and landlessness tend to depress subsistence wages and incomes still further. Another result is that a few large producers may begin growing crops which have traditionally been produced by smallholders, and displace the latter with their greater bargaining power in the markets. Thus the *peasantry becomes more and more marginalized—a strange result for a program which, in Rostow's terms, is designed to bring about greater integration in the economies.* From the vantage point of the peasants, today's "Modernization" of agriculture is anti-social. We must also note the impact of mechanization on the outlook and values of the peasants. The propaganda in favor of mechanization that accompanies the spreading of costly equipment which peasants cannot afford to buy tends to distort their views of their problems, so that they themselves are inclined to believe that if they only had access to tractors, their problems would be solved.[23] When peasants have access to tractors, on a rental basis, for example, their costs of operating their smallholdings increase. The same would be true were they to purchase this equipment, whose costs are disproportionate to their incomes. *They do not clearly understand that under the prevailing conditions the tractor becomes another mechanism for keeping their incomes at subsistence levels.*

A similar reasoning applies to the increased use of improved seeds and fertilizers. The increased distribution of better seeds, such as improved varieties of corn, cotton or rice, usually implies the distribution of seeds for crops grown by large-scale

---

[23] The craze for mechanization is systematically fostered, beginning with schoolchildren in rural areas and towns.

producers. As demonstrated by the successful and much advertised Mexican program for improved wheat varieties and hybrid corn—which resulted in the production of exportable surpluses in this country—benefits accrued almost exclusively to the large hacendados, particularly in the new irrigation districts.

Research on crops grown principally by smallholders is practically unheard of, in Mexico as well as in other Latin American countries. The distribution of fertilizers is also geared to the landed elite—usually through credit, in which the smallholders have only a very small share. In Peru, for example, some fertilizers are used almost exclusively by large producers of commercial crops of the coast. They purchase them at relatively low prices, with the government subsidizing their sales. Between 1959 and 1963 the average annual subsidy to large-scale farm operators for guano amounted to 4.8 million dollars—a tidy sum for a tiny group of hacendados![24] What counts is not only the annual gift of the nation to the landed elite, but the resulting cumulative disadvantage to the peasants over the years. If new fertilizer plants were to increase the availability of this important input, it is highly probable that Latin America's peasants would obtain only a minute share of it, unless government policies were focused on distributing it to the small producers. Such policies are unthinkable in an agriculture dominated by a small landed elite with its influence on domestic agricultural institutions.

In this context it is noteworthy that lately a growing literature has been extolling the virtues of the Green Revolution, to be brought about by magical HYV (high yielding varieties), the new miracle grains, developed by ingenious agronomists. The Green Revolutionaries see in the development and distribution of HYV a way to eradicate hunger throughout the world; they practically equate progress and the modernization of agriculture with the spread of the new miracle seeds. So far, the most unsophisticated piece of literature on the subject is Lester Brown's *Seeds of Change* (London: Pall

---

[24] CIDA, Peru Report, op. cit., pp. 330 ff.

Mall Press, 1970) whose claims for what HYV can accomplish cannot be taken too seriously. In fact, it might be said that in light of the adverse impact of the Green Revolution on the agricultures of the Third World, and particularly on the peasants, Lester Brown has created a veritable credibility gap. However, *Seeds of Change* is by no means ingenuous, nor testimony of a passing intellectual fad. It is written for and on behalf of big business. It reflects the dangerous belief, already put into practice through national and international development strategies, that the development of the Third World agricultures is a matter for the big agricultural industries and financiers to tackle. According to this belief, more and better inputs, on a global scale, produced, marketed and financed by the fertilizer or machinery manufacturers with the aid of the industrial countries, *coming in the wake of* HYV (as Brown has us believe it) will abolish hunger and malnutrition, unemployment and social conflicts in agriculture.

The Green Revolutionaries of the Brown variety err in several ways. First, as Barraclough pointed out, "similar impressive technological revolutions have been occurring with considerable regularity during the past three or four centuries, beginning with the agricultural revolution in seventeenth century western Europe."[25] None of these innovations has reduced hunger and poverty. Thus the glorification of HYV lacks historical perspective. A more crucial error seems to lie in Brown's timetable. It is true that the spread of HYV will, and in fact *must,* call forth more of the other "sophisticated" (i.e., expensive) inputs produced by big business, because HYV thrives best under conditions where these inputs are also used. But the manufacturers of heavy farm equipment had been swamping the agricultures of the Third World with tractors or harvesters before the spread of HYV. The overwhelming majority of this equipment is used by large producers. The tractors and fertilizers have long preceded the seeds. They have displaced rural labor and increased the wealth and income gap in agriculture. It is precisely the adverse impact of mechanization or modernization in develop-

[25] Barraclough, "Why Land Reform?", *Ceres,* p. 21.

ing countries which will make it impossible for HYV to undo the damage already done and eliminate hunger and poverty. The conditions under which HYV will be spread make a more rapid marginalization of the peasants seem unavoidable.[26] The Green Revolution approach is also lopsided, with its over-emphasis on irrigation. There are few countries where irrigation agriculture is more than a small portion of all agriculture. But apparently what happens to the non-irrigation sector and the peasants who live in it does not concern the Green Revolutionaries greatly. Finally, their argument that the spread of HYV will increase rural employment is not very convincing. Even if it were true that some farming operations would now require more labor inputs (assuming no labor-saving equipment), the overall impact on employment is bound to be negative.

Will HYV result, as it is claimed, in crop diversification? It is possible. But it is no less likely that producers will want to exploit the new miracle seeds to the fullest extent possible, for maximum profits, and ignore crop diversification, particularly if the governments subsidize the production and marketing of HYV. If this were to occur, it would considerably weaken one of the arguments for increased employment through HYV.

The glorification of HYV seems to originate mainly with those who have a vested interest in developing the big input industries. This calls for extra caution. A large number of experienced and objective observers see in the Green Revolution a way to magnify economic, social and political conflicts.

Let us now turn to another recommendation of the Modernizers. There are many social scientists and politicians who are enamored of the theory that *education for the peasant masses* is an "input" which will benefit the peasants in terms of higher incomes. The argument is based on the positive relationship, found in developed as well as developing countries, between education and income. For example, a recent publication stated that "agricultural college education improved the managerial ability of the farms [in highly industrialized countries] which led to efficient running of the farms

[26] See, for example, W. Ladejinsky, "The Green Revolution in Punjab, A Field Trip," *Economic and Political Weekly* (Bombay), 28 June 1969.

and higher output per ha."[27] This is not surprising, since the aim of education is precisely that of enabling students to perform better, once education is terminated. It is like saying that when it rains, it gets wet. To apply this statement as a basis for strategies of "economic development" is absurd if the social structure is as inimical to education as is a latifundio agriculture. Latifundismo and agricultural education for the peasant masses are incompatible, as witnessed by the systematic and obstinate refusal of the landed elite to increase educational facilities by voting larger budgets for agricultural colleges or vocational schools, and by their control over local schoolteachers. We are not suggesting that efforts to educate the rural masses ought to be stopped until latifundismo disappears. Even a little education assists in undermining the "establishment." But we must recognize that, under present conditions, progress for the peasants in terms of "higher incomes through education" would come about just as slowly as waiting for latifundios to diminish their average size through the inheritance process, that is, it would take forever. It is doubtful that it would ever solve the problems of the peasants.

Curiously enough, those who sponsor education for the rural masses conveniently overlook the fact that members of the landed elite also lack "education," though in an entirely different sense. The landed elite are well educated in the sense that they have high school, college or university degrees from domestic or foreign schools and universities and are, by definition, much better educated than the rural masses. In Latin America, agricultural colleges and universities are almost entirely geared to the education of the children of the landed and urban elite. They are not for the children of the campesinos.[28] Most of the graduates from the agricultural colleges obtain jobs as government officials or in privately owned

[27] United Nations Research Institute for Social Development Report No. 5, Ram Dayal, "The Impact of Selected Economic and Social Factors on Agricultural Output," Geneva, November 1966, p. 51.

[28] See, for example, CIDA, "La Educacion, la Investigacion y la Extension Agricolas en el Peru," *PAU*, Washington, D.C., 1967. This revealing study demonstrates, among other things, that the very entrance requirements of the agricultural college of Molina precludes sons and daughters of campesinos from attending. See particularly pp. 190 ff.

plantations or processing industries, and become part of the establishment which tries to keep the campesinos from education. Whether all this education of the rural well-to-do has an impact on the performance of the latifundio sector has never been clearly shown. But it is a moot question. If it were to have any impact on the peasants and agricultural progress, the "education" of the landed elite would have to be focused on entirely different subject matters than those now taught in agricultural colleges and universities: on social responsibilities, on sense of justice, on knowledge of peasant living and working conditions and an understanding of their problems. In all these issues, the landed elite is sadly lacking in knowledge, interest or sympathy. Although an education of this type is obviously mere wishful thinking, we cannot omit it from a discussion of education in agriculture, as so many economic developers do.

We conclude, therefore, that "education of the peasant masses," as advocated by some economic developers, might theoretically erode the power of the landed elite in future generations, but as a strategy of development today, it puts the cart before the horse. Education of the peasants to enable them both to carry out their farm work more efficiently and to become integrated with the rest of society can be visualized only after radical land tenure reforms have set the basis for full employment of physical and human resources and for scientific agriculture, and have provided the assurance that the peasants will benefit from these reforms.

Let us now turn briefly to so-called "land tenure programs" which national governments, inspired and encouraged by the Technocrats, Green Revolutionaries and Food Drivers will offer the frustrated peasantry during the 1970's. These programs are thought to be necessary to prevent peasant frustration from becoming rebellion, and the landed elite has learned by experience that marginal or fake measures, if implemented, with sufficient publicity, can pacify the peasantry for a little while longer.

A program which is dear to the Technocrats is "increased taxation." It falls midway between the strategy of pumping more inputs into the landed elite sector and land tenure improvements. Its alleged purpose is to serve as an economic incentive for estate owners to produce more and enable them to pay higher taxes. But some even argue that it assists in the break-up of latifundios when their owners do not increase production and default in their tax dues. Both arguments are unrealistic, which may be exactly why they are so popular with the Technocrats. In a country dominated by a small landed elite, a proposal to increase taxation—and the increase should be significant to be an effective incentive—is as unrealistic as carrying out a land reform in favor of the peasantry. There is no historical experience to indicate that the wealthy have ever taxed themselves for the benefit of the masses. The only way is to pressure them to do so through democratic processes. What is more, taxes are usually raised only *after* output and profits have risen. In Latin America there is reluctance to raise taxes and implement tax laws effectively even then. And what is to prevent a bankrupt hacendado from selling out to another latifundista? But if we imagine for a moment that taxes were raised, it would have little effect on output and an adverse effect on the peasantry, as the hacendados would recuperate their higher taxes by paying lower wages (or not raising them). The Brazilian Estatuto da Terra of 1964, for example, uses tax incentives on the theory that taxes are "an important determinant of reform"—which is only another way of saying that reforms are not under consideration. Taxes were not raised significantly in Brazil after 1964 and their collection remained as haphazard as in the past.[29] Nor has increased taxation resulted in the peasantry's easier access to land or more land reform projects. The taxation feature of the statute might just as well never have been written at all.[30]

[29] It is not well known that in the state of São Paulo, in the early 1960's, a similar "land reform law," based on increased taxation, was a dismal failure because of the systematic sabotage of the law by the landed elite. Why it should work on the national scale when it failed on the state level is still unexplained.

[30] The cadastral survey of IBRA, Brazil's land reform agency, was to set the basis for the higher taxes. Actually the survey turned out to be a Technocrat's dream of how a "land reform" should be carried out. The survey, which was not a cadastral survey at all but an agricultural census of sorts, was extremely costly and time-consuming, although it used modern computers. It lasted for

The greatest popularity and most of the resources are re-
served for colonization or settlement schemes as the Technocrats' "solution" to the agrarian problems of Latin America.
There are different types of colonization schemes: in frontier areas far away from civilization; in valleys that need expensive multipurpose irrigation, drainage and power schemes
for their further development; some projects are financed by
public funds or international loans; a few are private undertakings, as private land companies subdivide and sell their
property to smallholders at enormous profits, often maintaining dictatorial control over land use and the marketing of the
product.

It is to be expected that in the next few years publicly financed colonization schemes will continue to enjoy the highest
priority with national governments and international financial
and technical assistance agencies, on the pretext that they are
a solution to the land problem. In reality, of course, they are
not. Even the largest settlement projects absorb only a few
landless peasants, and often plots are given to non-peasants.
They do not modify the social, economic and political structure of agriculture and are therefore anti-land reform measures.

Colonization projects are always extremely costly, particularly when they are planned in new irrigation and drainage
projects. But the high costs of these schemes, which benefit
the construction firms or the cement industry much more
than the peasants, have never been a deterrent to planning
new ones. This demonstrates that costs do not matter when
the preservation of the status quo is involved. Scarcity of resources is alleged only when it comes to effective programs
to assist the peasants. Nor is it a deterrent that most colonization schemes have been dismal failures for the peasants. They

---

years and is not yet completed. In the process, IBRA spent three quarters of a
million U.S. dollars for a small five-passenger, two-jet plane for the use of
IBRA officials. The plane became symbolic of Latin America's agricultural
programs for the benefit of the peasants, directed entirely from above so that
the campesinos were not visible from an altitude of 20,000 feet. IBRA poured
more resources into the cadastral survey than into land distribution or settlement, but the program was ideally suited to gain time and establish a large
bureaucracy in order to make it appear that something was being done for
the campesinos.

are usually showpieces for governments eager to make it appear that they are willing to help the peasants up to a point. In most cases, they are poorly planned, inadequately executed and forgotten after an initial effort, and many peasants are obliged to leave the schemes after a period of time. Taken by themselves, settlement schemes introduce an element of economic equality and social justice into agriculture, but within the framework of a latifundio agriculture, they are insignificant little cells of egalitarianism, and given the hostility of the landed elite, the probability of their survival as effective production units is small. Besides, as we have demonstrated earlier, there is no need in most Latin American countries to resort to colonization schemes, as there are more than adequate land resources available for distribution to the peasants in the now existing multi-family farms. Only in the distant future will colonization of unused farming areas become a necessity, when the agricultural population increases. Settlement schemes will be beneficial to peasants only after the traditional agricultural structure in the established farming communities has been abolished.

In our view, the policies pursued by the Technocrats will therefore have no salutary effect whatever on the existing social, political and economic imbalances which now characterize Latin America's latifundio agriculture. On the contrary, an accentuation of these imbalances by their policies seems unavoidable. We may even claim that in the recent past, since Reformers and Technocrats began their giant battle over the issue of progress, the advance of science and technology in Latin American agriculture has already tended to increase sharply the inequalities in the distribution of income and wealth, rural unemployment, the bitterness of the peasantry and the potential of violent class conflicts.

The issue of social justice in agriculture does not entirely exhaust the question of what may happen to Latin American agriculture in the coming years. Industrial nations, in collusion with a few progressive members of the landed aristocracy, continue to pour more and more science and technology into a strengthened landed elite sector. We view the development of latifundismo in the near future as a composite of two opposite trends. A small but slowly growing sector will be devoted to commercial agriculture, to the use of modern equipment and farm management methods, increasing numbers of seasonal (part-time) and migratory labor. This sector will produce a growing proportion of the agricultural output, for both export and domestic consumption, and operate at increasingly larger profits, benefiting from government subsidies, price supports, low wages, and all the other advantages that accompany the forced spread of science and technology. This small sector will then form a *technocratic latifundismo*, in which the owners will have the best of two worlds: the benefits of modernization, and the advantages of an excess labor supply. The contribution of this sector to rural employment is likely to be considerably smaller than its contribution to output, and the same will be true with respect to its contribution to the overall intensity of land use, since much of commercial agriculture is going to be located on relatively small areas of irrigated land. The most likely result will be that the output of a small number of specialized crops will be raised to sufficiently high levels to yield exportable surpluses (as happened in Mexico), but without raising domestic diets and rural welfare. Hunger will accompany surpluses.

But latifundismo as a whole is an agriculture of unemployment, and we must not expect the forced increase in the use of science and technology to improve sharply overall performance of the agricultural sector. We must not expect that aggregate agricultural output, as opposed to the output of a few specialized crops, will be raised in any spectacular manner, over and above historic growth rates. It is more than likely that the remaining latifundio sector, in continuation of past trends, will not participate in the modernization process and will turn, as in the past, increasingly to extensive land uses in new and old farming areas such as cattle operations, as their soil becomes exhausted and yields decline. Increasingly extensive land uses are the best mechanism to continue monopolized ownership of land. As a result, its contribution to total output is likely to fall, although probably not as rapidly as the contribution to rural employment. This does not necessarily imply less monetary returns, since cattle and other

Index

Absentee land ownership and management, 84–92, 115 ff., 121 ff., 125 ff., 149, 178

Act of Bogotá, 184–85

Administrators (administration; farm managers and management), xvii, 85–92, 111, 120–24, 153–54; social and political functions of, 125–28

Affonso, Almino, 161 n

Agrarian reform, ix–xi, 171–73 (see also Agriculture; Land reform; specific aspects, countries); achievements of 1960's, 239–51, 252–53, 254–58 ff.; failure of latifundismo system and need for, 261–92; land needs and availability, 47–106; land use patterns and unemployment, 61–106; legislation and, 171–73, 191–213; progress and, 174–79; Technocrats (Modernizers) vs. Reformers and, 270–92

Agricultural production (agricultural development programs): absentee landlordism and management and, 84–92, 115 ff., 121–24, 125 ff., 149, 178; lack of capital investment and, 96–101; latifundismo system and unemployment and, 1–106; Reformers vs. Technocrats (Modernizers) and, ix–xi, 270–92; re-

sistance to technology and change in, 63–84, 95; unemployment and land use patterns and practices, 61–106

Agriculture (see also Agrarian reform; Agricultural production; Farm workers; specific aspects, crops): Alliance for Progress and, 175–76, 184–90, 191; failure of latifundismo system and, 1–106, 261–92; land reform and (see Land reform); land resources, needs, and distribution, 47–106; latifundismo system and arbitrary harshness in treatment of peasantry, 109 ff.; manifestations of rural unemployment and, 29–45; subsistence levels of rural employment and, 129–55, 156–67; Technocrats (Modernizers) vs. Reformers and, 270–92; unemployment and land use patterns, 61–106

Algolán estate (Peru), occupation by peasants of, 43

Alienation of workers, 269

Alliance for Progress, x, xi, 175–76, 184–90; CIDA, 188 (see also CIDA); Committee of Nine, 186–87, 243, 246; inconsistency of policies and downfall of, 188; Inter-American Committee (CIAP), 175–76, 187, 271 ff.;